THE MOTORIZATION OF
AMERICAN CITIES

THE MOTORIZATION OF AMERICAN CITIES

———————— *David J. St. Clair* ————————

 PRAEGER

New York
Westport, Connecticut
London

Library of Congress Cataloging-in-Publication Data

St. Clair, David James, 1950–
  The motorization of American cities

  Update of thesis (doctoral)—1979.
  Includes index.
  1. Transportation, Automotive—United States—
History—20th century. 2. Interstate Highway System.
3. Roads—Government policy—United States—History—
20th century. 4. Local transit—United States—
History—20th century. 5. Automobile industry and
trade—United States—History—20th century. I. Title.
HE5623.S617   1986   388.4′1321′0973   86-523
ISBN 0-275-92126-3 (alk. paper)

Library of Congress Catalog Card Number 86-523
ISBN: 0-275-92126-3

First published in 1986

Praeger Publishers, 521 Fifth Avenue, New York, NY 10175
A division of Greenwood Press, Inc.

Printed in the United States of America

∞™

The paper used in this book complies with the Permanent Paper Standard issued by the National Information Standards Organization (Z39.48-1984).

10 9 8 7 6 5 4 3 2 1

For Seda and David

Acknowledgments

This book has evolved, over many years and through more drafts than I care to remember, from a doctoral dissertation at the University of Utah. Many professional and personal debts have accumulated, which I would like to acknowledge here and express my thanks.

William Carlisle, Lawrence Nabers, and Ernest Randa all served on my dissertation committee at the University of Utah and provided many helpful comments and criticisms. William Carlisle was particularly generous with his suggestions and in the editing. Peter Lindert and Allan Olmstead, both of the University of California, Davis, read the dissertation and offered invaluable criticism, suggestions, and encouragement. James Seal of Santa Monica, California, unselfishly shared his wealth of research materials and knowledge. The California State University, Hayward, also assisted with small grants, travel funds, and release time.

On a personal note, I would like to thank my parents for more than can be listed here, but especially my mother for her gift of intellectual enthusiasm.

Finally, the biggest debt and the most thanks go to my wife Seda. She worked on the book, encouraged it, helped type it, and most importantly, put up with it. It could not have been done without her. A very special gratitude.

To all those who have helped me on this project, I offer my thanks. The remaining errors and shortcomings in the book are mine alone.

Contents

List of Tables

TABLES

1

The Changing Face
of Urban Transportation

Traveling in the United States in the 1920s was an experience very different from that of today. Then an American traveling between cities, or any long distance for that matter, would most likely have taken a train or a ship. Commercial air travel was as yet unknown, and travel by automobile was still only for the adventurous. Poor roads, unreliable automobiles, and a lack of motoring services generally limited such travel to short trips about town, commuting, and country outings. To get about in cities and towns across the country in 1920, our traveler would probably have walked, or taken a streetcar, a jitney, or perhaps a taxicab. In a few of the larger cities, subways and elevated railways were also available.

In 1920 the age of mass-produced (and consumed) autos was dawning. Private cars were increasingly plying the streets of both large and small cities and towns across the country, and commuting by auto was on the increase. It didn't take a lot of autos to clog roads that had not been built for such traffic and that were already congested with wagons and streetcars.[1] Public transit, essentially streetcars, still constituted the backbone of urban transportation in all but the smallest cities and towns.

Suburbs were already with us in 1920, most having developed around streetcar and interurban rail lines. Since these suburbs were still very dependent upon public transit, population densities were generally higher than the light densities that we associate with suburbia today. The auto-suburb still awaited a network of highways and expressways that would make widespread automobile commuting practical. Outside of the cities and the suburbs, the automobile held out its greatest promise to rural Americans who were still isolated on farms and in small towns across the country. Overcoming this rural isolation would take much more than the automobile, however; it would take a system of roads that would get the farmer out of the mud. The United States in 1920 did not yet have such a

1

road network, and the farmer as well as the intercity motorist had to contend with poor and often impassable roads.

Over the next five decades, this scenario was dramatically altered. By the early 1960s, an American traveling from one city to another would probably have flown or gone by automobile. In most cases, a traveler would have been hard pressed even to arrange a convenient trip by rail or ship. Most of the interurban commuter railroads had long since expired, and the mainline railroads had steadily reduced passenger service as patronage declined. By the 1960s a trip by automobile would most likely have been made over a network of multilane, limited-access freeways and highways that by then crisscrossed not only the countryside but also the cities as well. The backbone of this network of freeways and highways was the Federal Interstate and Defense Highway System. Serious construction of this freeway network, the world's largest construction project, had begun following the passage of federal legislation in 1956.[2] On the Interstate System one could travel hundreds of miles without a stoplight or cross traffic. The mud that had isolated farm dwellers was gone, as was much (although not all) of the "mud" of urban congestion that had earlier made urban and suburban commuting by auto so very difficult. The urban freeway system could "speed" a commuter or intercity traveler around or through urban areas that had previously been accessible only through traffic-congested city streets.[3]

By the 1960s, travel in the rural and small-town United States had become almost exclusively an automobile affair. Transit systems that had once served just about every small town had been early casualties of the automobile and/or the Great Depression. Transit systems in larger cities had fared better. But while they generally survived the depression, they did not escape the plague of declining patronage and financial distress. At the same time, the nature of public transit changed dramatically. Most of the old electric streetcars were gone—only a few survived in a handful of cities.[4] Once the ubiquitous mode of urban public transit, these electric streetcars had been steadily replaced by motor buses and, to a lesser extent, by electric buses and modern electric streetcars. (These will be discussed later in this chapter.) The financial distress continued to worsen, however, and by the 1950s privately owned transit companies were being replaced by public transit agencies. Transit districts were usually able to maintain only minimal, subsidized transit services.

In essence, by the 1960s a network of freeways and highways (made possible largely by federal financing) and a growing stock of private automobiles had replaced the privately owned local streetcar systems as the backbone of U.S. urban transportation. In addition, this same network of freeways and highways, along with the development of commercial airlines (again with considerable federal assistance), had replaced the privately owned passenger railroad network in this country. In terms of our getting about, we had certainly undergone a radical transformation since World War I.

The consequences of these changes were not confined to the transportation field. As our transportation patterns changed, so too did our life-styles, our surroundings, our consumption patterns, and even our culture. Social commentators have long noted, praised, lamented, and argued about the impact of the automobile and freeways on U.S. culture and life-styles. However one feels about these social changes, there can be no denying their significance. Nor is there any denying the economic impact of the automobile. Since the 1920s the production and sale of automobiles, the provision of automobile services and maintenance, the construction of roads and their servicing and maintenance, and the provisioning of other auto-related services have grown dramatically. One U.S. job in six became directly dependent on the automobile.[5]

CONTRIBUTING FACTORS

This far-reaching transformation in urban transportation can be seen as the result of changes in five related areas. First, urban automobile ownership grew immensely, and the automobile was increasingly used in urban transportation. Second, suburbanization increased and population densities declined, as the automobile freed the suburbanite from public transit. Transit patterns as well as the level of ridership changed as a result of this exodus to the suburbs. Third, public transit systems lost patrons, atrophied, and either expired or were rescued through public ownership and subsidies. Fourth, motor buses generally replaced the old electric streetcars as the backbone of our urban transit systems. Some modern streetcars and electric buses were also used as replacements for the aging streetcars, but motor buses, both gasoline and diesel, came to dominate the field. Fifth, government policy relating to urban transportation underwent radical changes. Public policy had originally emphasized providing public transportation through regulated transit franchises. This policy was generally replaced by one that emphasized the construction of urban expressways and freeways to solve urban transportation problems. This policy change was also accompanied by a dramatic increase in federal participation in the planning and funding of highways in general and urban highways in particular.

All of these developments were certainly interconnected, and while many of the relationships are undisputable, there are controversies or differences in interpretation in at least two areas. One controversy revolves around how the motorization of transit systems was related to their decline, and involves a very fundamental dispute as to whether buses were a help or a hindrance to transit firms in their competitive struggle with the automobile. The other issue involves differing interpretations as to the causes of the changes in federal transportation policy. The question here does not involve so much a factual dispute (as is the case in the bus controversy), but rather a disagreement over how to assign responsibilities (or blame) for political events. Both of these issues will take center stage in the analysis that follows. Each of the changes in urban transit discussed above will be considered primarily as it relates to these two issues.

MOTORIZATION AND DECLINE OF PUBLIC TRANSIT

Before 1920 just about every U.S. city and town of notable size had a public transit system, and the vast majority of transit vehicles used in these systems were electric streetcars. By 1920 the stock of streetcars was already getting old, with most cars dating from the early years of this century or earlier.[6] Even the newer streetcars being built were still using essentially the same technology as the older cars. There was, as yet, no really good alternative to the streetcar. This situation changed rapidly in the 1920s as two new types of transit vehicles were developed—the motor bus and the electric bus (or trolley coach). In addition, a newly designed streetcar was also developed in the mid-1930s as a replacement for the old streetcars.

The first of these new vehicles, the intracity motor bus, was a self-propelled vehicle that utilized either a gasoline or diesel internal-combustion engine. Gasoline buses were developed during the 1920s and were originally simply converted automobiles. Diesel buses were perfected by General Motors during the 1930s and were available after 1938. General Motors also perfected the other major technological change in the field, the automatic bus transmission, which was also available by the late 1930s. The intraurban motor bus should be distinguished from the interurban bus and the school bus. The intracity bus was lighter than the intercity bus and was not built to meet open-road conditions. In addition, since intracity buses operated in a stop-and-go urban environment, engine specifications, gear ratios, and soon were different from those of intercity buses. Operating costs, as well as vehicle prices, were correspondingly different. In contrast, school buses were generally cheap, light-weight, less durable vehicles, unsuited for use by either urban or interurban transit systems. The urban motor bus was built to operate in the same urban settings as the streetcar and trolley coach. The primary technological difference was in the type of motive power employed. Being self-propelled, motor buses were free of the overhead power transmission structures required by electric vehicles. Both streetcars and trolley coaches were self-propelled vehicles utilizing electric motors, but they drew their electricity from a power transmission grid. As such, neither trolley coaches nor streetcars could leave their power grid, as motor buses could. Their routes were thus circumscribed. Motor buses consequently enjoyed a flexibility that was not possible with the electric vehicles.[7]

Streetcars operated on tracks that generally ran down the middle of city streets. Entry to and exit from the cars therefore usually took place in the middle of the street. Streetcars were confined to their tracks and could not serve new areas until tracks were laid. In addition, they could not maneuver through traffic nor could they pass one another (thus express routes and local routes could not operate over the same track). Power was generally transmitted through an overhead cable system, but could be transmitted through a third rail. The two rails on which the streetcar operated served as the negative ground in each case. Streetcars had their motors mounted over the wheels in the truck assembly and utilized DC electricity. Either AC or DC power could be used, but if AC was transmitted, transformers along the route had to be employed. Track maintenance and, in most cases, the maintenance of the road surface around the tracks, was often the responsibility (and expense) of the streetcar transit company.

As noted, a new streetcar, the PCC car, was developed between 1929 and 1935.[8] The 1920s was a period of turmoil for streetcar companies, but as is often the case, it was also a period of significant innovation in streetcar technology. In 1929 an organization of street railroad officials met and formed a committee to create a radically improved streetcar design that would become the industry's standard. This committee, called the Electric Railway President's Conference Committee (or PCC), was headed by Dr. Thomas Conway, Jr., a well-known executive in the streetcar industry. Research was carried out under the direction of Professor C. F. Hirshfeld of the Detroit Edison Company. The committee spent more than five years and over one million dollars in their research and design efforts.

The product of their work was truly impressive. The new PCC cars were larger than the old streetcars, yet much lighter. They utilized the latest high-tensile steel and had streamlined bodies. Their acceleration was faster and smoother. The brakes were superior, as were the heating, lighting, and ventilation systems. The overall riding comfort was vastly improved; rubber-cushioned wheels and extensive rubber insulation made for a much quieter and smoother ride. In short, almost every aspect of the streetcar was significantly improved with the PCC car, including a reduction in both operating and power costs.

Following their introduction in 1935, PCC cars (or similar models brought out by other firms, such as Brill and Pullman-Standard, to compete with the PCC) soon dominated new streetcar sales, but never replaced or even outnumbered the older streetcars. This is an important point, since the available historical statistics on streetcar costs reflect not so much the costs of the newer PCC cars as they do those of the older cars. For example, the maximum number of PCC cars (including the Brills and Pullman-Standards) in use in North America in 1950 was 4,915,[9] out of a total of 13,800 electric streetcars in use that year.[10] Nonetheless, the PCC car was a significant technological breakthrough, and it was the only streetcar alternative available for modernizing transit systems.

The trolley coach (or electric bus) sought to combine the best of motor buses with the best of streetcars. It was essentially an electric bus that drew power from an overhead power system like a streetcar, but ran on rubber tires over city streets like a motor bus. The trolley coach was confined to its overhead system but was able to maneuver through traffic and to load and unload passengers at curbside, like a motor bus. This freedom was accomplished by having the power-collecting mechanism (a pole with a shoe on the end) swivel, thus allowing the vehicle to move up to 15 feet to either side of the overhead. Trolley coaches did require an additional overhead wire that was not needed by streetcars in order to serve as the negative ground. This could usually be inexpensively added to existing streetcar overhead when a streetcar system was being converted to trolley-coach operations.

The first trolley coach was run in 1911, but enjoyed only limited popularity through the early 1920s. Problems with tires, among other things, made it uneconomical. After the early 1920s the trolley coach disappeared, only to be revived when Salt Lake City installed a line in 1928. When Chicago began installing them in 1930, the trolley coach was back to stay and its use quickly spread. It was, however, never used as extensively as the motor bus (see Tables 1.1 and 1.3).

The basic characteristics of these three urban transit vehicles, which will be considered below,[11] can be summarized here. Streetcars, especially PCC cars, were larger and better able to handle large loads. They were, however, tied to their tracks and overhead and had to incur the construction and maintenance costs associated with these structures. Motor buses were completely free of overhead and tracks, both physically and financially. They were, however, generally recognized as more noisy, foul smelling, rougher riding, and generally less comfortable than either streetcars or trolley coaches. They were also generally smaller and less durable than the other two types of vehicles (particularly prior to World War II and the development of suspension systems that made large buses possible). Trolley coaches were not tied to tracks, but were constrained by electric overhead. Trolley coaches generally had the smoothness and the comfort of streetcars. They were smaller than the PCC car, but were as a rule larger than motor buses. In addition, trolley coaches had the speed and maneuverability through traffic of the motor bus, so that both motor buses and trolley coaches were superior to the streetcar in this regard. The trolley coach does seem to have been very successful in combining the best of both motor bus and streetcar.

In addition to the above, a few other points should be considered. An electrical failure would shut down all of the vehicles on a streetcar or trolley-coach line. The motor bus was immune to this problem. Good traffic managers could often do wonders in routing streetcars and trolley coaches around problem areas, but as the electric grid was reduced through motorization, this flexibility was reduced. On the other hand, cold weather might keep most of the buses (especially the diesels) from starting in the morning, so that transit operators often had to build storage sheds for them. The electric vehicles did not have this problem, since they could easily be stored outside.

In terms of operating characteristics, the electric vehicles enjoyed a power reserve that made them well suited to service on hills, and especially, able to handle peak overloads. Both San Francisco and Seattle, for example, found the trolley coach very practical. In addition, there seems little doubt that motor buses required more frequent maintenance and had lower life expectancy.

Urban transit systems were in a state of flux from the mid-1920s on. The outline of the major changes in the industry are shown in Tables 1.1, 1.2, and 1.3. Table 1.1 shows the replacement of streetcars by both motor buses and trolley coaches in terms of route miles and equipment. Only *urban* streetcar and motor-bus route miles are shown in Table 1.2. Interurban railway and intracity bus data are excluded. Table 1.3 clearly shows the overall decline in public transit ridership, as well as the substitution of motor buses and trolley coaches for streetcars. Only the war briefly forestalled the decline in streetcar ridership, while motor-bus and trolley-coach ridership increased dramatically into the late 1940s and early 1950s. One point should be made about the streetcar ridership figures in Table 1.3. These figures do include interurban ridership figures, and since

TABLE 1.1. Urban Transit Route Miles and Equipment

Year	Route Miles (Dec. 31)			Equipment (Dec. 31)		
	Railway Track	Trolley Coach	Motor Bus	Railway Cars	Trolley Coaches	Motor Buses
1970	2,081	583	112,700	10,600	1,050	49,700
1965	2,173	766	120,900	10,664	1,453	49,600
1960	3,143	2,196	108,700	11,866	3,826	49,600
1955	6,197	3,428	99,800	14,532	6,157	52,400
1950	10,813	3,513	98,000	22,986	6,504	56,820
1945	17,702	2,313	90,400	36,377	3,711	49,670
1940	19,602	1,925	78,000	37,662	2,802	35,000
1935	26,700	548	58,100	50,466	578	23,800

Source: U.S. Department of Commerce, *Historical Statistics of the United States, Colonial Times to 1970, Part 2* (Washington, DC: U.S. Bureau of the Census, 1975) p. 721.

TABLE 1.2. Streetcar and Motor Bus Route Miles

Year	Urban Street Railway Track Miles in Service	Urban Motor Bus Route Miles in Service
1922	28,906	1,370
1926	26,872	36,900
1930	23,898	60,900
1935	19,441	58,100
1940	15,163	78,000
1945	13,816	90,400
1950	8,071	98,000
1955	5,478	99,800

Source: Donald N. Dewees, "The Decline of American Street Railways," *Traffic Quarterly* 24 (October 1970): 564.

TABLE 1.3. Transit Ridership by Mode (in Millions of Passengers)

Year	Motor Bus	Trolley Coach	Streetcar
1923	661	—	13,569
1928	2,468	3	12,026
1932	2,136	37	7,648
1937	3,489	289	7,161
1942	7,245	898	7,290
1947	10,200	1,300	8,100
1955	7,250	1,202	1,207

Source: Donald N. Dewees, "The Decline of American Street Railways," *Traffic Quarterly* 24 (October 1970): 565. The figures are compiled from American Transit Association, *Transit Fact Book*, New York, 1944 and others. These data differ from statistics found U.S. Department of Commerce, *Historical Statistics of the United States. Colonial Times to 1970, Part 2* (Washington, DC: U.S. Bureau of the Census, 1975) p. 721. Since the above data exclude subway and elevated systems, they are preferable.

interurban ridership fell much more sharply than streetcar ridership, the decline in streetcar ridership is somewhat exaggerated, especially in the early 1930s. This does not, however, alter the basic trend in streetcar ridership.

Transit's decline can also be seen in the reduction in rides per capita. Rides per capita in cities with over 25,000 population fell dramatically during the depression. At mid-decade in the 1920s, rides per capita had stood at about 385 per year.[12] This fell to about 355 in 1929, but plunged to below 230 in 1933. Recovery over the next four years brought ridership back up only to about 255. By 1942, however, rides per capita had risen to about 340 and were still climbing rapidly as war production accelerated. As will be shown below, the decline was much less pronounced in larger cities, but the problem was the same.

A large part of the decline in ridership in the 1920s must certainly be attributed to the increasing use and ownership of the automobile. In addition, the curtailment and abandonment of transit services in smaller towns and on interurban lines must also have been factors. This reduction in transit services was itself the result of competition from the automobile. The precipitous decline in the early 1930s is hard to explain, however, in terms of automobile competition. Many of the systems most vulnerable to auto competition had already folded. Furthermore, the decline in automobile sales during the depression was equally dramatic (see Table 1.9 p. 14). Even the stock of automobiles declined at the depth of the depression. Between 1920 and 1929 automobiles per 1,000 population had increased 146 percent, but the increase between 1929 and 1938 was only 2 percent.[13]

The depression was probably most responsible for the decline in transit ridership in the 1930s. Declines of similar magnitude, or even greater, were not uncommon in other industries during those years. The transit industry seems to have followed rather closely the movement of the economy. For example, *Transit Journal* reported in 1936 that an index of transit passenger traffic (1928 = 100) had declined from about 97 in mid-1929 to a low of about 65 in the first quarter of 1933.[14] It also reported that the U.S. Bureau of Labor's Industrial Employment Index (1928 = 100) had declined from about 108 in mid-1929 to a low in the first quarter of 1933 of about 58. Industrial employment thus fell farther and faster than passenger traffic during the depression. Both indexes bottomed in the same quarter. Employment rebounded faster and more robustly than transit, but by mid-1935 the transit index was hovering around 75, while the industrial employment index stood at slightly above 80. Table 1.4 shows a similar pattern for Los Angeles transit. In addition to depressed business conditions, the increasing use of the five-day workweek during the depression hindered transit's recovery, since it effectively eliminated about 16 percent of the commuter ridership, transit's strength.

TABLE 1.4. Los Angeles Transit Ridership, 1929–1935

Year	Business Index	Passenger Traffic Index
1929	118	108
1930	100	100
1931	85	89
1932	68	75
1933	64	69
1934	68	77
1935	78	85

Source: California Railroad Commission, *Report on the Local Public Transportation Requirements of Los Angeles, Case No. 4002*, Los Angeles, CA, December 16, 1935, p. 12.

One additional factor in the decline ought to be stressed here. Aggregate transit figures generally fail to distinguish between trends in smaller cities and towns on the one hand, and trends in large metropolitan cities on the other. As will be shown later, the spread of the automobile definitely lagged in larger cities. The available evidence also suggests that transit fared quite differently in these two environments. For example, Table 1.5 shows how rides per capita per year in 1944 varied with the size of the community served. The overall average ridership two years earlier (1942) had been about 340. In 1944, larger cities greatly exceeded this average, while smaller cities had far lower ridership per capita. Table 1.6 shows the same dichotomy in terms of operating revenue. Again, larger cities fared better, actually increasing operating revenue in the late 1930s. The pace at which motor buses replaced streetcars during this period also varied with the size of the city. Table 1.7 shows the change in vehicles employed by transit companies between 1938 and 1948.[15] Again, the resilience of the streetcar in the larger cities is the salient point.

TABLE 1.5. Revenue Rides per Capita

City Population	Revenue Rides Per Capita
Over 1,000,000	423
500,000–1,000,000	420
250,000– 500,000	372
100,000– 250,000	302
50,000– 100,000	254
25,000– 50,000	118

Source: American Transit Association, *Transit Fact Book* (Washington, DC: American Transit Association, 1945), p. 4.

TABLE 1.6. Operating Revenue (thousands of dollars)

	Urban Population				
Year	Over 500,000	100,000–500,000	25,000–100,000	Under 25,000	Inter-Urban
1936	455,018	178,288	57,000	8,900	66,550
1937	459,303	181,000	59,100	9,250	70,500
1938	440,179	172,000	56,150	8,787	66,975
1939	452,910	176,300	57,500	8,990	67,000
1940	475,633	176,420	61,410	8,035	63,500
Change, 1936–1940 (percent)	4.5	–1.0	7.7	–9.7	–4.5

Source: *Transit Journal*, various years.

TABLE 1.7. Percentage Change in Vehicles, 1938–1948

City Population	Streetcars	Trolley Coaches	Motor Buses
Over 500,000	−26.9	+298.2	+146.6
100,000–500,000	−63.9	+143.9	+ 86.5
Less than 100,000	−60.6	+216.5	+131.3

Source: American Transit Association, Transit Fact Book (Washington, DC: American Transit Assiciation, 1949).

This last point should not be surprising, but it is often obscured in the aggregate figures. In addition, some writers seem to have failed to note the streetcars' resiliency in large cities, and have consequently been too quick in pronouncing the streetcar dead. For example, John Rae, a noted automobile historian, has argued that in regard to central city streetcar lines, "most were gone by the Second World War."[16] This certainly seems a bit premature. Tables 1.1, 1.2, and 1.3 also belie this conclusion.

Other writers have noted this distinction between large and small cities.[17] For example, Donald Dewees took note of this factor in his analysis of transit's decline in the 1920s:

> While the interurban railways lost half their passengers and 23 percent of their track miles, the urban systems were only undergoing an adjustment, with the elimination of a few marginal firms and some lightly traveled lines in smaller cities but little change for many companies. Track miles for urban systems decreased by only 13 percent, and revenue passengers by less than ten percent. The decrease affected primarily cities of less than 500,000 population, with passengers in cities of 50,000 to 500,000 inhabitants decreasing 25 percent during the period. From 500,000 to one million the reduction was 18 percent and in cities of over one million population it decreased only 4 percent.[18]

Another writer noted that it was not until 1933 that any large city was converted to an all-motor-bus system.[19] In that year San Antonio, Texas, with a population of about 200,000, became the first large city to completely motorize. The first small-city conversion had taken place in 1923.

In summary, the historical record regarding transit is fairly clear on a number of points. First, three new transit vehicles were generally available to transit companies that sought to modernize their old streetcar operations in order to meet the growing competition from private automobiles. Second, motor buses were most successful in replacing streetcars, especially in smaller towns and on outlying routes. This motorization, which began in the 1920s in smaller cities and towns and in the outlying areas of larger cities, continued through the 1950s. Streetcars on central-city lines in larger cities generally held out until after the Second World War, but only a handful of streetcar systems have continued to survive. Third, apart from the increase during the war, transit ridership declined during this period. This was accompanied by financial distress in the industry. Privately owned and operated transit systems disappeared and were often replaced with public agencies providing subsidized service. These trends are fairly uncontroversial; the real controversy begins with explanations of these events.

EXPLANATIONS: THE TRADITIONAL INTERPRETATION

The traditional explanation of the decline of urban transit has generally argued that it was the increasing popularity of the private automobile—and the resulting increase in automobile ownership and use—that was the root cause of all of these changes.[20] For example, John Rae essentially summarized the principal argument with the following:

> In spite of the handicaps under which it had to function, the motor vehicle in a surprisingly short time became the dominant element in urban transportation and therefore in urban development. Its first conspicuous effect was on existing transit systems. Two forces were at work here. First, as automobile ownership increased, people used their own cars for trips that they would formerly have made on public transportation. Second, railborne transit, especially streetcar and interurban lines, found itself in a losing contest with the motor bus, which was cheaper to operate and also enjoyed a flexibility that no railborne system could have.[21]

According to this generally accepted version of events, as lower prices and consumer installment credit brought the automobile within reach of the common man in the 1920s, the public enthusiastically took to the new machines. Almost every year, Detroit would set a new auto production record, only to surpass it the following year. This explosion in auto sales can be seen in Tables 1.8 and 1.9. As auto ownership grew, the auto was increasingly used for trips in both the urban and the rural United States (see Table 1.10). The increasing use of the private auto, it is argued, reduced the demand for public transit to the point where the latter became unviable. Patronage fell as people substituted their cars for streetcars. Falling patronage led to falling revenues. Costs could not be reduced as fast as revenues fell because of the substantial fixed costs associated with streetcar operations. Consequently, profits dropped, and chronic financial distress resulted.

In this interpretation, the substitution of motor buses for streetcars is explained as a reaction to this financial distress. As transit patrons forsook

TABLE 1.8. Motor Vehicle Sales and Registrations

Year	Factory Sales Passenger Cars		Factory Sales Motor Trucks and Buses		Motor Vehicle Registrations		
	Number (thousands)	Wholesale Value ($ millions)	Number (thousands)	Wholesale Value ($ millions)	Automobiles (thousands)	Buses (thousands)	Trucks (thousands)
1970	6,546.8	14,500	1,692.4	4,500	89,279.8	379.0	18,748.4
1965	9,305.5	18,380	1,751.8	3,733	75,257.5	314.2	14,785.7
1960	6,674.7	12,164	1,194.4	2,350	61,682.3	272.1	11,914.2
1955	7,920.1	12,452	1,249.1	2,020	52,144.7	255.2	10,288.8
1950	6,665.8	8,468	1,337.1	1,707	40,339.0	223.6	8,598.9
1945	69.5	57	655.6	1,181	25,796.9	162.1	5,076.3
1940	3,717.3	2,370	754.9	567	27,465.8	101.1	4,886.2
1935	3,273.8	1,707	697.3	380	22,567.8	58.9	3,919.3
1930	2,787.4	1,644	575.3	390	23,034.7	40.5	3,674.5
1925	3,735.1	2,458	530.6	458	17,481.0	17.8	2,569.7
1920	1,905.5	1,809	321.7	423	8,131.5	—	1,107.6
1915	895.9	575	74.0	125	2,332.4	—	158.5
1910	181.0	215	6.0	9	458.3	—	10.1

Source: U.S. Department of Commerce, Historical Statistics of the United States, Colonial Times to 1970, Part 2 (Washington, DC: US Bureau of the Census, 1975) p. 716.

13

TABLE 1.9. Domestic Automobile Sales (millions)

Year	Domestic Sales
1921	1.55
1922	2.42
1923	3.80
1924	3.31
1925	3.84
1926	3.91
1927	2.93
1928	3.78
1929	4.62
1930	2.95
1931	2.15
1932	1.25
1933	1.74
1934	2.44
1935	3.61
1936	4.11
1937	4.33
1938	2.16
1939	3.26
1940	4.21
1941	4.43

Source: Automobile Manufacturers Association, *Automobile Facts and Figures, 1947* (Washington DC: Automobile Manufacturers Association, 1947), p. 14.

the streetcars for their cars, transit companies sought to offset their lower revenues by reducing their costs, especially their heavy fixed costs. The motor bus, it is argued, was the solution both to the problem of large fixed costs and to the problem of inflexible streetcar routes in growing cities.[22] Motor buses were generally smaller vehicles, were priced lower than streetcars, and did not require electric overhead power lines or expensive tracks for their operation. These savings in capital costs, along with purportedly lower operating costs, made the motor bus an attractive alternative to the streetcar and a natural response to declining patronage. Consequently, the number of motor buses grew, while the number of streetcars fell. It was, however, according to this argument, too little, too late. The best that could be done was to delay the inevitable. For example, Mark Foster, discussing the decline of transit ridership in the 1920s, saw the bus in these terms: "A tapering off of street railway patronage concurrent with rapid urban growth signaled the beginning of the industry's decline; however, the robust health of the motor bus, a new means of public transportation, shrouded the

TABLE 1.10. Miles of Travel by Motor Vehicles (millions of vehicle miles)

Year	Total Travel	Urban Travel	Rural Travel
1921	55,027	—	—
1925	122,346	—	—
1929	197,720	107,409	90,311
1935	228,568	118,327	110,241
1940	302,188	149,993	152,195
1945	250,173	130,161	120,012
1950	458,246	218,248	239,998
1955	605,646	275,105	330,541
1960*	718,845	331,585	387,260
1965*	887,640	423,853	463,787
1970*	1,120,705	577,373	543,332

 * Includes Alaska and Hawaii.
 Source: U.S. Department of Commerce, *Historical Statistics of the United States, Colonial Times to 1970, Part 2* (Washington, DC: U.S. Bureau of the Census, 1975), p. 718.

impending demise."[23] Automobile competition was, according to this view, simply too formidable. Patronage continued its decline, revenues continued to fall, profits vanished, and the fate of viable public transit was sealed. In this interpretation, the substitution of buses for streetcars is viewed as a valiant but unsuccessful attempt at salvaging transit operations in the wake of the automobile.

This is essentially the conventional or traditional interpretation of these events. The reader is no doubt familiar with the argument in one form or another. Admittedly, there is an undeniable element of truth in this scenario, a very large element indeed. That the automobile was popular is undeniable. Suburbs did in fact grow rapidly, and the roads did become intolerably congested. Motorists did demand more roads, at least more of the roads that each intended to use. As roads were improved, automobile commuting became more practical, thus adding to the popularity of the auto. Transit firms did lose ridership, revenues, and profits to the auto, and the motor bus certainly must have been a viable alternative to the streetcar in many instances, especially on the lightly patronized lines.

All of this undeniable truth may not, however, constitute a full picture of the events, nor even an entirely accurate one. The extent of the damage done to public transit systems by the spread of the automobile has not been determined, it has only been assumed. In addition, a diametrically opposite view of the role of the motor bus in transit's decline has argued that this traditional explanation is incorrect on a number of key points. This makes for an interesting challenge to at least part of the traditional argument.

A "CONSPIRACY" TO MOTORIZE TRANSIT

Motor buses were considered to have been excellent alternatives to expensive and unprofitable streetcar operations in the traditional interpretation sketched above. A counterinterpretation holds that these buses were in fact a contributing (and probably major) factor in the financial distress that beset transit firms. Furthermore, this motorization, it is argued, was the result of a willful campaign designed to debilitate transit operations in this country, that is, a "conspiracy."

The most recent and controversial proponent of this challenge to the conventional argument is Bradford Snell.[24] Writing in *American Ground Transport* and testifying during Senate hearings in 1974, Snell argued that General Motors Corporation, along with its coconspirators, had purposefully sought to destroy electric public transportation systems in the United States by forcing an inferior technology on them—that is, the motor bus.[25] These electric transit systems had been, according to Snell's analysis, viable competitors with the automobile. They were therefore a major source of competition for General Motors in that company's principal area of interest, that is, in selling automobiles. Specifically, Snell contended that beginning in the 1920s and increasingly after 1930, General Motors diversified first into motor-bus production and then into operating transit systems. This ultimately led to the destruction of about 100 electric transit systems through its program of scrapping electric vehicles for inferior motor buses.[26] This program was carried out through various "front" organizations, such as National City Lines, Pacific City Lines, American City Lines, and others. These companies were created for such purposes by General Motors and its coconspirators, Standard Oil of California, Firestone Tire, Phillips Petroleum, and Mack Truck. Snell summarized the motorization campaign as follows:

> Due to their high cost of operation and slow speed on congested streets, however, these buses ultimately contributed to the collapse of several hundred public transit systems and to the diversion of hundreds of thousands of patrons to automobiles. In sum, the effect of General Motors' diversification program was threefold: substitution of buses for passenger trains, streetcars and trolley buses; monopolization of bus production; and diversion of riders to automobiles.[27]

This is essentially a "conversion-for-destruction" thesis, since the conversion to allegedly inferior motor buses was promoted in order to destroy one of the automobile's competitors. The argument in regard to public transit was that General Motors acquired transit properties and then forced its inferior products on the transit systems in order to destroy alternatives to the automobile. In a related charge Snell argued that General Motors exploited its monopoly in rail locomotive production, and its position as the largest railroad shipper, to force inferior diesel locomotives on railroads.[28] Only the streetcar/bus argument will concern us here. Both arguments, however, are diametrically opposed to the standard view that motor buses replaced streetcars and trolley coaches, and diesel locomotives (as opposed to electric locomotives) replaced steam locomotives because of their efficiency and lower costs. General Motors, in its reply to Snell, entitled *The Truth About American Ground Transport*, denied Snell's charges, arguing that "street railways failed for economic and demographic reasons which had nothing to do with a plot by General Motors. . . . Financial failure, of course, is precisely what spurred the conversion from streetcars everywhere. Buses were not a destructive force; they were largely credited by transit companies with staving off the collapse of many systems which survived."[29] General Motors also expressed a similar view about the beneficial effects of conversion to diesel locomotives.[30]

These allegations of conspiracy, if substantiated, should cause us to reevaluate our view of the decline of public transit.[31] They should also raise questions as to how such a thing could have occurred. What happened to our market and nonmarket safeguards against such abuse? Furthermore, if the parties involved actually pulled such a thing off, then they would certainly have to be "credited" with (or "acknowledged to possess," if the first term is offensive) an entrepreneurial talent that ranks up there with the best of them.

Before evaluating these charges, we will sketch the dimensions of the other issue, the formation of highway policy, which will also be of concern in this study.

URBAN TRANSPORTATION POLICY

Urban transportation policies in 1920 fell into basically two categories: policy regarding public transit systems, and road and highway policy. Public transit policy in 1920 was generally based on the franchise system. The transit franchisee, a private transit company, acquired a legal monopoly over public transit operations in the area covered by the franchise. In exchange for this monopoly, the transit company paid the city a franchise fee, often a percentage of gross receipts. It also had to provide additional services to the city, for example, maintaining the street around streetcar tracks, providing for snow removal, and furnishing free transportation for firemen and police personnel. Transit companies were willing to pay rather high franchise fees and to provide these extra services to the cities so long as the expected benefits from the transit monopoly justified the expense. Prior to the widespread use of the automobile, a franchise did assure the firm of a virtual monopoly over transit in the franchise area. Transit revenues, land grants, and real estate development profits, as transit brought new lands into the city, were often sufficient to make the transit franchise lucrative. The increasing use of the automobile, however, eroded the value of the monopoly, and the land profits were a one-shot deal. By the end of the 1920s the franchise could assure a monopoly in public transit but not an actual transit monopoly as people took to their cars. The value of the franchise thus declined, although many long-term contracts locked firms into franchise requirements no longer justified by the eroded monopoly. In addition, transit properties often issued bonds backed by their anticipated revenues, which often saddled companies with debt obligations far in excess of what had been necessary to build the system. Of course, this debt became unpayable when the monopoly was lost and revenues declined.

These factors often became a source of financial distress as well as conflict between many cities and their franchise holders during the 1930s and 1940s. They may also have influenced the choice of transit vehicles if, by changing vehicles, the terms of the franchise would be changed.

In addition to the fees and requirements paid to the city, the transit franchise generally operated under state regulation (and often local regulation as well). State regulation was generally carried out through a railroad commission (later, a public utilities commission). The railroad commission was charged with regulating fares, operating practices, safety, schedules, routes, and equipment.

As transit systems found themselves in worsening financial straits, this franchise system became increasingly untenable. Changes, however, either did not take place or did not happen fast enough to keep private transit alive. Transit operations were either discontinued or taken over by public transit agencies. The formal monopoly was still there, but it had become economically meaningless. Transit districts that replaced the private operators could provide only limited service, subsidized through general tax revenues. By the 1960s the goal of many transit districts was merely to provide minimal transit services for those unable to travel by private automobile.

The structure of transit regulation did not change significantly during the 1920–1960 period, so this aspect will not concern us. Regulatory bodies did have to deal increasingly with the changing nature of public transit and the problems of declining patronage, obsolete equipment, and so on. More important, the replacement of old streetcars did require regulatory approval, so the substitution of motor buses for electric vehicles had to have received regulatory approval. Questions regarding the performance of regulatory agencies in this regard will therefore be considered as they relate to the motorization.

The second area of urban transportation policy involved road and highway policy. With some exceptions, roads and highways had traditionally been the responsibility of state, city, and county governments. This was dramatically altered in the early years of this century, as the federal government got involved with highways. The two most important changes in highway policy in this regard were the increasing participation of the federal government in highway planning and construction; and the reorientation of federal highway policy away from an exclusively rural highway program to a program that emphasized urban highway needs. A review of the federal highway program through the 1920s clearly shows this increasing federal role. It also shows the beginnings of the second change, that is, the reorientation of federal policy to accommodate urban highway needs.

HIGHWAY POLICY TO 1930

The first major step toward an active federal participation in roads in the modern period began in 1893 with the formation of the Office of Road Inquiry (ORI) within the Department of Agriculture. As the name implies, this branch of the Department of Agriculture was primarily involved in collecting and disseminating highway information, conducting road research, and promoting good rural roads. The orientation was decidedly rural, with research to be carried out through the agricultural colleges and the agricultural experimental stations. One of the accomplishments of the ORI was the publication of a "Good Roads National Map" showing all macadamized and gravel roads in the country. In 1905 the ORI and the experimental stations that were doing research on rural roads were merged to form the Office of Public Roads and Rural Engineering. The rural emphasis was maintained.

The first federal road legislation was enacted in 1912, when $500,000 was appropriated for the purpose of aiding the states in improving rural postal roads. This continued the federal interest in rural roads that had begun with the Rural Free Delivery (RFD) service (begun around Charleston, West Virginia, on October 1, 1896). The RFD then spread rapidly until it was nationwide by 1900. This development was significant, because it provided the basis for increasing both state and federal participation in road finance. Roads had been, for quite some time, almost completely a local responsibility. State governments had only begun to get back into road improvements with the enactment of legislation in New Jersey in 1891. The spread of RFD had also increased this state participation. More important, however, the RFD provided a rationale for federal participation, because the mail was a federal responsibility. Through a need for rural postal road improvements, the federal government moved after 1912 from an information gathering and disseminating stage to active participation in road improvements.

This new federal participation was more firmly established in 1916 with the passage of the Federal Aid Road Act of 1916, better known as the Good Roads Act. For all practical purposes, this legislation began the active federal highway program. The legislation of 1912 was precedent setting, but clearly underfunded. The 1916 legislation established a 50 percent matching-funds funding formula, which was to characterize federal-state financing arrangements for the next 40 years (with a few exceptions). The legislation of 1916 authorized and appropriated $75 million to be spent over the next five years, $5 million in the first year and increasing to $25 million in the fifth year. The 1916 legislation also "created" state highway departments. Funds were dispensed to the states on condition that they establish and maintain working highway departments, which all of the states quickly did.

The 1916 legislation was called the Goods Roads Act not only because it provided, for the first time, a sound program for providing good roads, but also because it represented the successful culmination of the "Good Roads Movement." A brief analysis of this first lobbying effort is informative. Agitation for good roads, carried out largely on an individual basis, had begun after the Civil War.[32] This agitation was, however, to remain isolated and scattered until the rapid spread and popularity of the bicycle. Bicyclists immediately encountered problems with poor roads and the same hostility toward their machines that was later vented on automobile users; for example, bicyclists received the same complaints about "scorching" (the then current term for speeding) and complaints that bicycles scared horses. In 1880 an organization of bicyclists, the League of American Wheelmen, was founded to promote the bicyclists' need for better roads, more roadside facilities, and the protection of their legal rights. The bicyclists soon became the dominant force in the Good Roads Movement.[33]

Joining the bicyclists in agitating for better roads were various rural and farm organizations. For example, the campaign for good roads was picked up by the National Grange and the populist movement. These rural interests, along with the bicyclists, founded the National League for Good Roads (NLGR) in 1892 and held the first "Good Roads Convention" in Washington, D.C., the following year. The expressed goal was to "lift our people out of the mud."[34] The formation of the ORI by the Department of Agriculture was hailed as a step in the right direction, and agitation for federal participation continued with the NLGR's promotion of the RFD program.

The same year in which the ORI was established, 1893, was also the year in which the Duryea brothers had operated the first American-made automobile on the streets of Springfield, Massachusetts. This event was certainly not the beginning of an automobile "industry" by any means. The automobile was still an experimental curiosity. By the end of the decade, however, both automobile drivers and producers had begun to take an active interest in the Good Roads Movement. These early efforts usually involved long-distance promotion trips designed to demonstrate both the potential of the automobile and the need for better roads. One such "exploit" was a trip from Detroit to the 1901 auto show in New York City, made by Roy P. Chapin, president of the Hudson Motor Company (and later one of the auto industry's chief lobbyists).[35] The trip took seven and one-half days, with Chapin driving 150 miles of the distance on the Erie Canal tow path, because it was better than the roads!

These early exploits soon gave way to increased and more practical commitments to better roads by automobile interests. One such effort was the Lincoln Highway. Conceived by Carl Graham Fisher, a promoter of the Indianapolis Speedway, the proposal called for a coast-to-coast, hard-surfaced highway.[36] This attracted considerable interest in the automobile industry, especially from Chapin of Hudson and Henry B. Joy, head of the Packard Motor Car Company. A Lincoln Highway Association was formally organized in 1913. Although segments of the highway were actually opened and marked, high costs and problems with different state and local authorities led to the disbanding of the group after passage of the 1916 legislation. Groups such as the Automobile Association of America and the Automobile Club of St. Joseph also became involved in the good roads movement. It is important to note, however, that the movement remained essentially rural, with automobile interests actively promoting rural road programs. This harmony of interests was to last until the early 1930s.

Meanwhile, the Post Office Appropriation Act of 1919 directed the secretary of war to transfer to the secretary of agriculture all surplus war materials suitable for highway construction. Between 1920 and 1927, equipment valued at $224.6 million, mostly trucks and road-working equipment, was turned over to the Department of Agriculture under that mandate. This piece of legislation is indicative of the strong connection between postal roads, rural interests, and highways during this early period. It is also of interest as an example of the developing relationship between highway interests and the War Department. Was there a connection between the automobile industry's extensive participation in the war effort, and these grants? The record is presently unclear, but it is an interesting possibility.

A second major piece of highway legislation was passed in 1921. The Federal Highway Act of 1921 set up what was later to become known as the Federal Aid Primary System. The act limited the use of federal funds to 7 percent of the total rural roads in a state. Funds were to be available to the states for the routes they selected for the primary system on a 50–50 matching-funds basis. Again, only rural roads were permitted in the system, with urban areas explicitly excluded. The 1921 act also authorized and appropriated $75 million for fiscal year 1922. This was the last year in which authorizations and appropriations were combined. Legislation in 1923 began the policy of authorizing funds, but of not actually appropriating them until needed. This allowed for contractual arrangements with the states for funds to be provided as work was completed. Over 200,000 miles of rural roads were provided for under the 7 percent provision.

Legislation in 1928 further defined the exclusively rural orientation of the federal highway program[37] and made federal funds available "within municipalities of 2,500 population or more, along those sections of highway on which the houses were . . . more than 200 feet apart on average."[38] This has been interpreted by some as a half-hearted beginning at urban aid.[39] Another interpretation, however, seems more valid. The 200-foot spacing of houses would virtually exclude *any* urban area from consideration. The legislation appears to me to have been simply an effort to further define the exclusive rural nature of the roads program and to allow for the construction of city approach roads that were essentially rural but were technically located within urban boundaries. Clearly, the funds could be used in cities only in this manner.

The federal aid highway program was quite successful through the 1920s. By the end of the decade the 7 percent limit was being reached, and there was general agreement that the rural roads program had accomplished its original goal of "pulling the farmer out of the mud."[40] For this reason, and due to the changes in highway activities brought about by the onset of the Great Depression, a qualitative change in the highway program (and the political forces behind the program) can be seen in the early 1930s. Many highway advocates began to recognize that there were limits on what further could be gained through a continuation of the rural roads program. This recognition began to weaken and divide the coalition of highway supporters that had been successful in getting the federal program started. For example, the automobile industry was one group of highway supporters that felt that the rural program had essentially outlived its usefulness. James Cope of Chrysler (representing the Automobile Manufacturers Association), when he testified during congressional hearings in 1953, summarized how the automobile industry's views had changed. As the industry saw it, "the great road-building era that began in the 1920s ended in 1931."[41] By 1939 the auto industry was openly complaining of the waste of resources that was occurring in the *rural* roads program, because in their view the point of diminishing returns had long since been reached in this area. For example, in 1939 Paul Hoffman of the Automobile Safety Foundation, an industry lobbying group, wrote glowingly of the success of the rural roads programs: "We have spent a mint of money for roads in this country in the last thirty years, and, on the whole, we have done a grand job. We have pretty well pulled ourselves out of the mud."[42]

He then went on, however, to criticize the continued construction of rural roads that would serve only limited traffic. "But along with these fine things, we've done silly and senseless things. Either because we didn't know better, or hadn't changed our ways of thinking fast enough from horse-and-buggy days, or perhaps because some petty politician who had the spending of our money willfully thought it would be jolly to put a road here, or there, or younder."[43] The real problem was now the "mud" in the cities, that is, the "mud" of urban traffic congestion.

The automobile industry was certainly not the only group to criticize the continuation of the rural roads program, although it was one of the first and one of the most vocal. The important point here is that by the onset of the depression, the rural roads program had been successful in overcoming the worst problems of rural isolation. Up until that time, just about everyone in the coalition seems to have been satisfied with, or at least tolerant of, the exclusively rural orientation of the highway program. By the early 1930s, however, a split began to develop between rural and urban interests, as urban interests balked at further extensions of the rural program. Rural interests, on the other hand, had sought just such an extension. They were successful in 1932 in effectively removing the 7 percent ceiling by enacting legislation that would progressively raise the ceiling by 1 percent increments.[44] This provided for an almost limitless expansion of the rural primary system, although funding remained a limiting factor.

The story of highway politics from the late 1930s to the early 1950s is essentially one of struggle between rural and urban interests. This conflict was then gradually superseded, prior to 1956, by intense struggles over highway financing. Each of these struggles also came to center on the Interstate Highway System, especially its urban components, and the expanded federal aid necessary for the construction of this new system. The Interstate System was established in 1944, but adequate funding was not provided at that time. Construction of the system was left to the states, which generally ignored it. Until the early 1950s, rural highway interests still had the strength to block increased federal aid to urban highway construction.

Highway politics from 1944 through 1956 came to be dominated by an intense political campaign to provide adequate funding for the Interstate System. This effort culminated in the enactment of a National System of Interstate and Defense Highways in 1956 and, more important, adequate funding provisions. The long standing rural versus urban dispute was essentially put to rest, as were the conflicts over the financing arrangements that had been the system's last hurdle. The reorientation of federal highway policy was basically (although not fully) completed.

Highway Policy: An Entrepreneurial Approach

Explanations of these changes in highway policy generally take two courses. One type of explanation tends to emphasize the public's increased demand for more and better roads. This "derived" demand, it is argued, stemmed from new suburban life-styles and the public's increasing use and ownership of automobiles. People wanted and needed more roads, and the government delivered. The freedom provided by the private automobile allowed people to escape the crowded city for the good life in the suburbs, suburbs that no longer had to be clustered around streetcar or commuter rail lines. People no longer had to live near their work, nor did they have to live near transit lines. And as the auto suburb became viable, a vigorous real-estate boom and economic expansion ensued in these areas, further fueling interest in them.

The change in road policy, it is held, was the inevitable consequence of the auto and this suburban migration. The logic of this quest for freedom and relief from city overcrowding through a flight to the suburbs was, however, flawed. It could not work if everyone were doing it, at least not without a vastly improved road system that allowed the auto to work its magic. But that did not deter the exodus. Since these road systems were not in place in the 1920s, the growth of automobile ownership and the suburban migration created a growing demand for more roads to relieve automobile congestion. Of course, providing new roads set off a "vicious circle" process: More roads made the automobile and the suburbs more useful and desirable; more autos were sold; ad infinitum. That initial decision to accommodate the automobile was indeed a momentous (or fateful) decision. Most urban planners apparently saw the automobile as the solution to city transportation problems, not to mention urban crowding and urban problems in general.[45] That they by and large failed to see, or chose to ignore, the nature of the problem in this relationship between roads, suburbs, and automobile ownership is a telling criticism.

Public transit was also adversely affected in this process. Population densities declined and the growth of new suburban areas changed transit patterns. This posed an urgent and critical question as to what to do with transit operations. Should transit be upgraded, extended to new areas, or should public transit be played down in favor of a transportation policy organized around new road systems? Proponents of this interpretation essentially argue that, given the growing popularity of the automobile, the choice was inevitable: more roads for more cars. There is no doubt, they argue, that the public freely chose the automobile. As John Rae put it,

> It should be unnecessary to make the point that the American people freely chose the mobility represented by the motor vehicle, but much of the criticism directed at the automobile suggests otherwise, although none of the critics has ever explained the process by which cars were imposed on reluctant recipients. People have bought and used automobiles

because they preferred this kind of mobility to alternative forms of ground transportation. The issue has been defined by Jerome B. Wiesner, formerly Science Advisor to the President of the United States and now president of the Massachusetts Institute of Technology: "The major exploitations of scientific ideas and inventions were done by individuals, and their ideas were accepted or not on the basis of a generalized vote by society. Society decided it wanted the automobile, and it bought the automobile."[46]

It is then argued that a political consensus emerged around this need to satisfy the public's demand for more roads. From a more-roads policy to a policy of more expressways and eventually to a call for urban freeways was simply a logical extension of the original argument. A few problems remained, however. First, urban expressways and freeways were prohibitively expensive for city and state governments. Consequently, federal aid became indispensable to the fruition of the auto-dominated transportation system. Second, in order to bring Americans the urban freeways they demanded, it was necessary to overcome political inertia, rural opposition to urban highways, and partisan political interests.

While part of this scenario is intuitively obvious, taking this for a full or even a primary explanation does not seem wise. This approach tends to ignore the actual political process. Few political processes are as spontaneous as this interpretation implies. Who initiated the process and why? Where was the "entrepreneurial spark," if you will? For example, Congress was ahead (no value judgment intended) of the public on the interstate issue. In fact, very few people knew of the system before 1956, let alone had an opinion on it. A poll taken after 1956 found that only 2 percent of the people polled knew what the Interstate System was.[47] So if the public was not clamoring for the interstate, who was? What motivated them? Were they successful in meeting some or all of their objectives? Focusing on the "derived demand" requirement of more roads tends to slight the entrepreneurial aspects of these promotional activities. The distinction being drawn here is similar to the distinction between "initiative" and "reaction."

The other type of common interpretation of these events generally seeks to show that the Interstate System, and especially its urban segments, were the result of a political conspiracy perpetrated by vested economic interests.[48] The Interstate System is seen as a system that the public either did not want or did not know about. It was nonetheless pushed through by bought-off politicians and lobbyists. Instead of being viewed as a positive political response to a popular demand for relief from traffic congestion, this interpretation views the passage of the 1956 legislation as a political travesty. It also tends to deny that the public's demand for automobiles and roads was as spontaneous or genuine as the first interpretation insists. This perspective essentially sees urban freeways as destroying traditional life-styles as well as public transit. Urban freeways therefore created a "derived demand" for automobiles by removing alternatives to the automobile.

In extreme form, this approach appears as naive as a crude version of the first type of explanation would be. Writers in this vein seem either shocked or concerned that people, industry groups, and lobbyists worked vigorously for political objectives that they considered in their best, selfish interest. When they encounter this, a conspiratorial interpretation is given. But if people will act in their best interest elsewhere, why not in the political arena? Could one reasonably expect less, or more? Of course, it is necessary to inquire into the political system's ability to perform in these kind of cases. For example, does our lobbying system break down in cases where the rewards are very high for specific groups or individuals, yet the costs of programs are to be dispersed over the general population? Or one might ask whether there is a counterpart to the check of market competition in the political arena? These are legitimate questions in the highway issue. Unfortunately, this interpretation does little to address these questions, being too preoccupied with conspiracy. In addition, entrepreneurial activities are again ignored.

Controversies in the area of highway policy center primarily on questions of interpretation, rather than on factual disputes. This study will proceed in these choppy waters under the conviction that there is benefit in trying to determine what people wanted, how they acted on their wants, and how successful or unsuccessful they were in accomplishing their goals. This conviction applies to all actions, those in the private sector as well as to those relating to the public sector and political issues. The fact that political issues and public policies entail collective actions does not negate any part of this conviction; it only makes the task more difficult.

In addition, this study will try to avoid slipping into either the *assumption* of conspiracy or the converse, the *assumption* of a harmonious pluralistic consensus. Either of these arguments should be seriously considered if they can be substantiated through empirical investigation, but they should not be simply assumed. Assuming either position tends to cripple the analysis. The assumption of conspiracy tends to exaggerate the power of the conspirators by underestimating the opposition as well as the safeguards in the system. The investigator therefore cannot follow the actual drama of events, because his or her world is populated by super-villains and incompetent victims. Entrepreneurship cannot be appreciated in such an easy contest. On the other hand, the assumption of harmonious consensus is equally debilitating, because it essentially assumes that all actions somehow resulted from some sort of collective appreciation of an objective problem. For example, the public needed roads and they got roads as soon as enough people (especially public officials) realized it. This seems to eschew entrepreneurship as well. This approach also seems to detract from efforts at determining which groups were most successful in getting what they wanted. Suggestions that it might be possible or even necessary to trace a political act back to the efforts of *some* of its backers are often rejected as automatically implying a conspiracy. It need not.

The study at hand will strive to document the activities of groups and individuals who played the role of entrepreneurs, political entrepreneurs if you will, in the successful promotion of urban highways. Of course, entrepreneurship is also present in the substitution of buses for streetcars. This is an essential link between these two events. Interpreting both of these events as the result of entrepreneurial actions will be a goal of this study.

PLAN OF STUDY

The study that follows will concern itself with a basic question: Why did all those streetcars disappear, and how and why did we get all those urban freeways and highways? This is a big question and one that cannot be entirely answered at this time. A complete treatment of this question, given the state of our knowledge of these recent events, would be premature. Consequently, attention will be focused primarily on the role of firms in the U.S. automobile industry in motorizing public transit and in influencing highway policy. It is hoped that this will broaden our knowledge of these events, as well as add to our understanding of the entrepreneurial aspects of these activities.

The following chapter will explore the economics of public transit as it relates to the motorization issue. Chapter 3 will consider the evidence supporting the existence of a conspiracy to destroy transit through motorization. Chapter 4 considers the conspiracy in view of other factors contributing to the decline of transit. The next two chapters (6 and 7) consider the highway policy issue. The closing chapter offers some conclusions and interpretations regarding both issues.

NOTES

1. For an interesting and readable account of the problems brought about by the early growth of automobile use and ownership in Chicago, see Paul Barrett, *The Automobile and Urban Transit* (Philadelphia: Temple University Press, 1983).

2. The Interstate System was inaugurated in 1944, but was grossly underfunded. Consequently, little of the system was contructed until legislation in 1956 resolved the funding problem.

3. The speed of traffic on urban freeways is debatable. Rush-hour traffic, as any commuter knows, can only rarely be characterized in such a fashion. On the curious side, motorists' disappointment with the ability of urban freeways to live up to their advance billing often generated a rather strange response, that is, a cry for more urban freeways.

4. For a description of some of the surviving systems, see Stanley I. Fischler, *Moving Millions* (New York: Harper and Row, 1979), especially pages 105–213.

5. *Automobile Facts and Figures, 1968* (Detroit: Automobile Manufacturers Association, 1968), p. 33. This figure is for 1963, but similar figures have been cited for earlier years, going back to World War II. For a fuller discussion of the impact of the automobile on the U.S. economy as a whole, or individual industries, see John Rae, *The Road and Car in American Life* (Cambridge, MA: M.I.T. Press, 1971), especially pages 44–49; 101–108.

6. For example, Steve Easlon, in a history of the Los Angeles Railway (LARY), reports that practically all of LARY's streetcars were considered obsolete in 1932. About 70 percent of the company's 1,130 streetcars had been in service for 25 years or more. Yet LARY could order only 90 new PCC cars before the Second World War. See Steve Easlon, *The Los Angeles Railway Through the Years* (Anaheim, CA: Easlon Publications, 1973) pp. 32–35. For a full description of LARY equipment, see California Railroad Commission, Transportation Department, Research Division, *Report on Urban Mass Passenger Transportation Facilities and Requirements of Los Angeles, Case No. 4461* vol. 2, 1940, especially pp. 223–39.

7. Technologically, the motor bus was such more flexible. The practical significance of this flexibility, however, is a more complex problem that will be considered in Chapter 4.

8. For an extended account of this development, see William D. Middleton, *The Time of the Trolley,* (Milwaukee, WI: Kalmbach Press, 1967), pp. 125–26. The discussion of PCC car characteristics here draws heavily from this source.

9. Harold E. Cox, *PCC Cars of North America* (Philadelphia: Philadelphia Community Press, 1963), p. 4.

10. American Transit Association, *Transit Fact Book* (Washington, DC: American Transit Association, 1951), p. 2.

11. Two other urban transit systems were subways and elevated railways. These systems were electric, but differed from streetcar operations in that they operated on a controlled right-of-way instead of on city streets. This increased their speed, but also greatly increased their construction costs. Subway construction was the most expensive, since structures had to be underground. Elevated railways had their track constructed *over* public streets. Costs of operation of both subways and the elevated rails were very different from those of streetcars. Neither of these two urban operations will be considered in the study that follows, since data were not available and because they are not directly related to the motorization issue.

Interurban electric railroads differed from streetcar operations in that they *connected* cities rather than operating within the city. As such, their operating costs and capital costs were different from streetcar costs. Interurbans often operated on private rights-of-way or along the *side* of highways. Capital costs often included right-of-way purchase costs. Track maintenance costs were probably lower than in streetcar operations, since the surrounding road surface usually did not have to be cared for. Power transmission costs were higher, however, since interurbans were almost always required to transmit AC to avoid serious line power losses. This necessitated DC transformers in practically all cases.

The principal differences between streetcars and interurbans, however, were in the areas they served and in their competitiveness. By the mid-1930s the interurbans wre uncompetitive in all but a few cases. They could not compete with the automobile or the interurban buses. As will be shown, this was *not* true of the urban streetcars, at least in the larger cities.

Finally, commuter railroads differed from all of the above. They were either steam, electric, or diesel (actually diesel-electric) and were trains in the true sense, that is, a locomotive pulling cars, as opposed to self-propelled cars. They always operated in the vicinity of an urban area and their beginnings were often to be found in a railroad's desire to generate extra revenue on its established long-haul lines. To generate additional traffic, the railroad would offer special reduced rates for travel between the city and its outskirts—the regular fares were "commuted." The commuter railroads differed from the interurbans on a number of other significant points. They often served a large, single metropolitan area, with a large traffic volume. Furthermore, the commuter railroads often remained competitive in their niche, which was not true of the interurbans.

12. ATA, *Transit Fact Book*, 1943, p. 7. Also, Donald N. Dewees, "The Decline of American Street Railways," *Traffic Quarterly* 24 (October 1970), p. 565, cites the following figures on rides per capita per year (drawn from ATA data):

1917	260
1925	270
1930	226
1935	171
1940	176
1945	305
1950	195
1955	124

These figures vary from those cited in the text. The probable reason stems from restricting the data to cities of 25,000 or more in the text.

13. "Transit vs. the Automobile," *Transit Journal* 84 (January 1940):4.

14. Morris Buck, "More Riding and More Revenue in 1935," *Transit Journal* 80 (January 1936):7. Figures here are from a graph on page 7.

15. It is likely that the decline in streetcars in cities with less than 10,000 population was *only* 60.6 percent because a large number of these streetcars had not survived the depression, or had already been replaced by motor buses in the 1920s and early 1930s.

16. Rae, *Road and Car*, p. 209.

17. On the prevalence of motor buses in smaller and mid-sized cities, see "Yellow Truck and Coach," *Fortune* (July 1936), p. 63. In addition, an American Transit Association summary of motorized properties and lines and streetcar abandonments through 1936 clearly shows that the conversion was almost entirely confined to small towns and outlying routes in larger cities. See letter from Guy C. Hecker, General Secretary, American Transit Association, to O. A. Smith, President, Pacific Electric Railway Co., Pacific Electric Exhibit No. 49 in Application Case 20567, filed July 1, 1937, before the California Railroad Commission.

18. Donald N. Dewees, "Decline of the American Street Railways," p. 569.

19. John Anderson Miller, *Fares, Please!* (New York: Dover, 1960), pp. 162–63.

20. We will sketch a "traditional" interpretation that cannot properly be attributed to any source or sources. It will be readily recognizable by the reader, who will have seen it before, but would probably be hard pressed to identify an original source.

21. Rae, *Road and Car*, pp. 208–9.

22. The argument that the trolley car (and presumably the trolley coach) was too "inflexible" is commonplace. See, for example, Rae, *Road and Car*, p. 277. This argument will be evaluated in Chapter 4.

23. Mark S. Foster, *From Streetcar to Superhighway* (Philadelphia: Temple University Press, 1981), p. 49.

24. These charges did not originate with Snell, although he is certainly the focus of the current controversy. In addition to the citations in the next footnote, see Washington Society of Professional Engineers, *A Request For Grand Jury Action in the Matter of The Seattle Transit System, Paper No. CA-166* (April 1968); also by the same authors, *An Analysis of Simon and Curtin's Report to the Mayor's Transit Study Committee of Seattle Dated September 1964, Paper No. CA-165* (December 1966); Walter Hatch, "Elmer Van Ness' Conspiracy Theory," *Seattle Sun*, May 21, 1980, p. 9; "City Lines," editorial, *Interurban* (February 1946); "N.C.L. Found Guilty," *Interurban* (June 1949).

25. Bradford Snell, *American Ground Transport* (1973), reproduced as an appendix to U.S., Congress, Senate, Committee on the Judiciary, *The Industrial Reorganization Act: Hearings before a subcommittee of the Senate Committee on the Judiciary on S. 1167, Part 4A*, 93rd Cong., 2d sess., 1974. Hereafter referred to as "Snell." Snell's testimony, as well as that of former San Francisco Mayor Joseph Aliotto and Los Angeles Mayor Thomas Bradley can be found in U.S., Congress, Senate, Committee on the Judiciary, *The Industrial Reorganization Act, Hearings before a subcommittee of the Senate Committee on the Judiciary on S. 1167, Part 3*, 93rd Cong., 2d sess., 1974. Both support Snell's allegations. Testimony by George Hilton refutes these allegations.

26. Snell, p. A-32.

27. Ibid., p. A-27.

28. Snell also argued that essentially the same conversion-for-destruction process had occurred in the railroad industry, whereby General Motors first diversified into the production of diesel locomotives (technically, diesel-electric locomotives) in the 1930s and then forced the railroads to convert their steam and electric operations to diesel power. General Motors thereby acquired a monopoly in the locomotive field and, even more important, purposely destroyed the competitiveness of the railroads, vis-á-vis automobiles and trucks, by forcing the inferior diesel technology on them. Again General Motors' alleged motivation was to increase its automobile sales by destroying transit alternatives to the auto.

29. General Motors, *The Truth about "American Ground Transport—A Reply by General Motors"* (1974), reproduced as an appendix to *The Industrial Reorganization Act*. Quoted from pp. A-112, A-123.

30. For General Motors' denial of Snell's allegations regarding diesel locomotives, see General Motors, *Truth*, pages A-110 through A-112.

. 31. The term "conspiracy" is used here in reference to this "conversion-for-destruction" argument. It is the term used by Snell and others. General Motors, Standard Oil of California, Firestone Tire, Philips Petroleum, and National City Lines were convicted of antitrust violations in 1949. "Conspiracy" here involves a conspiracy to monopolize the motor-bus market and the motor-bus supply market. On the antitrust case, see *United States v. National City Lines, Inc., et al.*, 186 F. 2 562, January 3, 1951.

32. Rae, *Road and Car*, p. 27.

33. See Rae, *Road and Car*, p. 29, on the dominant role of the bicyclists in this campaign for better roads.

34. Ibid., p. 30.

35. Ibid., p. 34.

36. Ibid., p. 36.

37. Public Law 478, 70th Congress.

38. George M. Smerk, *Urban Transportation: The Federal Role* (Bloomington: Indiana University Press, 1965) p. 123.

39. Ibid.

40. Philip H. Burch, Jr., *Highway Revenue and Expenditure Policy in the United States* (New Brunswick, NJ: Rutgers University Press, 1962), p. 220.

41. Testimony of James Cope in U.S., Congress, House, Committee on Public Roads, *National Highway Study, Hearings before a Subcommittee on Roads of the House Committee on Public Roads*, 83rd Cong., 1st sess., 1953, p. 415.

42. Paul G. Hoffman, "American goes to Town," *Saturday Evening Post*, April 29, 1939, p. 1. Reproduced and circulated by the ASF. Citations are to the reprint.

43. Ibid., p. 1.

44. Burch, *Highway Revenue and Expenditure Policy*, p. 230.

45. On how and why planners felt and acted in this regard, see Mark S. Foster, *From Streetcar to Superhighway*.

46. Rae, *Road and Car*, p. 153. Quote from Jerome B. Wiesner, "The Impact of Scientific Technology on Industry and Society," *Conference on Space, Science, and Urban Life*, (Washington, DC: National Aeronautics and Space Administration, 1963), p. 69.

47. This poll was apparently taken in the mid-1950s, after all of the extensive lobbying and public relations campaigning for the interstate. See Burch, p. 259, citing William L. Garrison, *Connectivity of the Interstate Highway System* (Seattle: Department of Geography, University of Washington, 1960), p. 1.

48. In this vein, for example, see Helen Leavitt, *Superhighway-Superhoax* (Garden City, NY: Doubleday, 1970); Ben Kelley, *The Pavers and the Paved* (New York: Donald W. Brown, 1971); A. Q. Mowbray, *Road to Ruin* (Philadelphia: Lippincott, 1969); Snell, *American Ground Transport*, pp. A-21 through A-27. These can be compared and contrasted with Mark Rose, *Interstate Express Highway Politics, 1941-1956* (Lawrence, KS: Regents Press of Kansas, 1979).

2

The Economics of
Urban Public Transit

The logical starting point in evaluating the allegations of a conspiracy to destroy urban transit is the charge of motor-bus inferiority. This is the crux of the argument, because the purported ill effects of motorization essentially rest on this point. The conspiracy argument holds that due to the inferiority of motor buses vis-à-vis electric transit vehicles, this forced motorization saddled already struggling transit firms with inefficient, unpopular, and costly transit vehicles. Costs therefore rose as revenues declined, thus compounding the problems of transit companies. This, it is argued, was enough to seal the fate of transit systems.[1]

It should also be obvious that acceptance of any evidence or data purporting to document the existence of such a conspiracy requires a prior demonstration that motor buses were inferior.[2] If motor buses were inferior, then a wholesale motorization campaign would be suspect, to say the least. But if the motor bus was not inferior, then such a motorization campaign could not be considered a conspiracy, regardless of how covert, devious, or suspicious other actions may have appeared. There would simply have been nothing to have conspired about.

At this point it is necessary to consider what would have constituted "inferiority." In what sense were motor buses inferior? While the question can be and has been approached in different ways, only one criterion appears legitimate—profitability. Suggestions that we use the public's preference for vehicles, or vehicle characteristics, or mechanical efficiency, or relative pollution levels, or revenues alone, or costs alone, or the compatibility of a type of vehicle with an urban master plan, are all unacceptable. While each of these is certainly of interest, and may have been of paramount importance in another context, our criterion must be economic efficiency, that is, profits. In the question at hand we are concerned with the purported financial weakening and, in many cases, the demise of urban transit as a result of motorization. The profitability of motor buses vis-à-vis the electric vehicles is therefore the relevant issue.

Finally, it should also be reemphasized that the traditional interpretation of the decline of urban transit and the conspiracy argument are in marked disagreement on this issue of motor-bus inferiority. In fact, the former argues that the motor bus was a superior vehicle that was—unfortunately—too little, too late. One writer has even turned the conspiracy argument around, maintaining that actually it would have taken a conspiracy to save electric transit.[3] Consequently, the clash of views is most pronounced on this point and provides an excellent first opportunity to assess the controversy.

THE STATUS OF THE INFERIORITY QUESTION

Although the inferiority question is so crucial to the larger argument, it is surprising how little attention has been paid it. Writers, both pro and con on the question, have espoused opinions with little or no supporting evidence. For example, this neglect is nowhere more conspicuous than in the analysis by Bradford Snell that reignited the controversy. While motor-bus inferiority is the crucial link in the argument, it is his weakest. Only one comparison of vehicle costs was presented, that of electric-bus and diesel-bus operations done in Toronto, Canada, in 1969.[4] However, the motorizations of electric systems that are relevant to the argument began in the late 1930s and continued to the mid-1950s. The conversions were essentially completed by the mid-1950s, well before the period from which Snell took his cost data. How much had transit operations changed since the 1930s and 1940s? Can Snell's data, drawn from the late 1960s, be relevant to the 1930s, 1940s and 1950s? Even if we feel that his data are indicative or suggestive of the historical situation during the earlier period, there can be little doubt that his thesis remains somewhat speculative as long as this glaring deficiency persists.

In addition, the sole cost comparison offered by Snell covered "operating costs." The Toronto Transit report put diesel-bus operating costs at 22.41 cents per mile and electric-bus operating costs at 16.02 cents per mile. The electric-bus costs were therefore 40 percent lower than diesel-bus costs. Electric buses would certainly have been the preferred mode on the basis of these operating costs. It is not clear, however, whether or not depreciation and other capital costs are included in these figures. This is an important point because these costs were often cited as one of the main problems with electric vehicles. In addition, these costs relate only to electric versus diesel buses. Since the conversion of electric operations to diesel operations generally involved the conversion of electric *streetcars* to diesel buses, it would be helpful to explore the economics of the new streetcar. As shown below, the electric bus was generally the chief competitor of the diesel bus, but the costs of PCC streetcar operations are also relevant to the conspiracy thesis.

In an attempt to compensate for the lack of cost data, Snell cited a number of engineering studies that showed that electric vehicles were superior to diesel buses. Snell noted that "engineering studies strongly suggest that conversion from electric transit to diesel buses results in higher operation costs, . . . loss of patronage and eventual bankruptcy. They demonstrate, for example, that diesel buses have 28 percent shorter lives, 40 percent higher operating costs, and 9 percent lower productivity."[5] We can summarize Snell's evidence in the following points:[6]

- The tractive efficiency of a General Motor's diesel bus was estimated to be only 10.6 percent, as compared to 83.4 percent for an electric bus.
- An electric motor with only one, perfectly balanced, moving part and operating at 300 degrees Fahrenheit could not possibly be more expensive to operate than a diesel engine with hundreds of moving parts and operating at 1700 degrees Fahrenheit.
- "Even if motor fuel were free, it would still be cheaper to power a trolley or even a streetcar."
- Diesel buses with their pollution, vibrations, and noise levels reduced patronage on public transit.
- Dieselization results in the "certain bankruptcy of urban transit systsms."

From the cost comparison and the engineering data, Snell argued his "conversion-for-destruction" hypothesis. Yet this argument is too heavy to rest on such weak foundations. The cost data are inadequate, and the engineering data are interesting, but incapable of resolving the economic question of motor-bus inferiority. While Snell's analysis generated considerable interest, support, and controversy, it has not, to my knowledge, evoked substantial supporting data on this point.

This neglect of economic analysis is by no means unique to Snell or his supporters. General Motor's denial of Snell's allegations, referred to in the previous chapter, was equally unsupported by any economic data. Likewise, those who have argued that the motor bus was a boon to transit rarely support their contentions with relevant economic data.[7]

There were probably many reasons why this economic issue has been so neglected over the years. First, the task was difficult. In addition, many writers must have felt no need to critically evaluate a position that to them was beyond dispute. This must have been the case with much of the trade literature that was written by "bus men," or "trolley-coach men," or "streetcar men"—that is, by individuals who had an undying devotion to a particular mode of transit. Since they had already made up their minds as to which technology was best, cost comparisons were not viewed as essential. They were rarely undertaken and only casual observations or references to cost data are to be found in their writings.

In other cases, the neglect of economic comparisons was due less to a bias toward a particular transit mode than to an overriding interest in writing a "popular" history of streetcars, buses, or trolley coaches. An antiquarian interest in these vehicles as a slice of bygone Americana dominates much of the transit-history literature. Economic considerations were certainly of secondary interest and received little attention. For example, William D. Middleton, in a large volume devoted to all aspects of the history of the streetcar, confined his entire discussion of the economics of the decline of the streetcars to two observations: "Its [bus] operating costs were low, and no costly maintenance of track and overhead systems was required."[8] The only other reference was the following observation: "Despite the superior qualities of the PCC car, the remaining street railway operations were becoming increasingly uneconomical. . . . The cost of new trolleys was substantially higher than that for mass-produced motor buses, and may cities found that growing traffic congestion made it almost impossible for the more expensive PCC cars to realize their superior earning potential."[9]

A different reason for neglecting economic issues is found in writers who thought that general economic comparisons were of little use, since specific local circumstances were always of overriding importance in the choice of transit vehicles. This view was expressed in a 1932 *Transit Journal* article: "Since each of the three types of vehicles has a specific field of application and is most economically operated in that field, there is no logical basis of unit cost comparison."[10] This is not an entirely unreasonable view, but it is too extreme, and it certainly does little to resolve a question that cannot be ignored.

Finally, some writers, as well as many readers, who encounter motorization allegations, either cannot or will not consider the possibility that our economic institutions failed to prevent such a perverse manipulation.[11] Since such things are not supposed to happen in our economic system, the charges must be unfounded. The motor bus must have been superior; otherwise, why did it replace streetcars? This view, unfortunately, begs the question. A contrary—although equally unsound—view is held by those who seem to have come to expect such sinister manipulation as common fare. They have developed a penchant for assuming that our economic institutions never work and that all charges of corporate impropriety must be true. In the extreme, this view tends to see virtually everything in conspiratorial terms. Both of these views, while very different, share a common disinterest in the economic question, because their position is held to be self-evident. Such faith in misplaced and inappropriate. The task of historical scholarship will not be served by glossing over the issue in either fashion.

The Economics of Transit Vehicles—A Review of the Literature

Because of this neglect of economic issues, a review of transit-industry trade publications reveals a very small quantity of data, much of which is not very useful. Scattered references to economic data can be found, but there is generally no way of knowing how the data were collected or how conclusions were arrived at. For example, a 1932 *Transit Journal* article cited Chicago's experience with one 7-mile trolley-coach line. The article put the savings from trolley-coach operations (over motor buses) at more than 5 cents per bus-mile.[12] No details or references were given. Another *Transit Journal* article in 1940 compared the results of 17 modernization programs underway on transit systems across the county.[13] Costs were reported in only 11 cases, yet in these cases there was no attempt to take into account differences in the size of the vehicles being compared, the age of equipment, and different methods of computing costs. Meaningful comparisons in these cases were impossible. Only one conclusion was possible—that *any* modernization program increased patronage and usually lowered costs (which was, in fact, the theme of the article).

Problems such as these predominate in the trade literature and tend to limit severely the usefulness of this source. One clear exception can be found in a 1949 article that compared a trolley coach with a diesel bus on the basis of costs, revenues, and rates of return. The trolley coach was shown to have been a vastly superior vehicle. The article will be discussed more fully in a later section of this chapter. Suffice it here to note the exception to the general rule.

Outside of the trade literature, the situation is only a bit better. The most rigorous and comprehensive study of the economics of transit vehicles can be found in a 1940 study by George Hoard.[14] Hoard developed a model that compared the profitability of a streetcar, a trolley coach, and a motor bus under different headways, passenger volumes, and under a number of different operating and financial assumptions. While it is not possible to repeat his analysis here, a number of his conclusions are of interest. First, Hoard determined that the PCC streetcar was the most economical vehicle for use in modernizing an existing streetcar line, *if* the volume of traffic was sufficient to warrant reasonably frequent service, and *if* the track had a remaining useful life equal to that of the new rolling stock. The key here was track rehabilitation requirements. If track rehabilitation was necessary, then either the trackless trolley (trolley coach) or motor bus would be warranted. If track rehabilitation cost $60,000 or less per double-track mile, or if annual passengers averaged over 5.5 million, then the PCC car was still the most economical. This "heavy traffic" could be expected only on the heavily traveled lines in the big cities. Hoard also put average track cost in 1940 at around $65,000, that is, right around the break-even point. At higher track costs and/or lower volume, the trolley coach would have been more economical. If track costs rose to over $100,000 per mile, the PCC car would be uneconomical, regardless of traffic volume. Hoard also concluded that unless track costs were brought down, streetcars would have to be gradually retired on all but the heaviest lines.[15]

As a replacement for the PCC car, Hoard generally favored the trolley coach. He concluded that "for the near future the backbone of the transit system appears to be the trackless trolley, with motor buses on the lighter lines."[16] The trolley coach was generally more economical than the motor bus and would tend to be the vehicle of choice for all traffic levels over 800,000 annual passengers.[17]

Hoard tried to draw the boundary lines for each vehicle in 1940. As such, his analysis is excellent. However, our ability to apply his model to the question at hand is limited by a lack of historical data. This drastically curtails the usefulness of Hoard's model, although his analysis of vehicle choice in 1940 is a valuable historical insight.

Donald Dewees, writing in 1970, relied heavily on the conclusions of Hoard and others.[18] In 1929, motor buses, he argued, were smaller and had higher operating costs than streetcars. There was, however, a minimum traffic level necessary for economical streecar operations. Dewees estimated that at 300,000 passengers per track-mile per year, streetcar costs were 4 to 6 cents per passenger.[19] Costs fell by only one-half cent if volume increased to 700,000 passengers. If volume fell to below 200,000 passengers, however, costs rose "steeply."[20] Dewees estimated average volume on urban lines to have been 300,000 in 1922, 335,000 in 1927, 255,000 in 1932, and 325,000 in 1937.[21] The increase between 1932 and 1937 reflected the decline of the streetcar in smaller cities, its survival in larger cities, and the economic recovery.

By 1939 motor buses had increased in size to the point where they were about 75 percent as large as the PCC streetcar. Dewees cited operating costs of 23 cents per vehicle-mile for the PCC car and 21 cents per vehicle-mile for the motor bus,[22] with the PCC car still enjoying lower seat-mile operating costs. But the competitiveness of the PCC deteriorated rapidly in the post-World War II period. Citing Chicago Transit Authority (CTA) data[23] for 1946, Dewees noted that PCC car prices had risen 40 percent since 1940, and had cost almost $10,000 more per vehicle than motor buses by 1946. PCC cars, however, were by then only 10 to 20 percent larger than motor buses, since motor buses had continued to increase in size. More important, streetcar operating costs in Chicago in 1946 were 48 cents per car-mile *higher* than bus costs.[24]

Dewees's use of Chicago data here serves to illustrate a problem often encountered in the literature. Can Hoard's cost data (cited by Dewees) be compared to CTA cost data? Did street car costs really increase from a level of 2 cents more than motor-bus costs per vehicle-mile in 1940 (Hoard's estimate) to a point where they were 48 cents higher in 1946, according to CTA data?[25] Or was part of this dramatic increase simply due, for instance, to different methods of cost accounting or to geographical variations in costs and operating conditions? There is reason to suspect that this was the case. For example, the CTA's method of calculating depreciation was somewhat unusual.[26] Total combined depreciation charges for *all* transit operations (streetcar, trolley coach, motor bus, subway, and elevated railways) were simply set at 8 percent of gross revenues. Total depreciation charges were then distributed over the various transit modes according to their percentage of total capitalization. This method would grossly exaggerate streetcar depreciation charges, since no account was taken of the longer life expectancy of streetcars. Obviously, costs calculated in this manner are not comparable with other cost data calculated in a more conventional manner.

In a 1973 study devoted entirely to trolley coaches in the United States and Canada, Mac Sebree and Paul Ward reported that operating costs for transit vehicles in the 1930s had been 12.32 cents per mile (vehicle-mile?) for trolley coaches, 14.72 cents per mile for gas buses, and 17.82 cents per mile for streetcars.[27] Sebree and Ward cited data from the 1940s in Fort William, Ontario, indicating that trolley coaches had cost 4.7 cents less per mile to operate than gasoline buses.[28] By 1952, however, diesel-bus costs were "generally claimed" to have been about 1.5 cents per mile lower than trolley-coach costs in the United States, although the trolley coach still maintained its superiority in Canada. Cincinnati, however, reported that its motor-bus and trolley-coach operating costs were still about equal in 1953.[29] The real problem for trolley coaches, they argued, came in the 1960s. The vehicles were getting old (none had been delivered since the early 1950s) and replacement parts were scarce.[30] Sebree and Ward cited 1970 figures showing that trolley-coach costs per mile exceeded motor-bus costs by a margin of 36.4 cents in Seattle, 18.8 cents in Boston, and 14.1 cents in San Francisco.[31]

Finally, John Bauer and Peter Costello,[32] writing in 1950, were vigorous advocates of the complete motorization of transit. Although they cited a number of comparisons of various types of vehicle costs, they never really developed a complete cost comparison. The closest thing to an overall comparison was their simple statement that "on the basis of valid comparisons, the superiority of bus economy stands beyond warranted challenge."[33] No figures or "valid comparisons" were cited. It was also interesting to note that, on the basis of the relative fuel costs, Bauer and Costello felt that the gasoline bus would continue to be more economical than the diesel bus.[34] It was, however, the diesel bus that figured so prominently in the replacement of the streetcar.

TRANSIT: AN ECONOMIC ANALYSIS

While all of these studies shed some light on the subject, a clear picture cannot be drawn. The available literature on the economics of transit vehicles is not sufficient to evaluate the inferiority allegation. Consequently, a cost-and-profit study was undertaken and is included herein.[35] Previous attempts at just such a study have generally been thwarted by a combination of severe data limitations and the highly localized nature of urban transit. This study seeks to overcome these problems by utilizing aggregate data published annually by *Transit Journal* and later by the American Transit Association (ATA) in its annual trade journal, *Transit Fact Book.* Data on revenues, expenses, vehicle miles, number of vehicles, miles of track and route, and so forth, were collected from transit companies across the country, aggregated, and presented by vehicle mode. The basic prodecure was to utilize this group of data, supplemented by additional data when possible, to provide a consistent and comprehensive comparison of costs and profits over the 15 year period 1935–1950. (Estimates for the year 1942 could not be made because of data limitations engendered by the switch from *Transit Journal* to ATA reporting that year.)

For the period 1935–1950 (except 1942, and 1935 in some cases) the following model was used to estimate costs, revenues, and profits:

$$C_t = C_0 + C_c$$

$$C_o = \frac{L}{V} + \frac{M}{V} + g$$

$$C_c = s + e + t$$

$$s = \frac{[d + .5(r)]S}{V/x}$$

$$E = \frac{[d + .5(r)]E}{V/z}$$

$$t = \frac{[d + .5(r)]T}{V/y}$$

$$P = \frac{R}{V} - C_t$$

where C_t = total cost per vehicle-mile; C_o = operating cost per vehicle-mile; C_c = capital costs per vehicle-mile; V = vehicle-miles run (annual); M = maintenance material costs (annual); L = annual payroll; g = power or fuel costs per vehicle-mile; s = vehicle capital costs per vehicle-mile; e = electric overhead capital costs per vehicle-mile; t = track capital costs per vehicle-mile; S = vehicle purchase price; E = total cost of electric overhead (either construction or conversion and refurbishing of existing overhead); T = total cost of track construction; P = profit per vehicle-mile; R = annual revenue; d = rate of depreciation, straight-line over estimated life of capital; r = rate of interest; x = number of vehicles; z = number of miles of electric overhead; and y = number of miles of track.

Estimates for each vehicle for each year were made with this basic model. It was often necessary, however, to interpolate, extrapolate, and otherwise supplement the cost model with various estimation techniques, where data were incomplete or unavailable from primary sources. These problems and procedures are presented in an appendix.

A few notes on the basic procedure and the nature of the estimates are in order here. First, all vehicles did not incur all of the costs identified above. Specifically, $e = 0$ for motor bus, since these vehicles were self-propelled, and $t = 0$ for both motor buses and trolley coaches, since no tracks were used. Second, the method of depreciating capital costs and estimating interest expenses is the method used by Paul David in his treatment of nineteenth-century mechanical-reaper capital costs.[36] The simplicity of this method was beneficial, and it was felt that little would be gained with a more complicated method. More important, this method seemed acceptable in view of the choice facing transit firms in the 1930s and 1940s. All three vehicles were clearly preferable to the old streetcars. The task facing a transit firm was to select a modernization program to replace its old streetcars. How should the firm evaluate capital costs in making this choice? More correctly, how can we treat these costs in a meaningful way, given the data limitations? It was decided to estimate these capital costs for each year on the assumption that a decision to purchase new vehicles, to construct or convert electric overhead, and to construct new track was to be made during that year. Obviously, no transit system did this every year. A cost comparison of the alternatives available to a transit firm that was considering modernization was what was desired. Consequently, this seemed to be the best procedure under these circumstances. David's method was used to approximate an "average" cost of capital (depreciation and interest) for each of the three vehicles, under the assumption that the firm was deciding which one to pick during that year. The reported capital costs, therefore, do not purport to show the actual capital costs incurred over successive years by any particular firm. Instead, the figures show the capital costs relevant to the modernization choice for each year.

Third, and most important, this method of estimating costs cannot identify cost, revenue, or profit functions. For example, it does not identify how costs varied with any variable that affected cost. Instead, the aggregate method utilizes reported aggregates reflecting the operating conditions, capital requirements, and so on, that were actually encountered by the reporting systems. Consequently, the costs and profits are historical averages for the reporting systems. Cost-and-profit functions for each vehicle and a comparison of all three in a specific historical situation would have been preferable to the aggregate method. Data limitations have, unfortunately, thwarted such analyses. With these considerations in mind, and the special estimation procedures left to an appendix, the results of the cost-and-profit study can be summarized.

Operating Costs

Operating costs and components—labor costs (including operating labor, maintenance labor, and overhead labor costs), maintenance material costs, and power (or fuel costs)—are shown in Tables 2.1 and 2.2. Table 2.1 shows that operating costs for motor buses were slightly lower than those for trolley coaches. Streetcars, however, had costs significantly higher than either of the other two vehicles. Over the 15-year period of the study, average trolley-coach operating costs were 7.2 percent higher than motor-bus operating costs, whereas streetcar costs were 55.3 percent higher than those of the motor bus.

It must be pointed out, though, as is shown in Table 2.3, that motor buses were usually much smaller than either trolley coaches or streetcars. For the period 1936–1950, I have estimated that newly purchased trolley coaches averaged 42.8 seats per vehicle, whereas motor buses averaged 33 seats per vehicle. The PCC streetcar averaged 57.5 seats per vehicle. As explained in the appendix, my estimating procedure probably tends to *overestimate* the size of motor buses and to underestimate the size of trolley coaches. Nonetheless, I estimated that over this period trolley coaches averaged 28.7 percent more seats than motor buses, whereas PCC streetcars averaged 74.2 percent more seats than motor buses. Consequently, although trolley-coach operating costs were 7.2 percent greater than motor-bus costs, the average trolley coach was at least 28.7 percent larger than the average motor bus. A similar situation prevailed with streetcars, that is, operating costs were 55.3 percent higher than bus costs, but the average PCC streetcar had 74.2 percent more seats. These differences in average vehicle size must be remembered in interpreting these and all other costs. Too often casual cost comparisons have neglected this point and have consequently overstated the cost advantages of the motor bus.

TABLE 2.1. Operating Costs (cents per vehicle-mile)

Year	Motor Bus	Trolley Coach	Streetcar
1935	15.5	18.2	23.1
1936	15.6	18.1	24.4
1937	16.3	16.7	24.4
1938	16.5	16.9	24.7
1939	17.0	16.0	24.9
1940	15.6	15.2	25.4
1941	17.0	17.4	26.4
1942	—	—	—
1943	18.6	19.7	29.0
1944	18.8	20.2	31.9
1945	19.9	21.2	34.7
1946	23.0	23.1	35.1
1947	26.0	26.3	38.8
1948	28.3	30.3	40.9
1949	29.4	32.4	45.5
1950	30.5	34.2	50.2
Average 1935–1950	20.5	21.7	32.0

Source: The source material used in compiling this and subsequent tables was primarily aggregate data published in various issues of *Transit Journal,* between 1935 and 1942, and *Transit Fact Book* published annually by the American Transit Association, 1943 through 1951. Reprinted by permission from David J. St. Clair, "The Motorization and Decline of Urban Public Transit, 1935–1950," *Journal of Economic History* 41 (September 1981): 579–600.

Looking at the components of operating costs, we find that labor costs were significantly higher on streetcars and lowest on motor buses. Trolley-coach labor costs were only slightly higher than motor-bus labor costs. The high labor costs on streetcar operations accounted for the largest part of their higher operating costs. It should be noted, though, that many streetcars were required by local ordinances to carry two operators, whereas buses and trolley coaches were not subject to this requirement. The high streetcar labor costs may have been attributable in large part to local regulations, rather than to the acutal operating characteristics of the streetcars. An example of such a situation will be given in Chapter 4.

Power costs and maintenance material costs were not essentially different for any of the vehicles. With power costs, the motor bus enjoyed a slight advantage over the trolley coach and a slightly larger advantage over the PCC streetcar.

In summary, trolley-coach operating costs per vehicle-mile were 7.2 percent higher than those for the motor bus, and streetcar operating costs

TABLE 2.2. Labor, Power, and Maintenance Material Costs (cents per vehicle-mile)

Year	Labor Costs			Power Costs			Maintenance Material Costs		
	Motor Bus	Trolley Coach	Street-Car	Motor Bus	Trolley Coach	Street-Car	Motor Bus	Trolley Coach	Street-Car
1935	9.2	9.7	16.4	2.8	3.9	6.0	1.7	3.2	2.9
1936	9.6	10.1	17.0	2.9	3.8	4.5	1.5	3.1	2.9
1937	10.0	10.5	17.6	3.0	3.8	4.4	1.8	2.5	2.4
1938	10.2	10.7	18.0	2.9	3.8	4.4	1.7	2.4	2.3
1939	10.6	11.1	18.5	2.7	3.7	4.3	2.0	1.3	2.1
1940	9.8	10.1	18.9	2.6	3.6	4.3	1.8	1.5	2.2
1941	10.4	10.8	20.0	3.2	3.6	4.2	1.9	2.5	2.2
1942	11.7	12.2	22.3	3.5	3.5	4.1	1.6	2.1	2.0
1943	12.9	13.9	23.1	2.5	3.4	4.0	2.1	2.4	2.1
1944	14.0	14.1	26.0	2.6	3.4	4.0	2.2	2.2	1.9
1945	15.1	15.5	28.2	2.0	3.5	4.2	2.0	2.3	2.1
1946	18.3	17.3	28.7	2.6	3.5	4.1	2.1	2.3	2.2
1947	20.3	20.0	30.6	3.1	3.7	4.4	2.6	2.6	2.4
1948	21.3	23.6	33.5	4.1	4.0	4.6	2.9	2.9	2.8
1949	22.7	29.3	37.3	3.6	4.3	5.1	3.2	3.2	3.1
1950	23.5	26.3	41.7	3.5	4.3	5.1	3.5	3.5	3.4
Ave. 1935–1950	14.4	15.3	24.9	—	—	—	—	—	—

Source: See Table 2.1.

43

TABLE 2.3. Vehicle Capital Costs and Average Vehicle Size (cents per vehicle-mile and average seats per vehicle for newly purchased vehicles)

Year	Motor-Bus Size	Vehicle Capital Cost	Trolley-Coach Size	Vehicle Capital Cost	Streetcar Size	Vehicle Capital Cost
1935	—	3.9	—	4.9	—	—
1936	28.0	3.7	41.0	4.8	55–60	3.9
1937	28.5	3.4	42.0	4.7	55–60	3.9
1938	29.0	3.5	42.0	4.7	55–60	4.0
1939	29.5	3.9	42.0	4.8	55–60	3.9
1940	30.0	4.0	42.2	5.4	55–60	4.0
1941	30.5	4.3	43.0	5.1	55–60	4.5
1942	32.9	—	43.0	—	55–60	—
1943	34.6	4.9	43.0	4.8	55–60	4.1
1944	35.0	5.5	43.0	5.1	55–60	4.4
1945	35.4	4.6	43.0	4.1	55–60	4.2
1946	35.3	5.0	43.0	4.3	55–60	4.4
1947	35.6	5.3	43.0	4.8	55–60	4.2
1948	36.4	5.3	43.3	4.7	55–60	4.3
1949	37.2	5.3	44.0	5.4	55–60	4.9
1950	37.8	5.6	45.0	5.2	55–60	5.4
Average 1936–1950	33.0	4.6	42.8	4.9	57.5	4.3

Source: See Table 2.1.

were 55.3 percent greater than motor-bus costs. Labor costs appear to have been the cause of the significantly higher operating costs of the streetcars. Trolley-coach operating costs were generally higher than those of the motor bus, but the difference was probably due to the larger size of the trolley coach. The same consideration applies to streetcar costs.

Capital Costs

There are three components of capital costs: vehicle, electric overhead, and track costs. In the case of streetcars, the capital costs were those of the new PCC car, since this, or a similar car, was the relevant option. A fourth capital cost, structure costs (office and garage costs, and so forth) were not considered, due to insufficient data. This should not significantly distort the relative costs, but how this omission affects the level of costs is not known. I suspect that the underestimation is slight. Of these three costs, motor buses incurred only the first, that is, vehicle costs. Trolley coaches incurred vehicle costs and electric overhead costs, and streetcars incurred all three costs. Trolley-coach electric overhead costs were calculated for cases where new overhead construction was required, as well as for cases where the old streetcar overhead could be converted to trolley-coach use. In addition, electric overhead costs for the PCC car were assumed to have been the same as trolley-coach costs. In the case of the PCC car, the counterpart to converting old streetcar overhead to trolley-coach operations was the refurbishing of the existing electric overhead for use by the new PCC car. Both the costs of constructing and converting (or refurbishing) electric overhead were made in order to approximate better the actual choices or options available to a transit company considering the conversion of old streetcar operations to either motor-bus, trolley-coach, or PCC-streetcar operations. Since the conversion option was almost always available, it would be misleading to consider only new overhead construction. The cost of converting the existing streetcar overhead to trolley-coach or PCC-car operations was almost always the relevant cost.

Track capital costs were calculated for the streetcar only. As will be seen, this was a significant cost component. Again, since we are interested in evaluating the choice between motor buses, trolley coaches, and streetcars within the context of a conversion of old streetcar facilities, the condition of the old track would have been an important consideration in determining the need for new track, and therefore the choice of vehicles. Despite this consideration, it was decided not to follow the procedure used in calculating electric overhead costs, that is, of calculating the costs of new track and also track refurbishing. Instead, track costs were calculated on the assumption that new track construction would be required with any conversion of old streetcar operations to PCC-car operations. This assumption was made in view of the general age and probable condition of most track during this period. If new track were not needed, streetcar costs would be correspondingly lower.

Finally, the interest rate used in determing all capital costs was 5 percent, an assumption based on the reported dealings of transit firms during this period. For example, in 1940 *Transit Journal* reported that the yield on transit company bond offerings ranged from 3 to 7 percent, with most around 4 to 5 percent.[37] This situation does not appear to have changed appreciably over the period in question. Consequently, 5 percent was used in all cases.

Table 2.3 shows vehicle capital costs on a vehicle-mile basis. Despite higher prices for PCC streetcars, streetcar vehicle costs per vehicle-mile were the lowest of the three vehicles. This was attributable to the much longer lives of these vehicles. Streetcar costs were also lower, despite the streetcar's generally smaller number of vehicle-miles logged per vehicle. It will be recalled that annual depreciation and interest charges were divided by the number of vehicle-miles *per vehicle*. This procedure was used to allow for the consideration of capital requirements, although the method only roughly approximates actual historical vehicle requirements.

Average motor-bus vehicle costs over the 1936–1950 period were 6.9 percent greater than streetcar costs. Average tolley-coach vehicle costs were 14 percent greater than streetcar costs. Trolley-coach costs, however, were only 6.5 percent greater than motor-bus costs. The difference between trolley-coach and motor-bus vehicle costs narrowed in the post-World War II period. This probably reflected the narrowing of the difference in vehicle sizes during this period, as average bus size grew faster than trolley-coach size, but it still must be remembered that significant differences in vehicle size persisted over the entire period. On the basis of vehicle-seat-mile costs, streetcars enjoyed an even more pronounced cost advantage. The ranking of motor-bus and trolley-coach vehicle costs, however, was reversed, when costs were calculated on this basis.

Table 2.4 shows electric overhead costs for both trolley coaches and streetcars and track costs for streetcars. All costs were depreciated over their estimated useful lives and, as was the case with vehicle costs, these costs were then divided by the number of vehicle-miles per mile of line or track in order to account for capital requirements. Table 2.4 shows how insignificant electric overhead costs actually were, and also how significantly track costs contributed to streetcar capital costs. The belief that motor-bus capital costs were always significantly lower than trolley-coach capital costs, simply because buses did not have electric overhead, is incorrect. On the other hand, not having tracks meant that both motor-bus and trolley-coach capital costs were much lower than those of the streetcar. Track costs were clearly the critical component of streetcar capital cost.

Table 2.5 combines all of these capital costs to show total capital costs on a vehicle-mile basis. Motor buses had the lowest capital costs, followed by trolley coaches with converted overhead. Next were trolley coaches with new overhead, followed by streetcars with refurbished overhead. Trolley coaches with converted overhead had capital costs only 10.9 percent greater than motor buses. Streetcars with refurbished overhead, however, had capital costs 210.9 percent greater than motor buses. Clearly, streetcar capital costs were significantly higher than both motor-bus or trolley-coach capital costs.

If we attempt to compensate for the differences in average vehicle size by expressing these captial costs on a vehicle-seat-mile basis, we find the following seat-mile costs: motor bus, 0.14 cents; converted trolley coach, 0.12 cents; and refurbished streetcar, 0.25 cents. In other words, on a vehicle-seat-mile basis, trolley-coach capital costs were 16.7 percent *lower* than motor-bus costs. On the other hand, streetcar capital costs per seat-mile were still 78.6 percent greater than motor-bus capital costs.

In summary, motor buses enjoyed a slight advantage over trolley coaches in the area of capital costs. Again, however, as was the case with operating costs, differences in vehicle sizes were probably responsible for

TABLE 2.4. Electric Overhead Capital Costs and Track
Capital Costs (cents per vehicle-mile)

	Trolley Coach		Streetcar		
Year	Converted	Constructed	Refurbished	Constructed	Track
1935	.2	.7	.3	1.4	7.6
1936	.2	.7	.3	1.4	8.0
1937	.2	.7	.3	1.3	8.9
1938	.2	.6	.4	1.4	9.4
1939	.2	.7	.3	1.3	9.0
1940	.2	.9	.4	1.7	9.0
1941	.2	.9	.4	1.7	8.8
1942	—	—	—	—	—
1943	.2	.8	.4	1.6	8.6
1944	.2	.8	.4	1.7	9.1
1945	.2	.8	.4	1.6	9.0
1946	.2	.8	.4	1.7	9.4
1947	.2	.9	.4	1.7	9.3
1948	.2	.9	.4	1.7	10.0
1949	.2	.9	.5	2.1	12.0
1950	.2	1.0	.6	2.3	13.5
Average					
1935–1950	.2	.8	.4	1.6	9.4

Source: See Table 2.1.

the cost difference. Trolley-coach capital costs were not significantly higher than motor-bus costs, despite higher vehicle prices and the necessity of electric overhead. This was no doubt due to the fact that trolley coaches had longer lives, and because electric overhead costs were relatively insignificant. Streetcars, on the other hand, had very high capital costs, which were primarily due to their large track costs. Longer equipment lives, larger vehicles, and lower vehicle capital costs were not sufficient to compensate for these high costs, even on a seat-mile basis.

Total Costs

Table 2.6 combines both operating costs and capital costs to show total costs for each vehicle. On a vehicle-mile basis, converted trolley-coach costs over the period 1936–1950 were, on average, 6.3 percent greater than motor-bus costs. The trolley coach with new overhead had costs 8.6 percent greater than bus costs, whereas refurbished streetcars had costs 84.3 percent greater than motor-bus costs. Streetcars with new overhead had costs 89 percent greater than motor-bus costs. Again, if we compensate for the

TABLE 2.5. Total Capital Costs (cents per vehicle-mile)

		Trolley Coach		Streetcar	
Year	Bus	Converted	Constructed	Refurbished	Constructed
1935	3.9	5.1	5.6	—	—
1936	3.7	5.0	5.5	12.3	13.3
1937	3.4	4.8	5.4	13.2	14.2
1938	3.5	4.9	5.4	13.8	14.8
1939	3.9	4.9	5.4	13.2	14.2
1940	4.0	5.6	6.2	13.4	14.7
1941	4.3	5.3	6.0	13.7	15.0
1942	—	—	—	—	—
1943	4.9	5.0	5.6	13.1	14.3
1944	5.5	5.3	5.9	13.9	15.1
1945	4.6	4.3	5.0	13.6	14.9
1946	5.0	4.5	5.1	14.2	15.4
1947	5.3	5.1	5.8	14.0	15.2
1948	5.3	5.0	5.6	14.8	16.1
1949	5.3	5.6	6.3	17.4	19.0
1950	5.6	5.4	6.1	19.5	21.2
Average 1936–1950	4.6	5.1	5.7	14.3	15.5

Source: See Table 2.1.

differences in vehicle size by expressing these total costs on a vehicle-seat-mile basis, the costs were as follows: converted trolley coach, 0.63 cents; trolley coach with new overhead, 0.65 cents; motor bus, 0.77 cents; refurbished streetcars, 0.82 cents; streetcars with new overhead, 0.84 cents. Once again, the trolley had the lowest cost on a vehicle-seat-mile basis.

Revenues

In the case of each of the costs discussed above, reference was made to the differences in average vehicle size. Indeed, when costs were expressed on a vehicle-seat-mile basis, the larger trolley coaches were generally the most cost efficient. The larger streetcars, though generally still not as cost efficient as the motor buses, compared much more favorably on this basis. But were the extra seats on these vehicles utilized? Carrying around surplus seats obviously was not a virtue, nor was it cost efficient, regardless of what the vehicle-seat-mile cost calculations indicated. So the critical question remains: Were the extra seats utilized?

Table 2.6 provides an indication, with revenues per vehicle-mile shown. It is clear that the larger trolley coaches and streetcars *did* generate

TABLE 2.6. Total Costs and Revenues (cents per vehicle-mile)

Year	Motor Bus		Trolley Coach			Streetcar		
	Total Cost	Revenue	Total Cost		Revenue	Total Cost		Revenue
			Converted	Constructed		Refurbished	Constructed	
1935	19.4	16.3	23.3	23.8	12.4	—	—	52.8
1936	19.3	20.0	23.1	23.6	34.8	36.6	37.7	41.3
1937	19.7	20.0	21.6	22.1	27.9	37.6	38.6	42.5
1938	20.1	20.8	21.8	22.3	25.4	38.5	39.6	42.1
1939	20.9	21.4	21.0	21.5	28.8	38.1	39.2	43.7
1940	19.7	21.7	20.8	21.5	33.4	38.8	40.1	43.3
1941	21.3	23.6	22.7	23.4	34.1	40.1	41.4	47.5
1942	—	26.3	—	—	45.5	—	—	47.3
1943	23.5	32.2	24.7	25.3	49.1	43.1	44.3	54.9
1944	24.3	33.5	26.2	26.8	51.0	45.8	47.0	57.5
1945	24.5	35.0	25.6	26.2	51.1	48.4	49.6	59.4
1946	28.0	34.5	27.6	28.2	50.1	49.2	50.5	60.4
1947	31.3	34.3	31.3	32.0	49.5	52.8	54.0	60.6
1948	33.6	37.0	35.2	35.9	50.8	55.7	56.9	67.5
1949	34.7	38.5	38.0	38.8	56.0	62.9	64.5	71.6
1950	36.1	39.7	39.6	40.3	59.3	69.7	71.4	78.1
Average 1936–1950	25.5	28.4	27.1	27.7	41.2	47.0	48.2	54.4

Source: See Table 2.1.

greater revenue. Over the period, average trolley-coach revenues were 44.9 percent greater than motor-bus revenues. It will be recalled that I had estimated that trolley coaches carried about 28.7 percent more seats than motor buses. Accordingly, a large part of the higher revenue was no doubt attributable to the larger carrying capacity of the trolley coaches. The remainder of the increased revenue was probably attributable to the relative concentration of trolley coaches in more highly urbanized areas.

Streetcars, which averaged 74.2 percent more seats than motor buses, generated revenues that were 91.3 percent greater than motor-bus revenues. Again, the larger size of the streetcar was reflected in larger revenues. As in the case of trolley coaches, the extra seats were being utilized, thus providing one indication that, in general, ridership levels had not fallen to levels that would no longer justify the use of these larger vehicles.

Profits

The larger trolley coaches and streetcars were producing greater revenues per vehicle-mile, but were the higher revenues enough to compensate for their higher costs? Table 2.7 shows net profits per vehicle-mile for the three types of vehicles. Net profits were calculated by subtracting total costs from revenues. In this way the larger vehicles with their greater revenue potential, but also higher costs, were compared with the smaller vehicles with their lower costs, but lower revenue potential.

Trolley-coach profits over the entire 1936–1950 period were consistently and significantly higher than either motor-bus or streetcar profits. The average converted-trolley-coach profit over this period was 407.6 percent greater than the average motor-bus profit. For the period 1936–1941 that comparison is even more pronounced; that is, the average trolley-coach profit was over seven times the average motor-bus profit. Because electric overhead costs were almost insignificant, profits of trolley coaches with *new* overhead were still 292 percent greater than the average motor-bus profits for the 1936–1950 period.

Trolley-coach profits were also superior to streetcar profits, but streetcars were more profitable than motor buses. The 1936–1950 average profit for streetcars with refurbished overhead was 107.7 percent greater than the average motor-bus profit. Even with newly constructed electric overhead, streetcar profits were 74.4 percent greater than motor-bus profits.

TROLLEY COACHES

The conclusion that the trolley coach was the superior vehicle available to transit firms for modernizing their operations may be somewhat

TABLE 2.7. Profits (cents per vehicle-mile)

Year	Bus	Trolley Coach		Streetcar	
		Converted	Constructed	Refurbished	Constructed
1935	− 3.1	−10.9	−11.4	—	—
1936	0.7	11.7	11.2	4.7	3.6
1937	0.4	6.3	5.8	4.8	3.8
1938	0.7	3.7	3.1	3.6	2.6
1939	0.5	7.8	7.3	5.6	4.6
1940	2.0	12.6	12.0	4.6	3.3
1941	2.3	11.4	10.8	7.4	6.1
1942	—	—	—	—	—
1943	8.6	24.4	23.8	11.8	10.6
1944	9.3	24.8	24.2	11.7	10.4
1945	10.5	25.5	24.9	11.0	9.8
1946	6.3	22.6	22.0	11.2	9.9
1947	3.0	18.2	17.5	7.8	6.5
1948	3.5	15.6	15.0	11.8	10.5
1949	3.8	18.0	17.2	8.7	7.1
1950	3.6	19.7	19.0	8.4	6.7
Average					
1936–1950	3.9	15.9	15.3	8.1	6.8

Source: See Table 2.1.

surprising. One usually encounters the motorization issue largely in a motor-buses-versus-streetcars context. Yet this conclusion should have an intuitive appeal, if one considers the hybrid nature of the trolley coach, that is, as an electric bus or as a streetcar without expensive track costs. As such, it does appear to have succeeded in capturing the best of both.

This conclusion is supported by a number of sources, such as Hoard, discussed above. In addition, an even stronger case for the trolley coach can be found in a 1949 *Mass Transportation* article by E. J. Mueller.[38] This is the article referred to above as a clear exception to the general dearth of economic data in the trade literature. Mueller provided a good systematic comparison of a trolley coach with a diesel bus on a six-mile line, with five-minute headways, and a peak load service of 800 passengers per hour. Both vehicles were 44-passenger vehicles, so the generally neglected disparity in vehicle sizes is rectified. Mueller's analysis strongly supports the use of the trolley coach on lines requiring peak headways of from two to ten minutes. The salient features of the analysis are shown in Table 2.8. The comparison of rates of return is quite dramatic here. A determination of rates of return was not feasible with the aggregate method presented above, so Mueller's figures provide complementary support for the trolley-coach case.

TABLE 2.8. Motor Bus versus Trolley Coach, Economic Analysis

	Motor Bus	Trolley Coach
Annual mileage (equal service)	$597,883	$583,300
Scheduled Vehicles	17	14
Spares	2	1
Total	19	15
Vehicle investment		
Motor Buses at $17,000	$323,000	—
Trolley Coaches at $18,500	—	$277,500
Storage, service, and maintenance	$100,000	$ 30,000
Overhead and Feeder		
(6 miles at $25,000/mile)	—	$150,000
Substations		
(750 KW at $70/KW)	—	$ 52,500
Total Investment	$423,000	$510,000
Depreciation (Annual)		
Buses (8 years)	$ 40,750	—
Trolley Coaches (12 years)	—	$ 23,125
Storage, service, and maintenance	$ 2,500	$ 1,100
(10 years tools, and 50 years building)		
Overhead and Substations (20 years)	—	$ 10,125
Total Depreciation	$ 43,250	$ 34,350
Total Cost (cents per vehicle-mile)	$ 46.9	$ 37.9
Total Revenue (cents per vehicle-mile)	$ 48.5	$ 52.2
Total Revenue (Annual Gross)	$290,000	$304,500
Total Expenses (Annual)	$280,610	$227,944
Gross Profit (Annual)	$ 9,390	$ 76,556
Investment Required	$423,000	$510,000
Rate of Return	2.2%	15.0%

Other citations in the trade literature, although not thorough or complete, also support this conclusion. For example, Winnipeg Electric Company reported to *Mass Transportation* in July 1946 their experience in running trolley coaches, motor buses, and streetcars during 1941–1945.[39] Both trolley coaches and streetcars turned a profit in each year, while motor-bus operations showed losses in two of the five years and smaller profits in the other three years. Trolley coaches consistently showed the largest profit per vehicle (as well as per vehicle-mile). Seattle's experience with trolley coaches was equally favorable. Between 1940 and 1948, Seattle Transit System farebox profits amounted to $12,099,185.[40] The trolley-coach operations contributed $15,904,925 toward this profit, while motor-bus operations lost $3,805,740. San Francisco reported in 1953 that its trolley coaches were the only vehicles to show a profit.[41] Toronto also reported in 1953 that the trolley coach was the most economical vehicle in the medium-density (1,000–2,000 passengers per hour) traffic range.[42] Upward of 3,500 passengers per hour, the PCC car was still the vehicle of choice. In a 1953 survey of 14 transit companies operating both trolley coaches and diesel buses, a *Mass Transportation* article reported costs per vehicle-mile of 17.11 cents for the trolley coaches and 20.08 cents for comparable motor buses.[43] These costs included maintenance, fuel, power, depreciation, administration, tires, injuries, and taxes (except gasoline taxes, inclusion of which would raise motor-bus costs). In addition, studies undertaken well after the period that concerns us here also support the superiority of trolley coaches.[44] While these studies cannot directly bear on the questions at hand, they do tend to lend support to the results obtained here.

CONCLUSIONS

The economic study of urban transit vehicles presented above, along with the supporting literature, makes a very strong case for the superiority of the trolley coach. It also suggests that the streetcar, too, was generally more economical than the motor bus, at least during this period and at least on the more heavily patronized lines. Consequently, strong confirmation of the motor-bus inferiority argument is warranted.

It should be pointed out here that this does not therefore validate the entire conspiracy argument. Inferiority is a necessary but not a sufficient argument in the conspiracy theory. We must now examine the evidence that supports the existence of such a conspiracy. We will turn our attention to that task in the following chapter, where we will analyze a campaign that sought to eliminate all electric streetcars and trolley coaches in favor of motor buses. In view of the above, that must appear suspicious, at best.

NOTES

1. The conspiracy argument has another important aspect. Where streetcar and interurban rail lines used private rights-of-way, motorization of these lines has resulted in the irreversible disposal of these rights-of-way, thus precluding their use as nuclei of rapid transit systems. The two systems that are often mentioned in this regard are the Pacific Electric Railway in the Los Angeles area, and the Key System in the Oakland, California, area. The right-of-way of the Key System, which operated trains on tracks over the San Francisco Bay Bridge, was originally considered for use as BART's transbay connection. It was disposed of, however, by the Key System, after its acquisition by NCL, but before such a move could be made. On the disposal of the Key System's transbay right-of-way, see Harre W. Demoro, "The Conversion of the Key System," *National Railway Bulletin* 44 (No. 6), 1979, especially pp. 18–24; also see the testimony of former San Francisco Mayor Joseph Alioto in U.S., Congress, Senate, Committee on the Judiciary, *The Industrial Reorganization Act: Hearings on S.1167*, 93rd Cong., 2d sess., 1974.

The Pacific Electric case often involves agreement among both pro- and anti-conspiracy writers. That is, most writers lament the loss of the private right-of-way, agreeing that this system could have served as the nucleus of an efficient rapid transit network. Writers disagree as to who is to blame for its loss—short-sighted public officials or conspiring auto-oil interests. See Snell, p. A–31–35; George W. Hilton and John F. Due, *The Electic Interurban Railways in America* (Stanford, CA: Stanford University Press, 1960) p. 409; also see the testimony of Mayor Bradley in *Hearings on the Industrial Reorganization Act* (cited above). Also see the testimony of George Hilton in the same hearings (especially p. 2263), where he disagrees with his co-author in *The Electric Interurban Railways in America* regarding the ability of the Los Angeles rights-of-ways to serve as the basis for a rapid transit system. The Pacific Electric is dealt with as a case study in Lyndon Henry, *A New Perspective on the Decline of Regional Public Transportation Services* (Austin: Texas Association for Public Transportation, 1974).

2. This refers to a conspiracy to destroy public transit systems. Other conspiracies—for example, a conspiracy to monopolize the bus market—are conceivable, but that is a very different allegation and one not requiring the demonstration of motor-bus inferiority.

3. David Brodsley, *L. A. Freeway* (Berkeley: University of California Press, 1981), p. 95.

4. Toronto Transit, *Commission Report No. 5* (November 5, 1969), cited in Bradford Snell, *American Ground Transport*, Appendix to *Hearings on the Industrial Organization Act*, pp. A–37, A–92.

5. Ibid., pp. A–37, A–38. Also see citations in Note 21 in Chapter 1.

6. See ibid., p. A–92, for a list of the various engineering sources and citations.

7. For example, General Motors' reply to Snell denies the charges, but does not provide supporting economic data. Also, the opinions of John Rae regarding the superiority of the motor bus were cited in the previous chapter, but he provides no economic data supporting his position.

8. William D. Middleton, *Time of the Trolley* (Milwaukee, WI: Kalmback Press, 1967), p. 374.

9. Ibid., p. 395.

10. A. B. Paterson, "The Trolley Bus: Wide Use Probable within Decade," *Transit Journal* 76 (October 15, 1932): 470.

11. See, for example, the testimony of George Hilton in Senate, *The Industrial Reorganization Act* (1974) pp. 2230–31. Hilton's economic data supporting his rebuttal of Snell's allegations are skimpy at best, and unable to resolve the economic question.

12. E. J. McIlraith, "Excellent Performance Forecasts Steady Growth," *Transit Journal* 76 (October 15, 1932): 482.

13. John A. Miller, "More Riders at Less Cost through Modernization," *Transit Journal* 84 (July 1940): 221–38.

14. George Hoard, "Modernization of a Transit System," *Engineering Experimental Station Series*, Bulletin No. 100 (Seattle: University of Washington, 1940).

15. Ibid., p. 61.

16. Ibid., p. 62.

17. Ibid.

18. Donald N. Dewees, "The Decline of American Street Railways," *Traffic Quarterly* 24 (October 1970): 563–81.

19. Ibid., p. 570.

20. Ibid.

21. Ibid., p. 568.

22. Ibid., p. 574. Dewees cited Hoard, p. 15, on this point.

23. Werner Schroeder, *Metropolitan Transit Research Study* (Chicago: Chicago Transit Authority, 1956).

24. Dewees, pp. 577–78.

25. Ibid., p. 578.

26. This discussion is based on the Chicago Transit Authority (CTA) Unit Cost Files, made available to me by the CTA in Chicago, Illinois, in 1976.

27. Mac Sebree and Paul Ward, *Transit's Stepchild: The Trolley Coach* (Cerritos, CA: Ira L. Swett, 1973).

28. Ibid., p. 63.

29. Ibid., pp. 63–64.

30. An official at CTA told me that the CTA had to resort to cannibalizing its trolley coaches during the 1960s because parts were not available. Sebree and Ward, p. 68, noted the same difficulties—the use of homemade parts and cannibalizing in Seattle.

31. Ibid., p. 64.

32. John Bauer and Peter Costello, *Transit Modernization and Street Traffic Control* (Chicago: Lakeside Press, 1950).

33. Ibid., p. 105.

34. Ibid., p. 88.

35. The following economic analysis draws extensively from David J. St. Clair, "The Motorization and Decline of Urban Transit, 1935–1950" *Journal of Economic History* 41, No. 3 (September 1981): 579–600. Reproduced here by permission of the *Journal of Economic History*.

36. Paul A. David, "The Mechanization of Reaping in the Ante-Bellum Midwest," in Robert W. Fogel and Stanley L. Engerman, eds., *The Reinterpretation of American Economic History* (New York: Harper and Row, 1971), p. 227.

37. "Financial Atmosphere Clearing," *Transit Journal* 84 (January 1940): 19–21.

38. E. L. Mueller, "Two Minutes to Ten," *Mass Transportation* 45 (April 1949): 60–62.

39. C. H. Dahl, "Winnipeg Opens Its Books on Trolley Coach Costs for 1941–45," *Mass Transportation* 42 (July 1946): 298–309.

40. Committee for Modernization of Electric Transportation, *The Truth About Transit*, February 1964, p. 10.

41. "358 Trolley Coaches Bolster San Francisco's New System," *Mass Transportation* 49 (July 1953): 16–17.

42. W. E. P. Duncan, "Trolley Coaches in Toronto," *Passenger Transport Annual*, 1953, p. 48.

43. L. W. Birch, "Trolley Coach Versus Bus," *Mass Transportation* 49 (October 1953): 36–40.

44. For example, see Southeastern Pennsylvania Transportation Authority, *Trolley Bus vs. Diesel Bus*, March 1977; and Carl L. Natvig, "The Economics of the Trolley Coach" (M.B.A. thesis, San Francisco State University, 1975).

3

The Conspiracy Evidence

Before considering the evidence that purports to show a conspiracy to subvert urban public transit, a separation of the questions and issues is in order. First, did motorization take place? Yes, the record is beyond dispute here. Second, did a motorization campaign, as alleged by Snell and others, take place? Again, the record is clear: These activities were undertaken. The remaining interesting questions involve motives and impact. First, what was the intended outcomes(s) of the motorization campaign? Second, how significant was this motorization campaign, among all the other contributing factors, to the decline of urban public transit? The first of these questions will be considered in this chapter. The second will be dealt with in the next chapter.

To seek an insight into the question of motives and intent, it will be beneficial to look at both the identity of the participants in the motorization campaign and their activities. Our efforts will be directed at hopefully surmising their intent, always keeping in mind the preceding economic analysis.

THE PARTICIPANTS

There were many participants in the alleged conspiracy: National City Lines, American City Lines, Pacific City Lines, General Motors, Standard Oil of California, Phillips Petroleum, Omnibus Corporation, Yellow Coach, Rex Finance Corporations, United Cities Motor Transit, Mack Truck, and numerous individuals associated with these companies, as well as Greyhound Corporation, and others.[1] The field is not really so large, however, since there is a considerable number of interlocking personnel and subsidiary relationships here. Identifying the players is a crucial task.

While it might seem logical to start with the company in the thick of the controversy—National City Lines—it would be more beneficial to start with activities that predate the 1936 formation of National City Lines, which are basic to an understanding of what NCL was, how it was formed, and what it sought to do. We will therefore start with these earlier activities, the most important of which centered around the General Motors Corporation.

General Motors' involvement in buses began in 1925, when it acquired Yellow Coach, the nation's largest manufacturer of both intercity and intracity buses. This acquisition began General Motors' expansion into public transportation. One year later, General Motors integrated forward into intercity bus operations, when it formed Motor Transit Corporation. The name of this $10 million holding company was soon changed to Greyhound Corporation. General Motors retained control of Greyhound, placing the president of Yellow Coach, I. B. Babcock, on the Greyhound Board of Directors.[2] He was replaced in 1936 by John A. Ritchie, who also replaced Babcock as president at Yellow. General Motors remained the largest stockholder of Greyhound until 1948. While at Greyhound, Babcock was instrumental in organizing, through General Motors, a holding company called the National Highway Transport Corporation (NHTC) to establish an intercity bus network in the southeastern United States.[3] Babcock, H. E. Listman, and H. C. Grossman (who was later treasurer of General Motors when he was convicted in the National City Lines antitrust case) were all placed on the board of directors of NHTC as General Motors' representatives. In 1931, NHTC was merged into Greyhound as Atlantic Greyhound Lines. General Motors did not relinquish control of Atlantic Greyhound, however, until 1934. General Motors and Greyhound, by mutual agreement, had agreed that Greyhound would buy only General Motors Yellow buses.[4] Snell has further argued that after 1928, Greyhound undertook a policy of pressuring railroads into replacing their commuter rail operations with joint Greyhound-railroad bus routes.[5] General Motors retained an active interest in and control of Greyhound, while Greyhound was undertaking these activities. For example, General Motors was responsible for arranging a $1 million cash loan for financially troubled Greyhound in 1932.[6]

This study is not directly interested in Greyhound or developments in the intercity bus operations field. The Greyhound case does, however, illustrate a typical pattern of personnel interconnections, and Greyhound representatives were active in both the formation of NCL and in its motorization campaign. For example, Stewart Moore, a Greyhound maintenance executive was placed on the board of directors at NCL to help with the rail conversions.[7] Glenn Traer, another Greyhound executive, tried unsuccessfully to raise money in mid-1937 for Pacific City Lines' (an NCL affiliate—see below) planned motorization of transit systems in western states.[8] Traer then reported to Babcock (of General Motors and Greyhound) his lack of success. Final financial arrangements for the western conversions were purportedly made at a meeting held in the Chicago offices of Greyhound Bus Lines.

In intracity bus operations, General Motors' direct activities began in 1932 with the formation of United Cities Motor Transit (UCMT). According to General Motors general counsel, Henry Hogan, the formation of UCMT took place when it was "decided that the only way this new market for [city] buses could be created was for it to finance the conversion from streetcars to buses in some small cities."[9] This holding company operated until 1935, motorizing a few smaller cities in Ohio and Michigan. As Hogan later observed, "In each case [GM] successfully motorized the city, turned the management over to other interests and liquidated its investments."[10] The UCMT was dissolved in 1935, after being censured by the American Transit Association for its attempts at motorizing Portland's electric transit system.[11] The dissolution of UCMT was part of an arrangement between General Motors and the Fitzgerald brothers, nominal founders of NCL, for them to take over UCMT activities and extend the conversions. With more acquisitions planned, the Fitzgeralds brought in an old friend, Foster G. Beamsley, for advice and support. Beamsley in turn brought in his old partners at Motor Transit Corporation (that is, Greyhound), C. E. Wickman and Glenn W. Traer. These three, along with General Motors, had been involved in the formation of Greyhound Corporation. They had also started City Coach Lines (CCL) in 1935. Beamsley would go on to become a vice-president and director at NCL and also serve as a director on NCL's four large properties.[12]

Even prior to the curtailment of UCMT activities, General Motors' efforts were being directed to other areas. For example, a separate firm, Omnibus Corporation, was used in the motorization of New York City's electric streetcars in 1935.[13] General Motors had acquired at least partial control of Omnibus in 1926, through its control of the Hertz Corporation. By 1930 it essentially controlled Omnibus.[14] In any case, John A. Ritchie served simultaneously as chairman at General Motors' Yellow Coach division and as president of Omnibus Corporation from 1926 until after the motorization.[15] The New York motorization, which Ritchie presided over, was completed in 18 months. The New York system was one of the world's largest, and its motorization is often cited as the turning point for electric railways in this country.[16] Ritchie was also later involved in the acquisition of the Los Angeles Railway in 1944 by American City Lines (ACL), an NCL affiliate.[17] As chairman of Fifth Avenue Coach, he received a 1939 survey of the Los Angeles Railway that was preparatory to its acquisition by ACL. This was one of numerous surveys of transit companies that were undertaken by NCL in the late 1930s. The survey sought to identify acquisition and motorization candidates. The report considered the "practicality of all bus operations" and was commissioned by the Chicago Motor Coach Company. This company, founded in 1922 by Ritchie and John Hertz,[18] was also very active in promoting all-bus conversions throughout the transit industry in the late 1930s.[19]

Another approach taken by General Motors, prior to the dissolution of UCMT, eventually led to the formation of National City Lines. This began with General Motors providing ad hoc financial backing to the Fitzgeralds in their acquisition of some midwestern city transit systems, beginning in 1933. It is interesting to follow these developments that preceded the formation of NCL in 1936.

The Fitzgerald brothers, nominal founders of NCL in 1936, had gotten into the bus operating business when Roy Fitzgerald began regular bus service in 1922, carrying miners to and from work in northern Minnesota, with his Range Rapid Transit Co.[20] Some of his brothers soon joined in. Until 1933 the Fitzgerald brothers had operated various interurban bus lines through various corporations they had formed. In all of these ventures, the Fitzgeralds had been involved in *intercity* bus lines in the Midwest and Rocky Mountain areas. It was not until the fall of 1933 that an urban or local transit system was acquired (Oshkosh City Lines, on November 1, 1933). A Yellow Coach salesman was apparently instrumental in suggesting and assisting the Fitzgeralds in this move into city transit.[21] In any case, the Fitzgeralds entered the local transit arena and began scrapping streetcars and purchasing transit buses, Yellow's in most instances. In early 1934, the Fitzgeralds purchased, through their Rex Finance Corporation, Illinois Power and Light's Galesburg transit operation. Transit systems in Joliet were acquired in August of that same year and the new Yellow buses were installed. In 1935 properties were acquired in East St. Louis and Montgomery, Illinois, and in Jackson, Michigan. As noted above, at about this time, General Motors (through Yellow Coach) began curtailing its program of buying and converting local transit systems directly through subsidiaries such as United Cities Motor Transit Co. As Albert Meier put it, "Seeing that someone else was now on hand to take over its job, Yellow Coach stopped making investments in United Cities Motor Transit Co. Its officers, Col. M. D. Mills, Thomas E. Bedford, and Charles A. Blaney, arranged to sell Kalamazoo Motor Coach Co. to Rex Finance Corp. effective January 1, 1936."[22]

Colonel Marmion D. Mills is a good example of the interchange of personnel in this saga.[23] He went to work for General Motors Truck and Coach after World War I as a sales engineer. From 1929 through 1932 he was a regional sales manager at Yellow. (Was he the "salesman" who suggested the purchase of local properties to the Fitzgeralds?) In 1932 Mills became president and general manager of UCMT. He was a founding member of

National City Lines and a vice-president of NCL until 1937. In 1937 he became a vice-president of Pacific City Lines (an NCL affiliate—see below). In addition to these positions, Mills was a director at Atlantic Greyhound, another GM firm.[24]

The change in General Motors' strategy, from backing UCMT activities to backing the Fitzgeralds, was informal at first. General Motors' financing of the Galesburg streetcar system by the Fitzgeralds in 1934 was provided on condition that Yellow buses be used to replace the streetcars.[25] To obtain financing for the acquisition of the Joliet system and the East St. Louis Railway, the Fitzgeralds began negotiations directly with Babcock, head of Yellow Coach.[26] By 1936 there was apparently a need for a more formal arrangement between the Fitzgeralds and General Motors, and a need for greater financing.[27] Meetings in Detroit between Roy Fitzgerald, Foster Beamsley, Babcock, and Herbert Listman (Yellow's sales manager) resulted in the decision to form National City Lines and to seek bank loans and a public stock offering to finance expansion.[28]

The actual formation of NCL occurred on February 5, 1936 and is best characterized as a combination of UCMT, CCL, the Fitzgerald's Rex Finance Corporation, the ubiquitous Yellow Coach, and various personnel from GM, Greyhound, and other bus products suppliers. From CCL (and Greyhound and GM) came Wickman and Traer; from UCMT (and Greyhound and Yellow) came Mills; from Yellow Coach, GM, and Greyhound came I. B. Babcock, E. P. Crenshaw, and E. J. Stone. Beamsley (from Greyhound and CCL) was also involved, along with his associate, J. M. Schramm. The Fitzgeralds were certainly involved in forming NCL, but it should be clear that NCL was certainly not of their own creation, not with this group of "associates." In addition, financing came from Yellow in the form of loans, and later from the sale of stock to GM, Firestone, Standard Oil of California, and others. Over $9 million came from these suppliers.[29]

In January 1938, General Motors and Standard Oil of California organized Pacific City Lines (PCL) as an affiliate of NCL.[30] This affiliate was organized to motorize transit systems in the West, beginning with the electric systems in Fresno, San Jose, and Stockton. The formation of PCL followed the unsuccessful efforts of Traer and Babcock at raising funds (described above). General Motors, Standard Oil of California, and Firestone put up the capital and undertook the direct management of PCL.[31] General Motors put $300,000 into PCL in 1938, and another $1 million was added between 1940 and 1946 for the acquisition of Pacific Electric properties in Glendale, Pasadena, Burbank, and San Bernardino.[32]

Pacific City Lines reveals the same pattern of extensive interlocking personnel. For example, a list of presidents and chairman of the board of PCL between 1938 and 1944 includes Roy Fitzgerald of NCL; V. F. Palmer, formerly of Standard Oil of California; and T. J. Manning, who served at the Los Angeles Railway before its acquisition by American City Lines (another NCL affiliate).[33] H. C. Grossman, an official at General Motors (later its president) and one of those convicted in the NCL antitrust case, was a director at PCL from January 17, 1943 until October 17, 1946.[34]

Jesse Haugh served as both president and as chairman of the board at Pacific City Lines during this period. He was also the third largest PCL stockholder in 1946, when PCL was merged into NCL.[35] Pacific City Lines stock was exchanged for NCL stock, so Haugh became an NCL stockholder. He does not appear to have held a formal position at NCL, although he figured prominently in NCL's acquisition of Oakland's Key System in 1946. In addition, Haugh was active in operating and motorizing other transit properties on his own, through such companies as Western Transit Systems (in San Diego) and Metropolitan Coach Lines.[36] The latter acquired the Pacific Electric System in Los Angeles in 1954 in order to motorize the remaining four rail lines. One line was motorized, but permission for the other three lines was denied by the state. In 1957 the Metropolitan Transportation Authority, a state transit district, acquired the properties from Metropolitan Coach Lines.

In August 1943, National City Lines, General Motors, Phillips Petroleum, Standard Oil of California (through its Federal Engineering Corp.), Firestone Tire and Rubber, and General American Aerocoach formed American City Lines. Capital and management came from NCL and the suppliers. In December 1944 ACL acquired the Los Angeles Railway for about $13 million. This was the type of large purchase that ACL had been set up to facilitate. Conversion of 19 of its 25 rail lines was begun within four months.[37] American City Lines was formally absorbed into National City Lines in July 1946. Pacific City Lines was sold by NCL in March 1940, but repurchased in April 1946. None of these transactions, however, altered the fundamental nature of any of the organizations.

In addition to these more or less direct or formal relationships in the motorization campaign, there were a number of indirect or informal ones that must be considered in order to gauge the full extent of the motorization effort.[38] For example, Colonel M. D. Mills, mentioned above in connection with UCMT, NCL, Greyhound, General Motors, and PCL, had also been the first general manager of the Seattle Transit System. He served from 1939 to 1941, when he was called up to active army service (1942–1945).[39] Seattle's transit system was publicly owned, so an acquisition by NCL was out of the question. There are, however, data that suggest that Mills strongly advocated conversion to motor buses and would have worked vigorously for that, if his tenure had not been cut short by his military service.[40] Mills did not return to his Seattle post after the war, but he did become vice-president and general manager of the Oklahoma Railway Co., in Oklahoma City in 1945. The Oklahoma Railway was motorized in 1946.

Connections of this sort often extended even to supposedly separate entities, which were ostensibly competitors. For example, Meier in his article devoted to National City Lines, described the formation of American Transit Corporation in 1949 as an NCL competitor.[41] Yet it is hard to see a very competitive relationship. American Transit Corp. was never directly involved with NCL, but the indirect connections were substantial.[42] National City Lines personnel and American Transit Corp. personnel comingled in eight separate firms, that is, NCL and ATC personnel served with one another as directors and corporate officers in these eight companies. How competitive could these firms have been in these cases? While this proves nothing, it suggests a lot, particularly about how the motorization campaign was extended far beyond the direct involvement of NCL and the others.

Finally, the conversion of the Minneapolis Transit System shows how a conversion was accomplished directly by General Motors, without recourse to "intermediaries," such as NCL. While there is nothing conspiratorial here, it is a revealing case. Stephan Kieffer described the attempts of Minneapolis Transit System President Ossanna at modernizing the Minneapolis system in the early 1950s, as follows:

> First attempts at gaining local capital for conversion were rebuffed; local bankers lacked confidence in the future of public transportation in the Twin Cities. Discouraged, but not ready to throw in the towel, Ossanna approached General Motors Corporation about the purchase of twenty-five new diesel coaches, which would have taken most of the company's available funds at the time. Roger Kyes of GM, later to be Assistant Secretary of Defense in the Eisenhower administration, was impressed with the determination of the new management to provide successful mass transit in the Twin Cities, and dispatched a team of experts to the Twin Cities to survey the local company situation.[43]

The team of experts was headed by B. M. Larrick, formerly of National City Lines and an expert on the conversion of streetcars to motor buses. Their recommendation was complete motorization. Ossanna had gone looking for 25 diesel buses and had ended up purchasing 525 buses from GM. This required that 700 streetcars be taken out of service, including 141 new PCC cars in good working order. Why the new PCC cars were scrapped is unclear, but it does appear that GM offered a package deal, with the sale of the PCC cars as a condition for GM financing of the deal.

We have sketched the background and the relationships between the various participants in the motorization campaign, but how does this figure in the conspiracy argument? First, this jungle of "front companies" might suggest a cover-up. For example, at least two of the supplier companies sought to disguise their involvement in the NCL et al. affair.[44] Court records indicated that Firestone Tire had endeavored to conceal its participation by investing in the names of two of its employees, acting as nominees. Standard Oil apparently used the same tactic, investing through two nominee companies. Testimony from Standard Oil of California's treasurer indicated that the company did not want Standard to be held accountable for the motorization. It is hard not to agree with Jonathan Kwitney's observation that this is "strange behavior from companies that defended themselves on the grounds that they had performed noble public service by hastening the advent of the bus."[45]

The creation of front companies is likewise a cornerstone in Snell's allegations. He argued that because motor buses were not as cost efficient as electric streetcars or trolleys, free buyers would have bought General Motors motor buses. Testimony from General Motors executives does confirm a significant resistance to large-scale motor-bus conversions.[46] The solution, from General Motors' standpoint, was to engineer a campaign whereby General Motors would set up front companies, which would acquire urban transit systems, convert them to General Motors motor-buses, and then sell them off to allow for new acquisitions. Front companies would be captive buyers of inferior buses. In these cases, motorization did not require market transactions, but rather involved one General Motors subsidiary, or GM-controlled company, dealing with another GM-controlled subsidiary. In other words, it was the company essentially doing business with itself.

The existence of "front companies" therefore suggests a clandestine atmosphere surrounding the motorization campaign. Both the economic analysis and the testimony of the participants themselves also suggest that the promotion of inferior buses could not have been carried out initially without them. The use of front companies also bears directly on an issue raised by the defendants in the NCL antitrust case. General Motors argued at trial, and in *The Truth About American Transportation*, that NCL had approached them, that the scheme was NCL's idea, and that GM had only provided financing to a struggling customer during the depression.[47] It was presented as a completely innocent relationship. The appeals court, in upholding the conviction in the NCL case, did note that it had been NCL that had "conceived the idea" and had "approached" GM, although it was GM and the other suppliers that had suggested the exclusive contracts. In view of the origins of NCL, however, this seems to be a moot point. To the extent that it influenced the verdict (the defendants were acquitted on some of the charges), justice was not served.

SUPPLIER CONTRACTS: VEHICLE FORECLOSURE?

As previously noted, the intent behind motorization activities of NCL, PCL, ACL, Omnibus, and others is the primary issue. We will discuss here those activities that suggest a conspiratorial intent. We will also consider other possible motives for these actions, motives that were not conspiratorial.

Much attention has been drawn to the exclusive provisions in the contracts between NCL and its suppliers/backers, which seem to go well beyond normal bounds (if there is a "norm"). National City Lines was required to purchase most (sometimes all) of its buses and supplies from the suppliers/backers. When the transit systems were sold by NCL after motorization, any return to electric vehicles was explicitly prohibited through contract provisions that prevented the new buyers from engaging in the purchase of any new equipment using any fuel or means of propulsion other than gas. Note that the provisions of this part of the contract did *not* require the purchase of General Motors equipment or Standard Oil petroleum, and the like. Only gasoline-powered vehicles were stipulated. The new buyers were free to purchase motor buses from someone other than General Motors, but electric vehicles were explicitly excluded.

General Motors, in its reply to Snell's accusations, denied Snell's charges that the contracts selling NCL properties carried any provisions requiring that the new buyer never replace the existing equipment with any equipment not utilizing gasoline (or diesel) engines.[48] There appears to be little doubt, however, that these contract provisions were common in NCL sales contracts. The review of the antitrust conviction of the defendants by the U.S. Court of Appeals, Seventh Circuit, cited as one of the *undisputed facts* of the case the existence of contracts with NCL providing for the exclusive use of the suppliers' (GM, Firestone, Standard Oil of California, and so on) products on NCL properties *and* the existence of contract provisions requiring that NCL, PCL, or any of their operating companies "not renew or enter into any new contracts with third parties for the purchase of such products or change any then existing type of equipment or purchase any new equipment using any fuel or means of propulsion other than gas."[49] Kwitney has observed that these contracts had to be altered to allow for the use of diesel equipment.[50]

There can be little doubt that the contract provisions went beyond simply obtaining exclusive rights to supply NCL with the suppliers' products. There seems to have also been a preoccupation with guaranteeing that other modes of transit be kept out. There is also little doubt that these contracts limited NCL to technologies that they themselves, as transit operators, felt were inferior. For example, in congressional testimony, William C. Dixon, the government's chief trial counselor during the NCL trial, presented testimony from a bus dealer, which he had presented to the grand jury.[51] The bus dealer had tried to sell new motor buses (not trolley coaches) to NCL's Los Angeles Transit Lines (LATL). He was turned down by the president of LATL, with the following suggestion: "Well, I don't think there is any point in our operating your buses. . . . You know our setup with General Motors, and they are probably going to build 50 or 55 passenger buses; and if they build them, we will probably have to buy them. I think your bus is as good or better than any other bus, but with this tieup we have, it is just out of the question. You might as well take your business to some other property with whom you can probably do some business."[52] In addition, while NCL was supposed to pay competitive prices for the buses that it purchased from General Motors, NCL admitted in court that they did not compare prices.[53]

AN INSIGNIFICANT MARKET?

Insight into the motives of the suppliers/backers might also be gained from a look at another line of defense that was employed at the NCL antitrust trial. One of the grounds on which the antitrust conviction was appealed was that the defendants had been unfairly limited in the kinds of evidence they were allowed to introduce in their defense. The defendants had wanted to show that their sales to NCL were not a large part of their market, nor was it very lucrative. For example, General Motors later testified in congressional bearings in 1955 that its sales to NCL between 1949 and the first 10 months of 1954 were only 4 percent of its bus sales.[54] Indeed, one would wonder why they had bothered with it at all. In a similar vein, Mack Truck, which was acquitted in the NCL trial, apparently backed out of the NCL arrangement early because it was not very lucrative.[55] Ford Motor Company sold out of the transit bus business in the late 1940s because of the "low profit potential."[56]

The appeals court noted that the lower court was correct in allowing the introduction of such evidence, but that it was also correct in limiting such "collateral evidence," since it was not directly relevant to the antitrust issue. This, however, would have been very interesting for the question at hand. If the defendants wanted to argue in their defense that the NCL arrangement was not that large or very lucrative, then what were their motives? There certainly was a much larger question than the simple antitrust question here, but one that the courts did not pursue.

While one should not automatically take every courtroom defense argument at face value, this point should not be dismissed too lightly. There are indications from other sources that the motorization campaign was not a lucrative venture, at least not as far as the sale of buses and bus supplies was concerned. Kwitney cites numerous indications in the court transcript that the motorization campaign was not considered very lucrative by the participants. For example, an internal memo at Mack Truck cited "probable loss" on the NCL investment, but indicated that the investment was "more than justified" by the expectation of increased business in the future.[57] As noted, Mack did pull out of the deal, apparently because they were unhappy with what they were getting out of the arrangement. Their pull-out tends to support the argument that the NCL deal was not made with the expectation of large profits from bus-system operations or from the sale of buses to NCL. Because of its size and product mix, Mack Truck was clearly not in a position to gain as substantially from any reorganization of urban transportation as General Motors would. In addition, other companies contacted about participating in the NCL campaign had also turned the offer down. We can only speculate about their motives, but a lack of financial incentive seems one likely reason.

This expectation of only a minimal return from the actual sale of buses and supplies seems to have extended even to GM. As Kwitney has noted,

> [It does not] appear that General Motors expected to make its principal profit from the sale of buses, the new form of mass transit. If it did, there is no satisfactory explanation in the trial record for why General Motors gave half of the prospective bus business away to Mack, its supposed competitor. Another explanation, of course, is that the real profits were going to be made from the sale of cars (in Mack's case, trucks) after the destruction of mass transit opened the way for a huge public network of streets and highways. That this is what happened offers some justification for the explanation that it was intended.[58]

In congressional testimony in 1955, General Motors recounted the reaction of its Yellow Coach president in 1939 to Mack Truck's participation in the NCL arrangement. Even though this would have given Mack 42.5 percent of the bus sales to NCL, the president voiced no objections, claiming "the more the better."[59] This is not exactly what one would expect from a company out to compete in, let alone monopolize, a lucrative bus market.

A FINANCING SCHEME?

This argument by the defendants, that their sales of motor buses and bus supplies were insignificant, seems to contradict another defense argument that the NCL arrangement was only a means of financing the sale of buses in a cash-strapped world. Why was financing crucial, if the market was insignificant? General Motors' general sales manager at its bus division, Herbert Listman, testified that the NCL deals had simply been "temporary finance plans."[60] According to Listman, GM dropped its interest in NCL as soon as the plans had "served their purpose." Financing problems apparently did arise. For example, as noted above, Glenn Traer had tried to raise money for motorizations in the West. As he reported to Babcock in 1937, "I talked to investment houses, brokers, and private capital. . . . I couldn't get the money."[61] Testimony by Babcock, however, indicated more than a financing problem. He testified that "we were having great difficulty in convincing the power companies to motorize and give up their streetcars."[62] Babcock's solution was to put $300,000 into the motorization of three small cities, Kalamazoo and Saginaw, Michigan, and Springfield, Ohio. This initial motorization eventually led to UCMT and to NCL. While financing may have been a part of the NCL campaign, the arrangement went far beyond the range of financing. Acquiring transit properties prior to their motorization put the bus sellers in the position of being bus buyers. In addition to financing the purchase of buses, they were also making the decision to purchase. This is an important distinction. Extensive financing was nothing new to GM. It had set up its GMAC subsidiary for that purpose (financing cars, and later trucks, buses and so forth) in 1919. But to argue that the NCL arrangement was principally a financing arrangement is to miss the essential nature of the arrangement.

NATIONAL CITY LINES EARNINGS

If the sale of buses and supplies to NCL was not very lucrative, and if the NCL's backers were not very interested in NCL as a market for their products, might they have been primarily interested in the NCL arrangement as an investment in the transit operating companies that were acquired by NCL? Likewise, were NCL profits so lucrative as to belie any ulterior interests on the part of NCL executives in pursuing their motorization campaigns? On the surface, it appears highly unlikely that General Motors or the others were so motivated. Indeed, the testimony of General Motors executives cited above seems to indicate a lack of interest in NCL operations. But can NCL earnings confirm or deny this?

National City Lines' earnings are available, but they are inconclusive in this regard.[63] Earnings were positive, but not spectacular. But what should they be compared with? They never approached the rates of return that General Motors became famous for. More important, NCL earnings do not address the critical issue: Was motorization profitable? Earnings don't help much here for a number of reasons. First, the correct question is counterfactual. What would NCL profits have been if they had not motorized, if they had used streetcars and trolley coaches where appropriate? This is counterfactual because, of course, they did motorize. Second, profits alone do not tell much. Any sort of modernization of old decrepit streetcars would have improved profitability. Everyone agreed that new buses were often preferable to old streetcars. The question was what to replace those old streetcars with—trolley coaches, motor buses, or new streetcars?

In addition, one should not think that NCL was the only profitable operation in the industry. Many transit systems were able to show operating profits even before modernization. For example, the operating income for the Los Angeles Railway and the Los Angeles Motor Coach Company (owned jointly by the Los Angeles Railway and Pacific Electric) are shown in Table 3.1, where the figures are presented by division. Table 3.2 shows the combined results (along with other financial data). The Los Angeles Railway not only earned a profit, but the source of the profit was definitely the rail division. (It must also be pointed out that bus fares and revenue per passenger were higher, and that various accounting practices favored bus operations.)[64]

The third reason NCL profits are unreliable gauges of the profitability of motorization stems from the fact that motorization was often accompanied by fare increases, reductions in operating schedules, route changes,

TABLE 3.1. Los Angeles Railway Corporation Operating Income

Year	Rail Division	Motor Coach Division	Share of Los Angeles Motor Coach Company	Total
1924	$2,470,682.64	$(76,865.84)	$(26,341.18)	$2,376,475.62
1925	1,657,788.17	(103,198.91)	(31,225.22)	1,523,364.04
1926	1,542,005.75	(211,193.50)	(49,304.14)	1,281,508.11
1927	1,649,099.01	(214,223.98)	(24,684.65)	1,410,190.38
1928	1,978,387.11	(186,456.54)	(2,049.93)	1,789,880.64
1929	2,710,293.07	(152,189.76)	95,853.29	2,653,956.60
1930	1,776,893.67	(207,694.81)	71,500.43	1,640,699.29
1931	761,827.59	(162,993.42)	131,340.98	730,175.15
1932	484,317.68	(160,589.81)	101,437.80	425,165.67
1933	647,554.30	(150,863.81)	101,929.43	598,619.92
1934	18,356.45	(160,076.34)	81,296.07	(60,423.82)
1935	107,251.73	(83,768.19)	124,243.22	147,726.76
1936	635,024.42	12,684.65	155,095.82	802,804.89
1937	618,561.48	(81,458.78)	168,690.52	705,793.22
1938	615,495.99	(109,546.07)	196,541.02	702,490.94
1939	191,215.87	12,216.88	248,685.95	452,118.70

Note: Figures in parentheses are deficit figures.
Source: California Railroad Commission, *Report on Urban Mass Passenger Transportation Facilities and Requirements of Los Angeles, Vol. 2,* Case No. 4461, October 17, 1940, p. 30.

TABLE 3.2. Los Angeles Railway Corporation Rate Base and Rate of Return

Year	Operating Revenue	Operating Expense	Depreciation	Taxes	Operating Income	Rate Base	Rate of Return (percent)
1924	$13,097,426	$8,575,060	$ 862,140	$868,054	$2,792,172	$37,200,000	7.5
1925	12,852,119	9,040,893	919,147	820,316	2,071,763	39,700,000	5.2
1926	13,021,482	9,365,098	964,474	807,925	1,883,985	41,100,000	4.6
1927	13,287,600	9,503,632	1,009,808	814,348	1,959,812	42,200,000	4.6
1928	13,626,231	9,431,621	1,036,490	833,675	2,324,445	43,400,000	5.4
1929	14,874,309	9,659,033	1,081,636	997,392	3,136,248	44,200,000	7.1
1930	13,732,651	9,553,016	1,108,015	953,714	2,117,906	44,800,000	4.7
1931	12,229,222	9,239,154	1,104,407	812,866	1,072,795	45,200,000	2.4
1932	10,338,587	7,777,217	1,102,435	678,295	780,640	45,300,000	1.7
1933	9,464,252	6,811,465	1,093,448	598,368	960,971	45,000,000	2.1
1934	9,804,745	7,842,441	1,117,989	589,410	254,905	45,000,000	0.6
1935	10,591,879	8,447,553	1,164,978	558,255	421,093	45,100,000	0.9
1936	11,817,815	9,909,930	1,196,810	655,461	55,614	45,700,000	0.1
1937	12,395,171	9,500,105	1,028,786	874,638	991,642	46,500,000	2.1
1938	12,189,129	9,159,327	1,071,891	927,775	1,030,136	48,000,000	2.1
1939	12,329,480	9,504,223	1,114,105	950,741	760,411	48,700,000	1.6

Source: California Railroad Commission, *Report on Urban Mass Transportation Facilities and Requirements of Los Angeles, vol. 2.* Case No. 4461, October 17, 1940, p. 214.

and a general rationalization of transit operations.[65] These certainly augmented profits, but they are irrelevant to the question at hand, since most would have been warranted regardless of whether buses, trolley coaches, or streetcars had been used in the modernization program.

In a similar vein, NCL acquisitions and motorizations were often combined with a much-needed financial restructuring of the transit properties. Excessive debt obligations were often written off, and overcapitalization was pared down. For example, the low rate of return for the Los Angeles Railway in 1939 (Table 3.2) was calculated on the $48.7 million rate base shown. In addition, in 1939, debt payments of $838,059 were charged only against the rail division's operating income, that is, against the $191,215.[66] (It should be noted that no debt obligations were charged against the motorbus operations, although the debt obligations would still have to be met, even after any motorization.) The Los Angeles Railway was acquired by American City Lines in 1944 for about $13 million. In 1954, Los Angeles Transit Lines (the name of the property after its acquisition) had $10,578,400 in outstanding common stock.[67] It also had only about $1.8 million in debt obligations (compared to over $26.7 million in the late 1930s). The details of how this financial transformation was accomplished, and the role of the ACL acquisition in it, are unclear at the present time. There can be no doubt, however, as to how the system's profitability was affected by this reorganization—but such a financial reorganization would have been just as warranted, and beneficial, regardless of the vehicle employed.

The final problem with evaluating NCL earnings stemmed from the tendency of NCL to buy and sell properties at a rather rapid rate. This certainly augmented their earnings with income from capital gains. We know that NCL bought and sold properties continuously, even buying and selling the same property more than once. For example, San Jose City Lines were acquired and sold by NCL on three separate occasions.[68] We also know that a number of properties were sold to local transit districts (usually when they could no longer pay their way), and that these sales often brought large capital gains to NCL. My count shows at least 18 properties sold directly to local governments. Most properties were ultimately sold to local governments even when NCL sold the properties first to other private parties. As an example of the capital gains from these sales, NCL realized $5,092,800 from its disposal of the Key System in Oakland in 1960,[69] and another $6,463,245 net gain, after taxes, on the sale of its St. Louis Public Service Company in 1963. The sale of its Los Angeles Transit Lines in 1958 brought an estimated $6,500,555 in after-tax gain. All three of these properties were sold to local transit districts, most of which had to subsidize the continued operation of the systems. With regard to the sale of these properties, neither the Oakland nor Los Angeles sales included the private rights-of-way, which had been important attributes of both systems. These had been previously disposed of.

THE BINGHAM FORMULA

While earnings cannot shed much light on the question at hand, NCL activities in the early 1950s do not look like a company reaping the rewards of motorization. In particular, National City Lines' vigorous support of the "Bingham Formula," as the means to rescue transit, seems inconsistent with its other activities. Under the Bingham Formula, NCL proposed to sell its properties to municipal transit districts in about half of the cities in which it operated.[70] National City Lines would then operate the properties under contract with the city. The formula would thus provide for public ownership with private management, ostensibly the best of both worlds. According to an editorial in *Bus Transportation* in 1951, NCL was interested in the Bingham plan because the "plain, unvarnished truth is that the investment in money and ability is not paying off. Under the circumstances, National City Lines cannot be blamed for 'wanting out' if it now is convinced that there are 'easier ways to making a living'."[71] An article in *Mass Transportation*, reporting on efforts by NCL to put the Bingham Formula into effect, was even more emphatic about what NCL's actions meant: "This move on the part of the Fitzgeralds makes it obvious that they feel there is no long term future in the transit industry the way it is headed today."[72]

While this realization in 1951 would explain NCL's interest in getting out of the transit business, it would not explain their continued purchase of transit systems after 1951. After a two-and-one-half-year hiatus in acquiring transit properties, NCL acquired the Davenport City Lines and the Rock Island–Moline City Lines on August 6, 1950.[73] Assuming that the conditions that prompted the Bingham Formula had not developed overnight, these purchases appear contradictory. Yet the purchases continued. Seven more transit systems were acquired from January 1, 1951 to January 6, 1970. In addition, controlling interest in the Philadelphia Transportation Co. was acquired on March 1, 1955. Although in 1952 Roy Fitzgerald, head of NCL, thought the Bingham Formula could be the "solution" to a problem of "crisis proportions" that would force the loss of transit services in many cities "within the next twelve months," his firm continued buying transit systems.[74]

A LOOK INSIDE NCL

While the level of operating revenues or profits on National City Lines properties is unclear, a revealing look at the source of these operating revenues is possible for the years 1954 and 1956. Internal reports on the operations of National City Lines' five large transit properties, the "Big Five," were sent to a select group of NCL executives (12 executives were sent copies in 1957) and marked *"completely confidential."*[75] Operating income figures for these properties are shown in Table 3.3. What is most interesting in this regard is that the electric streetcars and electric trolley coaches that NCL continued to operate after acquisition, but prior to their motorization, were generally their biggest net revenue producers. These experiences with trolley coaches, streetcars, and motor coaches appear to be at odds with their motorization policy. Even though the method of assigning some cost items "on the basis of revenue" probably favored the motor bus, the figures hardly support a program of rapid and complete bus substitution.

ONLY DIVERSIFYING?

Could the suppliers/backers have been interested in the NCL campaign because of the diversification it provided? Diversification has long been recognized as a means of reducing risk, as well as positioning the firm in potential growth markets. Might their backing of NCL, for example, be interpreted as a legitimate diversification effort untainted by ulterior motives?

TABLE 3.3. National City Lines' "Big Five" (operating income in cents per vehicle-mile; costs include depreciation)

Property	Year	Motor Bus	Trolley Coach	Streetcar
St. Louis	1954	2.45	—	18.90
Los Angeles	1954	3.14	11.35[a]	8.82
Baltimore	1954	6.25	3.61[a]	—
Key System	1954	4.32	—	.32
Philadelphia	1956	3.24	15.27	11.67
St. Louis	1956	2.30	—	21.03
Los Angeles	1956	6.44	20.54	12.65
Baltimore	1956	8.14	—	(5.83)
Key System	1956	4.76	—	(3.42)[b]

[a] Streetcar and trolley coach combined.

[b] Transbay rail operations.

Source: National City Lines, *Big Five: Comparative Statement of Income*, for the years 1954 and 1956. These were confidential internal reports sent to a small group of NCL officers. They are both available in the Southern California Rapid Transit District Library in Los Angeles County.

In view of what we have considered thus far, this seems unlikely. Urban transit does not look like a very fertile field for diversification. And as we have seen, it appears that the suppliers/backers thought about the same. In addition, Alfred Sloan, Jr., in his memoirs, described at length General Motors' diversification into such areas as airlines, aircraft, diesel locomotives, and refrigerators, but barely mentioned Yellow Coach, and avoided NCL entirely.[76]

As far as General Motors is concerned, diversification to exploit a profitable transit or transit bus market seems unlikely. Diversification into transit, however, in order to protect or enhance the automobile market does seem consistent with General Motors' attitude. For example, Sloan's description of General Motors' interest in and motivation for acquiring aviation companies is quite revealing. Sloan described the reasoning behind GM's decision to vigorously enter the field in 1929, as follows:

> During the 1920s it became steadily clearer that aviation was to be one of the great American growth industries. . . . As automobile producers, we were especially concerned about one possible use of the airplane. There was in the late 1920s a great deal of talk about developing a "flivver" plane—that is, a small plane for everyday family use. . . . Our conviction grew that the flivver plane was at least a possibility. The development of such a plane would have large, unforeseeable consequences for the automobile industry, and we felt that we had to gain some protection by "declaring ourselves in" the aviation industry.[77]

The interest in aviation seemed to last only as long as the "threat" to the automobile industry lasted. Describing the decision to get out of the aviation field, Sloan explained that "by the end of the 1930s our perspective on North American and Bendix had changed considerably. Our original motive for investing in the aviation industry—the feeling that the industry might somehow produce a flivver plane which could compete with the automobile—came to seem less relevant as the years passed. No plane suitable for "family use" was ever developed."[78]

All of this seems to suggest that in diversification, General Motor's prime consideration always remained with the automobile market and how these developments might affect that market. The interest in aviation was primarily motivated by a concern over possible competition for the auto from a flivver plane. When this did not materialize (and GM did not try to develop it), the interest disappeared.

Unless we assume that GM approached the manufacture of buses and the acquisition of public transit systems in a completely different manner (and this seems highly unlikely), then it is reasonable to expect that an overriding concern for the giant automobile market again dominated its decision to enter the rather small bus and public transit markets. If so, the conversion-for-destruction argument is certainly consistent with this approach.

GENERAL MOTORS AND TROLLEY COACHES

In trying to evaluate General Motors' motivation in organizing and financing the activities of National City Lines, a rather curious fact assumes a certain degree of importance. Yellow Coach, General Motors' wholly owned subsidiary, had been producing trolley coaches between 1932 and 1938! Sales were particularly brisk in 1935 and 1936, after which sales fell off through 1938, the last year of production. Sebree and Ward summarized Yellow's record by noting that "Yellow quickly became the traditional leader of the bus industry but never amounted to much in the trolley coach field. Indeed, its total production of 456 TC's places it well down the list of builders of this type of vehicle."[79]

Sebree and Ward's discussion of Yellow's position in the industry is, however, confusing and somewhat misleading. First, it is misleading to say that Yellow never amounted to much in the trolley-coach field. If we look at the entire period over which trolley coaches were produced (roughly 1928 through 1955), we find Yellow ranked seventh among the eight significant producers of trolley coaches. But Yellow produced only from 1932 through 1938. In 1936, when NCL was formed (and the last big year of trolley-coach production at Yellow), Yellow was the *largest* producer of trolley coaches. Its market share in 1936 was almost 43 percent of the trolley-coach market. In 1935 its market share had been almost 61 percent. Yellow Coach was a major producer of trolley coaches—in fact *the* major producer—while it remained in the field. In 1938, the last year in which any Yellow trolley coaches were produced, Yellow was still the second largest producer, although it produced only 41 that year.

This makes the abrupt halt in production after 1938 all the more interesting. It also makes the contract provisions requiring only petroleum-fueled vehicles on properties sold by NCL all the more curious. Was this a situation where Yellow (that is, GM) simply shifted to a superior technology? Or was the discontinuation of production simply part of a larger plan for forcing less competitive motor buses on transit systems? If GM was simply interested in selling buses, why would it not have continued to produce *both* diesel buses and trolley coaches? That would have provided even greater diversification. National City Lines could have been required to buy GM vehicles, electric, diesel, or gasoline, *if General Motors' desire had been only to sell buses.* As noted, however, it is an established fact that NCL would not (or could not) purchase trolley coaches. Sebree and Ward had also noted this: "Not once did NCL propose trolley coaches for their newly acquired properties."[80] Only in one case, its 1945 acquisition of the Los Angeles Railroad, did NCL change its exclusive use of General Motors' motor buses in a conversion program. In 1947 NCL purchased 40 new PCC cars and a number of trolley coaches (most were vehicles from NCL's recently acquired Key System Transit Lines in Oakland) for the Los Angeles Railroad. Sebree and Ward were suspicious of the motives for breaking the trend in Los Angeles: "While proof would be difficult to establish beyond reasonable doubt, there are those who firmly believe that the 1947 purchase of trolley coaches and PCC cars by NCL for Los Angeles was an effort to take the wind out of the government's antitrust charges."[81]

In any case, General Motors discontinued producing its trolley coach, and National City Lines, with few exceptions, motorized their properties. There is little doubt about either's aversion to what E. P. Crenshaw, general sales manager for General Motors' truck and coach division, referred to in 1953 as the "mongrel vehicle."[82]

TROLLEY COACHES AND THE KEY SYSTEM

The story behind the NCL trolley coaches that ended up in Los Angeles is of further interest. The motorizers' absolute aversion to trolley coaches and streetcars and their total commitment to motorization is perhaps best illustrated by the fate of the proposed (and partially constructed) trolley-coach lines on Oakland's Key System.[83] Prior to its acquisition by National City Lines in May 1946, the Key System was planning to acquire PCC cars for four heavily traveled lines.[84] The remaining streetcar lines were to be abandoned in favor of motor buses and trolley coaches. In addition, the Key System was going to acquire new electric transbay trains to operate over the Bay Bridge. There is no doubt that while the PCC cars were planned, only tentative steps were taken to implement this part of the plan. This was definitely not the case with the trolley coaches. In 1945, 40 trolley coaches and the necessary overhead were ordered for conversion of the College Avenue and Arlington-Euclid streetcar lines in the summer of 1946, which had been planned for sometime. Numerous studies of these and other lines for possible conversion to trolley-coach operations had been made, the first in 1940. At least 15 trolley coaches were actually delivered to the company's shops for painting, another 25 had been ordered, and work was already under way on the installation of the overhead on the Broadway-College Avenue line, when NCL purchased the Key System on May 14, 1946. The same day, NCL announced that all streetcars would be abandoned in favor of motor buses and trolley coaches. The Key System's new president, Jesse Haugh (president of PCL) confirmed the company's intention to use the 40 trolley coaches on the lines already scheduled for trolley-coach conversion. One month later, the 15 trolley coaches were shipped to ACL's Los Angeles Transit Lines. Within weeks the other 25 trolley coaches were sold to Los Angeles Transit Lines. The trolley-coach plan was deferred by Haugh on July 19, 1946, because of the "high cost of electrification and the inability to obtain the rest of the electric buses."[85] General Motors buses began to be placed on these routes, although Haugh said that the deferment was not an abandonment. But by December 1946, the trolley-coach plans were abandoned as "impractical."[86] While Haugh cited an inability to get the electric buses in time as one of the main reasons for the "deferment" in July 1946, the 40 trolley coaches that were sent to Los Angeles were in operation in Los Angeles prior to the motorization of the Oakland streetcar lines that they were intended to replace. Likewise, the excuse of "high costs of electrification" is difficult to take seriously in the light of the fact that considerable work on the overhead had already been completed. This episode seems difficult to explain in any manner except as an intense effort to preclude the use of trolley coaches. They had been ordered, some had been received, work was already under way on the conversion, and the selection of the routes for trolley-coach conversion had been well studied and considered. The explanation given for not using them was feeble.

A SUGGESTED RATIONALE

Some have tried to identify more precisely why General Motors could not possibly have been interested in the motor-bus market. For example, Snell argued in 1973 that the sale of one GM bus, at a price of $40,000, would lose General Motors approximately $466,200 in lost car-sale revenue.[87] This was based on an average automobile price of $3,700 and an average life of 5 years for the car and 18 years for the bus. The crux of the argument was that one bus could replace 35 cars.

While I share the conviction that General Motors' automobile operations were its most profitable and most important operation, and that public transit did in fact compete with auto sales, these calculations are too contrived and too arbitrary to be taken as anything more than an illustration. There is no reason to suppose that some of those 35 cars would not have been sold anyway, even if 35 commuters utilized public transit. Some of those customers would have bought an automobile and still have used viable public transit for commuting to work and for other purposes. The 35 lost sales is therefore too high and confuses the bus's capacity to carry 35 commuters with lost automobile sales.

While these figures cannot be accepted, the basic proposition still seems sound. How could we expect General Motors not to have been more concerned with an auto market that was measured in millions (and turned over rather rapidly) than in a small bus market measured in thousands or an even smaller transit industry?

CONCLUSION

One must conclude that alternative explanations of the intent of the motorizers are weak. The activities of those alleged to have conspired to motorize and destroy public transit reveal a pattern that, when considered in the light of the preceding economic analysis, is highly suspect, to say the least. It must be stated that our knowledge of these events is still incomplete, and that there is no "smoking gun." There is, however, a growing body of evidence that, taken as a whole, does strongly support the allegation.

NOTES

1. Not all of these were indicted or convicted in the antitrust suit, although all were involved in the motorization in one way or another.

2. Bradford Snell, *American Ground Transport* (1973), reproduced as an appendix to: U.S., Congress Senate, Committee on the Judiciary, *The Industrial Reorganization Act, Hearings before the Subcommittee on Antitrust and Monopoly on S.1167, Part 4A,* 93rd Cong., 2d sess., 1974, p. A-29.

3. Ibid., p. A-89. The discussion of General Motors and Greyhound is based on Snell, p. A-89, unless otherwise noted.

4. Ibid., p. A-29.

5. Ibid.

6. Ibid.

7. Jonathan Kwitney, "The Great Transportation Conspiracy," *Harper's* 262 (February 1981): 20.

8. Ibid. The account of these events involving Traer, Babcock, and the meeting in Chicago are from this source.

9. Henry Hogan (general counsel—General Motors), Statement of the Facts from the Court Records Regarding General Motors in the National City Lines Cases, as reported in U.S., Congress, Senate, Committee on the Judiciary; *A Study of the Antitrust Laws—General Motors,* 84th Cong., 1st sess., 1955, p. 3920. Cited in Snell, p. A-30.

10. Ibid.

11. Snell, *American Ground Transport*, p. A-30.

12. Institute for Research in Biography, *Business Executives of America* (New York: Institute for Research in Biography 1950), p. 47. Cited in Washington Society of Professional Engineers (WSPE), *A Request for Grand Jury Action in the Matter of The Seattle Transit System,* Paper No. CA-166 (April 1968) p. 54.

13. Snell, *American Ground Transport*, p. A-30.

14. Ibid., p. A-89.

15. Ibid.

16. Ibid., pp. A-30, A-87.

17. Letter to J. A. Ritchie from B. Weintraub, vice-president and general manager, Chicago Motor Coach Company, January 26, 1940. The report, "All Motor Coach Operations for Los Angeles Railway Corporation and Los Angeles Motor Coach Co," survey by Messrs. Sherwood, Isaacson, and Lorentzen, August 1939, accompanied the letter. Copy in author's possession.

18. Glenn Yago. *The Decline of Transit* (Cambridge: Cambridge University Press, 1984) pp. 59, 246.

19. For example, see Arthur Jenkins, "Comparative Operating Costs: Buses vs. Streetcars, Los Angeles Railway, 1940." Copy in author's possession. Copy also available in the Jenkins file in the Transportation Research Library, University of California, Berkeley.

20. Albert E. Meier, "National City Lines," *Motor Coach Age* 26 (February 1974): 4–20. The account is based primarily on this source.

21. "Statement of the Facts from the Court Records Regarding General Motors in the National City Lines Cases" (Statement of General Motors), in U.S., Senate, *A Study of the Antitrust Laws* (1955). Excerpted in U.S., Senate, *Industrial Reorganization Act* (1974), p. 1822. Also see Meier, "National City Lines," p. 5.

22. Ibid., p. 6.

23. The background of Col. M. D. Mills is from WSPE, *Request for Grand Jury*, p. 47.

24. Snell, *American Ground Transport*, p. A–89.

25. Kwitney, "Great Conspiracy," p. 18.

26. Ibid.

27. Ibid.

28. Ibid.

29. Snell, *American Ground Transport*, p. A–89.

30. Ibid., p. A–31.

31. Ibid., p. A–90.

32. Ibid., p. A–89.

33. Pacific City Lines, intracompany correspondence, F. Triffin to J. L. Haugh, February 16, 1944. Copy in the author's possession.

34. Snell, *American Ground Transport*, p. A–90.

35. U.S., Senate, *The Industrial Reorganization Act*, p. 2239.

36. For an account of Haugh's activities in San Diego, see Stanley I. Fischler, *Moving Millions* (New York: Harper and Row, 1979), pp. 74–75. Also, see Meier, "National City Lines," p. 13. The discussion of Metropolitan Coach Lines in Los Angeles is from the statement of John F. Due in U.S., Senate, *The Industrial Reorganization Act*, p. 2266.

37. Snell, *American Ground Transport*, p. A–90.

38. In addition to the examples cited here, see Yago, *The Decline of Transit*, p. 247, notes 19 and 20.

39. WSPE, *Request for Grand Jury*, p. 47.

40. Ibid., p. 6.

41. Meier, "National City Lines," p. 16.

42. The account of the relationship between NCL and American Transit is from WSPE, *Request for Grand Jury*, p. 19.

43. Stephen A. Kieffer, *Transit and the Twins* (Minneapolis: Twin City Rapid Transit Company, 1958), p. 47.

44. Testimony of William C. Dixon, in U.S., Senate, *Study of the Antitrust Laws* (excerpted in Senate, *The Industrial Reorganization Act*, p. 2425. Also, see Kwitney, "Great Conspiracy," p. 20.

45. Kwitney, "Great Conspiracy," p. 21.

46. For example, see Kwitney, "Great Conspiracy," p. 20, and the testimony of H. Hogan, cited in note 9 above.

47. See *U.S. v. National City Lines, Inc. et al.*, 186 F. 2d 562, January 3, 1951, pp. 565–66.

48. General Motors, *The Truth About American Ground Transport* (1974), p. A–114. Reproduced as an appendix to U.S., Senate, *The Industrial Reorganization Act.*

49. *U.S. v. NCL* (cited above at note 47), p. 565. The antitrust case provides a wealth of data and insight into the motorization campaign, but it must be remembered that the defendants were not on trial for motorizing transit or attempting to destroy transit. They were on trial, and were convicted on the main charges, of monopolizing the motor-bus market.

50. Kwitney, "Great Conspiracy," p. 20.

51. William C. Dixon, in U.S., Senate, *A Study of the Antitrust Laws—General Motors*, (1955). Excerpted in U.S., Senate, *The Industrial Reorganization Act*, p. 2430.

52. Ibid. For General Motors' rebuttal, see the Statement of General Motors, p. 1823, cited in note 21 above.

53. Dixon testimony, p. 2424.

54. Statement of General Motors, p. 1819 (cited in note 21 above).

55. Dixon testimony, p. 2422.

56. "Reply of Ford Motor Co. to Letter from Senator Hart," reproduced in Senate, *The Industrial Reorganization Act*, p. 2714.

57. Kwitney, "Great Conspiracy," p. 20.

58. Ibid.

59. Statement of General Motors, p. 1822 (cited in note 21 above).

60. Quoted in Kwitney, "Great Conspiracy," p. 21.

61. Ibid., p. 20.

62. Ibid., p. 18.

63. NCL earnings can be found in Moody's (year by year). Also, see Meier, "National City Lines," p. 16, for a summary of the 1945–1950 period. Also, see NCL annual reports.

64. For example, see California Railraod Commission, Transportation Department, Research Division, *Report on Urban Mass Passenger Transportation Facilities and Requirements of Los Angeles*, vol. 2, Case No. 4461, 1940, esp. pp. 45, 52–53.

65. By 1946, NCL had raised its fares on about half of its properties. See Meier, "National City Lines," pp. 4–20. Some writers have suggested that NCL generally lowered fares. See, for example, "Selling Transportation Direct," *Transit Journal* 84 (August 1940): 227–28. This article in 1940 may have been based on an initial impression of NCL's operations (the company was only 4 years old). There appears little doubt, however, that fare increases were far more common. For example, in 1950, NCL requested and received 19 separate fare increases on its 43 wholly owned properties and 4 large properties. In addition, advertisements for GM buses often promoted the use of new buses in getting fare increases approved. For example, see the advertisements for GM buses in *Passenger Transport* 126 (December 6, 1963).

66. California Railroad Commission, *Report on Urban Mass Passenger Transportation*, 1940, p. 45.

67. Statement of T. Stein, "Financial Position of Los Angeles Transit Lines and Metropolitan Coach Lines." Exhibit No. 55 in Application No. 35601 before California Public Utilities Commission, Division of Utility Finance and Accounts, Los Angeles, California, October 8, 1954.

68. Meier, "National City Lines," p. 11.

69. These figures are from National City Lines Annual Reports, various years.

70. For a description of the Bingham Formula, see Colonel Sidney H. Bingham, "The Municipal Transit Problem and One Suggested Solution," *Mass Transportation* 48 (June 1952): 30–33.

71. "This is 1951 Not 1900," editorial, *Bus Transportation* 30 (December 1951).

72. "National City Lines Climbs Aboard as the Bingham Formula Begins to Roll," *Mass Transportation* 47 (December 1951): 18.

73. Meier, "National City Lines," p. 11.

74. Quotes from Roy Fitzgerald, "E. Roy Fitzgerald and the Bingham Formula," *Mass Transportation* 48 (January 1952): 41.

75. National City Lines, *Big Five: Comparative Statement of Income*, 1954 and 1956. Available in Southern California Rapid Transit District Library, Los Angeles County.

76. Alfred P. Sloan, Jr., *My Years with General Motors* (Garden City, NY: Doubleday, Anchor Books, 1972).

77. Ibid., p. 424.

78. Ibid., p. 431.

79. Mac Sebree and Paul Ward, *Transit's Stepchild: The Trolley Coach* (Cerritos, CA: Ira L. Swett, 1973), p. 152.

80. Ibid., p. 58.

81. Ibid.

82. Quoted in *Seattle Daily Journal of Commerce*, July 31, 1953. Reproduced in Committee for Modernization of Electric Transportation, *The Truth About Transit*, February 1964, p. 20.

83. The discussion that follows is drawn from Harre W. Demoro, "The Conversion of the Key System," *National Railway Bulletin* 44, No. 6 (1979): 4–31.

84. Ibid., p. 13–14, for a description of these plans and the ensuring events.

85. Ibid.

86. Ibid.

87. The discussion of Snell's analysis of GM's motives is from Snell, *American Ground Transport*, pp. A–2, A–7, A–87, and A–92.

4

The Significance of the
Motorization Campaign

The two previous chapters have dealt with the question of whether there had indeed been a concerted attempt to cripple urban transit through a motorization campaign. This chapter will endeavor to ascertain the significance of this campaign. Raising the question of significance at this juncture does not require that the skeptical surrender their disbelief or objections. The question is interesting and important in its own right, although those who find merit in the charges will certainly find it especially so.

It must be emphasized that this is a basic question, because demonstrating that a campaign of this sort took place does not demonstrate that it was important. Might this be the equivalent of arguing that someone left the portholes open on the *Titanic*? At least one author has indeed made this point, writing off the entire discussion as being essentially "irrelevant," because transit was doomed.[1]

While the significance question is important, it has been the least-developed aspect of the discussion. It probably seems unnecessary to those who find the conspiracy charges unfounded. Unfortunately, those who have found the charges credible also seem to have either ignored this question or felt it unnecessary to explore it. Consequently, little has been done in this regard. We will attempt not only to rectify this oversight but also to broaden the discussion to include other factors contributing to the decline of urban transit.

The limitations to the following discussions ought to be identified at the outset. First, the breadth of the question would require a more or less complete history of the decline of urban public transit. That is not feasible at this time; we can only hope to survey the terrain here. Second, determining the relative importance of all the various factors that contributed to an event is often difficult or impossible with any degree of accuracy.

Consequently, we will often have to be satisfied with identifying relevant factors, and with some rather crude impressions. This, however, will at least give a more accurate description of the events and is preferable to ignoring the question.

THE POPULARITY OF THE AUTOMOBILE

Perhaps no other single factor has been cited as much as has the automobile as a cause for the decline of urban transit. It was discussed somewhat in Chapter 1, where we noted that the increase in automobile ownership and traffic was an unmistakable trend in the period, and we will therefore not go back over this familiar ground here. Instead, we will try to put the trend into its proper context, revelant to the question at hand.

Opinions on the role of the automobile in the decline of transit seem to congregate around two extremes. Many writers have essentially argued that the decline was mainly (or even solely) a case of changing market preferences. Sovereign consumers simply exercised their freedom of choice, choosing the automobile and forsaking public transit. The fact that automobile use and ownership increased, while transit ridership decreased, is taken as proof of the public's preference. The growth of auto suburbs, transit's low-income elasticity, and so on are taken as additional proof. The opposite approach ignores, either explicitly or implicitly, the question of buyer preferences and consumer sovereignty.[2] The emphasis here is on the artificial molding of preferences and/or the elimination of alternatives. The rising ownership and use of automobiles is taken to reflect the elimination of choice as much as any expression of preferences, artificial or otherwise. Evidence of preference manipulation and/or the elimination of alternatives, including the conspiracy at hand, are taken as proof positive that people were forced to buy autos.

At times, the evaluation of these two positions often boils down to a question as to whether people did or did not "prefer" or "like" automobiles. Extreme positions are not uncommon here, since the question is often cast as a "yes" or "no" proposition. It certainly is not, and nothing will be served by casting the question in these terms.

The relevant question is not whether people did or did not prefer the automobile, but rather to what extent, for what purposes, and at what cost they preferred the automobile. A cursory glance at history should convince the honest observer that the automobile was indeed popular. We can therefore dismiss as ludicrous any argument that rejects this point or somehow makes light of the public's affinity for autos. We must stress, however, that while Americans liked or "preferred" automobiles, we cannot therefore conclude that transit was inviable. Two points need to be considered here. First, what were automobiles "preferred" for? Weekend trips? Daily commuting? Pleasure driving? Daily errands? Buying an automobile cannot be readily construed as an expression of a preference (or equal preference) for all of these different uses. I may strongly prefer an automobile for pleasure drives on weekends, yet be totally frustrated with "racing" down the freeways to work at five miles per hour. There is a logic to the argument that, given the large fixed costs and low marginal costs of using an automobile, it would be used well beyond its original purposes. It seems unwise, however, to dismiss the entire issue on these grounds alone. We therefore must take care in reading the message that those sovereign buyers were sending.

The second factor relates to the field of choices open to the urban commuter/traveler, who might be a potential transit rider and/or automobile owner. The choice, where individuals may act on their preferences, is conditioned in two important ways. First, the attributes of an automobile cannot be divorced from the social infrastructure and public policies necessary for accommodating (or restricting) its use. For example, the availability of roads and the degree of traffic congestion certainly influenced not only the overall preference for automobiles, but also preferences as to the kinds of automobile use. Public policy therefore conditioned the demand for and the use of automobiles. It also seems most likely that the daily commuter would have been the most sensitive to this consideration, since this entailed a peak-load problem, a problem to which automobile use was not particularly geared well suited.

In consequence, it seems inappropriate to discuss the public's preference for the automobile apart from the policy of accommodation. Lest we overstate the case, all this is not to suggest that there was no grass-roots interest (if that is the appropriate term) in the automobile. The intention here is to suggest only that an accommodating road policy would tend to encourage the use of automobiles and discourage the use of transit.[3] In addition to road policy, the demand for automobiles was dependent on, at least to some extent, the alternatives available. Curtailing the availability of transit as an alternative to the automobile, however, is the very essence of the conspiracy argument.

The increasing use of the automobile could therefore be interpreted as a *consequence* of the demise of public transit, rather than as a cause of the demise. In the extreme, this proposition seems unfounded, but there is no denying that this was a factor, and perhaps even a significant one.

This discussion does not resolve the question. Perhaps it cannot be resolved. What it and the related discussion in Chapter 1 have sought to do is argue the case for the middle ground; that is, that the automobile was popular, but that that alone was probably insufficient to explain the fate that befell transit. This is admittedly more an historical judgment than a documented conclusion, but it seems more tenable than the alternative explanations.

FLEXIBILITY AND VEHICLE CHOICE

Might the choice of transit vehicles have depended more on vehicle characteristics than on economic considerations? For example, it has often been maintained that the motor bus was the vehicle of choice by virtue of its purportedly superior flexibility. In the extreme, it has even been claimed that electric vehicles were incompatible with the development of cities. For example, John Rae has argued that "one certainty in American urban transportation is that the trolley car is too cumbersome and unmaneuverable to survive in our changing urban environment."[4] Were electric vehicles that bad in this regard? Were buses consequently the only real alternative?

There is a certain intuitive appeal in this argument, as well as an undeniable element of truth. Yet a closer examination of the issues suggests that this advantage has been blown out of proportion. The principle reason for this exaggeration appears to have resulted from confusing technical characteristics and capacity with practical operating requirements. For example, one type of flexibility involves the freedom from tracks and/or overhead. A trolley coach cannot leave its overhead and a streetcar cannot leave its track and overhead. A motor bus can, and is therefore more "flexible" *to the extent* that it might be necessary and practical to do so. This last point must be emphasized, if one wishes to gauge the degree to which this flexibility is a practical advantage. All three vehicles were tied to their routes, that is, transit services were always provided along fixed routes. The bus's capacity to be flexible was therefore irrelevant, to a large degree. It is true that a bus could temporarily change its route to avoid an accident, but the advantages of flexibility would then be limited to this kind of temporary departure from the norm, since the route still had to be maintained. It is interesting to note that efforts at utilizing this flexibility have generally been unsuccessful and/or repressed. The jitneys did use this potential, yet they were either regulated out of existence or confined to specified routes, again limiting their flexibility. Likewise, dial-a-ride programs that essentially provide door-to-destination service have rarely been allowed to realize the potential that many have seen in them.[5]

A completely different type of flexibility entails the ability to reroute or extend routes quickly and inexpensively. It is often argued that streetcars or trolley coaches cannot keep pace with the ever-changing pattern of traffic and/or a growing, changing city. There can be no doubt that the motor bus enjoys a technical advantage over the electric vehicles in this regard. It can be argued that the advantage is probably not very significant in the case of trolley coaches, but this aside, the significance of this advantage still depends on the frequency with which routes would have to be changed or extended. That frequency has probably been greatly exaggerated, for a number of reasons. First, in the case of service extensions (rather than reroutings), the motor bus affords only a shorter lead time required to inaugurate the extended service (and a lower *initial* cost). In rerouting, the value of the motor-bus flexibility depends on the degree to which transportation patterns change. In general, these patterns appear to have changed far less than is generally believed. For example, Los Angeles is essentially a city in which the original horse-drawn wagon trails were replaced by steam railroads that operated over the same routes.[6] These rail lines were eventually replaced with electric interurban rail and streetcar lines. Finally, freeways essentially replaced the streetcars and interurban lines, often acquiring the streetcar or rail right-of-way. The point here is the continuity of basic travel patterns in this rapidly growing city. The pattern of travel in Chicago seems also to have remained essentially the same since the turn of the century.[7] Even a city like San Jose, California, one of the fastest-growing cities in the United States since World War II, has maintained its original transit patterns during its spectacular growth. Of course, the pattern of travel has been greatly expanded, as it was in both Los Angeles and Chicago, but a radical change in the pattern of traffic has been relatively rare.

This observation is supported also by those authors who have noted that the "fixed" transit systems seem to have fared better over the years than have the "flexible" bus lines.[8] In fact, the "most-fixed" systems—the subways and the rapid transit systems—seem to have fared best. Of course, the fixed systems may have tended to fix transit patterns, but that does not negate the argument here.

Consequently, the need for frequent rerouting was probably not great. In addition, a reduction in traffic that resulted from the decline of an inner-city neighborhood and/or the growth of suburbs would not necessarily result in extensive rerouting. It is far more likely that the frequency of service and the rolling stock would be reduced to handle this reduction in patronage. Franchise requirements and/or regulatory authorities may have precluded such adjustments, but the greater flexibility of the bus would not have helped in that case. Indeed, it is hard to see how the motor bus's flexibility could have been expected to have dealt better with declining patronage.

Considering yet another type of flexibility, perhaps the expectation of an eventual (or early) abandonment of transit service would have made investment in overhead and track uneconomical. For example, in the event that changing transit patterns were expected to dramatically reduce patronage, a point might be reached where the larger fixed investment in electric operations would no longer be financially justified.[9] In such cases, the motor bus's flexibility, that is, its lower financial commitment, would be advantageous. This consideration must, however, be tempered by a few observations. First, the advantage was limited to those cases where substantial reductions in patronage were expected. We should also note that we are not talking about the advantages of buses on lightly traveled lines. It is assumed that electric vehicles would not have been considered on those lines in any case. We are referring to heavy lines that were reduced to lightly traveled lines, and how flexible buses might have better dealt with that transition. In these cases, the motor bus would have had an advantage, but the impression is that these rather extreme cases were not common.

It is curious or ironic that perhaps the most legitimate flexibility argument is one that has received little if any attention. While "fixed" systems, such as streetcars or trolley coaches, seem not to have been incompatible with growing and changing cities, it appears that the direction and uncertainties of public transportation policies did, in fact, cause many transit operators to prefer to stay as "flexible" as possible. Certainly the most important consideration in this regard was the promotion of freeways and the reroutings that they required. The motor bus's flexibility, essentially its lower investment commitment and its easier rerouting, were very compatible with this policy. This aspect of the flexibility argument will be considered when we return to the question of freeways.

In summary, there is no denying that the motor bus was technically more flexible, or that it could have been more flexible. This flexibility has been exaggerated, however, because its technical characteristics have been viewed apart from the practical circumstances that governed its use. It is as if one were to argue that a bus capable of speeds of 100 miles per hour would have better served transit. That capacity would have been irrelevant in any urban transit environment.

REGULATION: THE ISSUES

The urban transit industry was generally a regulated franchise monopoly. The role of regulation in the decline of transit will be considered here and will take two directions. First, we will try to show that the success of the motorization campaign was probably dependent, to a considerable extent, on the regulated-monopoly structure of the industry. This "failure" of regulation made it an important, although unwitting, factor in the motorization campaign.

Second, the question of regulatory failure will be pushed further to enquire as to how well regulators carried out their responsibilities. Regulation is essentially the application of political review and oversight as a substitute for nonexistent or ineffective market competition. In other words, for some reason the market is considered incapable of providing an effective competitive check on asocial economic activity in an industry. Consequently, regulation replaces the market check. By the nature of this process, regulators must assume some of the responsibility for subsequent developments in the industry, because they had to approve the regulatee's actions. In the case at hand, motorization had to have had regulatory approval. Consequently, it must be considered a factor, and indeed a very important factor, in this story.

In this connection, we will be looking for indications that regulatory officials did not adequately discharge their oversight duties and/or did not have the power to do so. We will return to this questions after considering the first point—how regulation facilitated the motorization campaign.

Market Foreclosure and Franchise Monopolies

The "conspiracy theory" is essentially a market-foreclosure argument, although one with a rather unusual twist.[10] The acquisition of local transit franchises by National City Lines (or one of the others) and the restrictive agreements that NCL had with its suppliers did effectively foreclose the market for transit vehicles and supplies in those areas where NCL operated. The success of the foreclosure does not appear to be in doubt. For example, the appelate court's review of the National City Lines antitrust conviction cited the successful foreclosure of the market as an undisputed matter in the case.[11]

The issues in the NCL case revolve around how effective market foreclosure was as a predatory strategy. Was foreclosure a means of attaining market power or was it a means of attaining economic efficiency? Critics of market-foreclosure arguments have criticized the feasibility, efficiency, and (by implication) the desirability of foreclosure. These criticisms have taken two directions.

First, Joseph Spengler has analyzed the positive effects of vertical integration in situations where successive market levels are characterized by market power.[12] Vertical integration could overcome the oligopolistic restrictions and thereby increase output and lower the price to the final consumer. (These effects may not occur if the vertically integrating firm has horizontal market power, but that would not be attributable to the vertical integration.) The implications of Spengler's analysis are that the quest for economic efficiency is the motivation behind vertical integration and that this integration has desirable market effects. What looks like the foreclosure of rivals would actually be a quest for economic efficiency. Is this relevant to the NCL case?

Spengler's analysis appears to lend itself to a simple test. If the vertical integration in the NCL case did overcome oligopolistic constraints, then fares should have been reduced after NCL acquired the transit system. Did this occur? The data are, unfortunately, unclear on this point. It appears that fares were reduced in some instances and raised in others.[13] For this and other reasons, a conclusive test of Spengler's argument is not yet possible,[14] but there is no evidence to suggest that his was the motivation for the NCL arrangement, in any case.

In addition to Spengler's argument, a second line of criticism has sought to refute the effectiveness of market foreclosure as a means to attaining market power.[15] It has been argued that wherever foreclosing the market could have increased a firm's market position, there always would have been alternatives that were distinctly superior to market foreclosure in obtaining the advantages of foreclosure, but without the costs specific to foreclosure.[16]

Foreclosing the market is costly to the foreclosing firm and can be successful only if it has a cost advantage or horizontal market power to begin with. But if it had a cost advantage, the firm could better attain market power without foreclosure by directly exploiting its cost advantage. The costs of foreclosure thus could be avoided. On the other hand, if the firm already possessed market power, foreclosure would be pointless and even counterproductive. The essential argument is that the costs of foreclosure could be avoided by pursuing alternative strategies better suited to advancing the firm's market power. Consequently, foreclosure as an important predatory tactic should not be expected.

These criticisms suggest that in the NCL case, foreclosure would have been too costly or would have been unnecessary. For example, if General Motors had had a cost advantage in producing transit vehicles, then it could have attained market power by exploiting its cost advantage without having to incur the costs of foreclosure. Or, with market power at the producer level, foreclosure would have been pointless and even detrimental. (If anything, General Motors did have market power here.) On the other hand, with a cost advantage in transit operations, General Motors could have monopolized that end of the market by exploiting its cost advantage directly, again avoiding the costs of foreclosure. In fact, General Motors would not have wished to ruin its transit monopoly by foreclosing its rivals, but instead would have exploited its position as a monopsonist vis-à-vis other vehicle manufacturers.

These criticisms of market foreclosure leave little rationale for General Motors or the other participants to have foreclosed transit operations, or any other market for that matter. What then of the motorization foreclosure argument and the economic analysis presented above? Are these allegations refuted a priori by these criticisms?

These criticisms of market foreclosure are not relevant to NCL activities, because of the historical circumstances in this case, which made a market-foreclosure strategy viable and effective. In the NCL case there were unique motives for foreclosure, and the institutional structure of the urban transit industry enabled the strategy to work. The circumstances will be considered briefly below.

Market foreclosure theories (and criticisms of these theories) assume that producers integrate forward in order to foreclose the market to their producer rivals. Their motivation is to attain market power in the producer market. The motorization foreclosure argument, however, is that the purpose of the NCL campaign had been to destroy the competitiveness of urban public transit vis-à-vis the automobile by excluding the most efficient vehicles, thus forcing uneconomical vehicles on transit systems.[17] The interests of General Motors, Standard Oil of California, and Firestone Tire, it is argued, were not in the minuscule (by comparison) transit vehicle and supplies market, but rather in the "automobile" market, broadly defined. Acquiring transit companies and then foreclosing the market appear to have been aimed not so much at the foreclosure of rival firms, but rather at the foreclosure of a rival technology. That is, foreclosure was an effective means to exclude electric transit vehicles, particularly trolley coaches, from urban transit systems. If technology foreclosure was the prime motive in the NCL case (as it appears to have been), then the criticisms of the lack of incentives for a market-foreclosure strategy are not relevant in this case.

This argument regarding unique motives is still predicated on NCL having had the ability to foreclose the market effectively. Why didn't competition from more efficient transit firms thwart any attempt at foreclosing an efficient technology from the market? In a competitive environment, this would have occurred. In this case, however, the regulated-franchise structure of the urban transit industry enabled the foreclosure campaign to be successful. When it purchased an urban transit company, NCL acquired an exclusive franchise to operate public transit in that area. Competition that might have prevented successful foreclosure in a competitive environment was nonexistent here. The exclusive franchise for transit operations not only shielded NCL from competition from other transit operators but also eliminated the possibility of an expansion of the vehicle and supplies market to compensate for the market lost through NCL foreclosure. This expansion would have been expected in a competitive market. Regulation replaced the market, yet a case for regulatory failure can be made here, because the exclusive-franchise structure of the industry actually facilitated foreclosure by restraining competition.

Effectiveness of Regulation

Before we try to determine if regulation was ineffective in the motorization case, we must inquire as to what would have been required for successful regulation. We want to go beyond concluding that regulation failed simply because the buses replaced the streetcars. That point has been made, and to continue here would only create a circular argument. We will attempt to get around this problem by inquiring into the manner of regulation, to see if it was carried out effectively. Consequently, an idea of the requirements for effective regulation is the first step.

Effective regulation requires that the regulators have the information necessary to arrive at consistent, optimal decisions. They must also have the power to regulate; that is, their regulatory decrees must be adhered to, and the scope of their regulatory powers must include all of the relevant areas of the regulated firm's activities. If regulators lack information or adequate powers to regulate, then a dangerous situation results: The illusion of regulatory protection is created, although substantive regulation is impossible. Whatever one believes about the merit, or lack of merit, of regulation as an economic policy, there can be no doubt that this is the worst of all possible worlds.

We must suspect regulatory failure if there are indications that regulatory decisions were being made without adequate information, or being made on the basis of irrelevant or inappropriate information. The latter certainly suggests a lack of competence, or worse, on the part of regulatory officials. A lack of information might also suggest the same—that is, it is necessary to ask for or insist on relevant information. Regulatory duties cannot be carried out on the basis of whatever data interested parties choose to submit. Likewise, indications that regulators lacked the power to effectively regulate must also suggest regulatory failure. The ability to enforce regulatory decrees was not generally the difficulty here. Rather, the scope of regulatory authority and the structure of regulation appears to have been the problem.

The popular consensus regarding regulation of urban transit appears to be that regulation was effective. This may be a somewhat inaccurate generalization, since very little has actually been written one way or the other on this topic. The only real exception is the regulatory suppression of the jitneys just prior to World War I.[18] The jitneys do not directly concern us, so the silence on the regulation of transit, particularly as it relates to the substitution of motor buses for streetcars, must be taken as a reflection of at least a tacit assumption that regulatory inefficiency was not an important factor. There are, however, numerous indications that this is an erroneous view. We will describe some of these problems by reviewing a few regulatory cases. This issue is too vast for a full treatment here, so the goal will be to use these cases to illustrate problems and to suggest how they could have affected transit. (The reader will note a preponderance of Los Angeles cases, which reflects the author's familiarity. The issues, however, are not unique to Los Angeles.)

Limited Regulatory Authority: The Pasadena Case

Two cases before the California Railroad Commission, involving local transit in Pasadena, California, and the commuter line between Pasadena and Los Angeles, show situations in which regulators seemed to have lacked adequate regulatory jurisdiction.[19] The first case, involving local transit in Pasadena (and adjoining Alta Dena), entailed a request by Pacific Electric to reorganize the entire local system through a series of route abandonments, conversions of rail lines to motor-bus routes, fare changes, and reroutings.[20] Local service had been provided by two rail lines, nine motor-coach lines, and two suburban Los Angeles rail lines (discussed below). The two local rail lines were heavily traveled arteries that had handled 51.4 percent of the total traffic carried by the entire local system in 1937. All of the bus lines had carried the remaining 48.6 percent. Pacific Electric's application included a request to abandon three "major" bus lines, along with two other bus lines that would be eliminated as part of a general rerouting. In addition to these changes, Pacific Electric requested the motorization of the two rail lines. The California Railroad Commission's engineers suggested an alternative to this part of the applicant's plan; they suggested that trolley coaches be installed to replace the rail lines, instead of motor buses. The rail cars used on the local lines were primarily old Birney cars, which were "conceded by all parties concerned to be obsolete and unsuited for further operation, and the desirability of immediate replacement by some other type of vehicle was agreed upon." Even with these old streetcars the commssion described the two rail lines as the "backbone of the local system, sustaining and providing support to the less profitable motor coach lines." In fact, in 1937, the two rail lines generated $25,207 in net operating income versus a loss of $97,594 on the bus operations. On a vehicle-mile basis, the rail lines incurred costs of 20.03 cents (or 16.02 cents with taxes excluded) versus 21.01 cents for the buses (or 20.18 cents with taxes excluded). Nor was flexibility an issue here, since the rail lines were "established beyond a doubt" and "except for extensions, no demand for change can be reasonably expected."

The commission noted that the trolley-coach plan "was vigorously opposed by applicant, based upon the contention, among others, that the cost involved was greatly in excess of that which would be necessary for motor coach substitution." On the other hand, the commission noted that the city of Pasadena "took a stand strongly endorsing the trolley coach installation and was opposed to any change in service, routing and fares unless, concurrently therewith, trolley coach substitution should be made."

The Railroad Commission sided strongly with the city of Pasadena on the choice of trolley coaches. The commission concluded that the "record indicates conclusively that the trolley coach installation, as recommended, would provide a superior type of service to that which would be possible by the use of motor coaches." The applicant had contended that the immediate financial requirements for trolley coaches to cover additional electrical distribution, track removal, and so forth would favor the motor bus. The commission pointed out, however, that this cost argument was not valid. The city of Pasadena had indicated that they would waive the track-removal provisions in their franchise agreement, provided that trolley coaches were installed. In addition, although the company had not considered it, company witnesses admitted that the rails could be used as a negative ground (this technique was not explained). With these provisions, the cost of trolley-coach installation would have been $470,000. Pacific Electric had estimated the cost of trolley coaches at $650,000 and the cost of the bus conversion at $346,000. Once again, however, the commission disagreed, insisting that the cost of the bus program would be $520,000, that is, $50,000 greater than the trolley-coach installation.

The commission concluded that the "trolley coach substitution would provide a larger measure of benefit to both the public, in the way of superior service and facilities, and to the company, in the way of greater net earnings." While this was a rather strong statement, the commission also admitted that it lacked jurisdiction regarding franchise terms, track removal, and apparently, vehicle choice. The commission seems to have abrogated its responsibility on the entire issue, stating simply that "applicant should be authorized to substitute, in lieu of presently operated local rail cars, either electric trolley coaches . . . or motor coaches." It went on to castigate Pacific Electric for not wanting to use the trolley coach, when it would have been in their own best interests to do so, but that was the extent of their actions.

The commission's decision in this matter was not consistent with its own views of the transportation requirements of both the community and the company. It either could not or would not act to ensure an optimal choice in transit vehicles. It cannot be determined which at this juncture, although something is seriously amiss with the regulatory process in either case. If it did not have the power, it certainly gave the impression in numerous cases, including this one, that it did and that it could protect the public in these matters. Of course, if it had the power but avoided the issue here, then it simply failed to fulfill its responsibilities. In view of the argument that the commission made in favor of the trolley coach, it seems a good guess that the former was the case, but we do not know for sure.

In the other case involving the two suburban lines between Pasadena and Los Angeles (the Short Line and the Oak Knoll Line), a similar problem involving the scope of regulation can be seen. Here the California Railroad Commission was asked to determine whether the service between Pasadena and Los Angeles was to be provided by rail or bus. The commission took the matter up with an eye toward resolving the issue on the "relative merits of rail versus motor coach service." Yet all action by the commission was deferred "due to the uncertainties of future developments." The most important of these "future developments" was the construction of the Arroyo Seco Parkway (Los Angeles' first urban freeway), which was scheduled for completion in July 1941.[21] The completion of the Arroyo Seco had held out the possibility of using buses on the freeway, providing some radiating streets could be constructed to distribute traffic at the Los Angeles end (to relieve traffic bottlenecks). Both the city of Pasadena and the city of South Pasadena, however, had opposed the use of the Arroyo Seco by any mass-transit vehicle, so the franchise issue was in doubt. In any case the Arroyo Seco was being constructed, with apparently little consideration given to its impact on transit, or even to whether transit could utilize a portion of the freeway when constructed.

The commission argued that rail service "possessed greater potentialities in the way of comfort, speed and satisfactory operation, if developed to the ultimate degree of refinement as to new, modern equipment operating over high-speed, congestion-free rights of way, but that construction of such facilities would require the expenditure of funds far in excess of the financial limitations of a private enterprise." In addition, the potential offered by the extensive rights-of-way on these two lines were "largely nullified" by the congestion on the Los Angeles end of each line, where congested city streets were used. For example, 33.3 percent of the total running time on the Pasadena Short Line was consumed in traversing the congested streets at the Los Angeles end, but this section of the line comprised only 16.6 percent of the route miles.

The essential point here is not a criticism of the commission's decision, but rather an attempt to point out the impossibility of effective regulation when so many developments were beyond the commission's jurisdiction. In fact, it appears that their input into the decision-making process was limited or nonexistent. All of the "future developments" that precluded commission action were outside the commission's jurisdiction. It is also apparent that the choice of vehicles was ultimately going to be determined by these events, and not by the relative merits of the vehicles in a more encompassing transportation plan. The freeway was the most important factor in this case, yet the commission could only wait and see what might develop there. The freeway would raise the cost of rail operations to a prohibitive level for a private company, but the commission could not act. It could not or would not help defray the costs, although the freeway, a public project, did not suffer from such limitations. The commission did not even know whether buses could be utilized on the freeway. Finally, the commission lacked the ability to secure or protect the rail's strong point, that is, its private right-of-way, from stifling congestion.

The Los Angeles Two-Man Car Ordinance

Another "limitation" cited in the above case was Los Angeles' two-man car ordinance. In 1939 the Los Angeles electorate, through initiative ordinance No. 81319, required all streetcars to conduct two-man operations, even PCC cars and other cars that were equipped for one-man operation. This had a disastorous effect. Since the mid-1930s, numerous studies by both the city and the California Railroad Commission had recommended the acquisition of one-man streetcars and the conversion of older streetcars to one-man operation. For example, the California Railroad Commission recommended in 1935 that the Los Angeles Railway (LARY) purchase 230 new PCC cars and convert 313 older cars to one-man operation.[22] In fact only months before the LA ordinance took effect, the commission granted approval to LARY to operate one-man PCC cars and to convert four types of older cars to one-man operations.[23] Los Angeles' Board of Public Utilities had also approved one-man operation.[24]

Company studies had shown that substantial cost savings could be obtained by a conversion to all one-man operations. For example, in 1936, the Los Angeles Railway undertook a study of the reduction in platform labor costs that could be expected from a total conversion to one-man operations.[25] On an annual basis, the company estimated that it could save $791,415 on its actual platform labor cost of $2,809,753. In other words, savings of about 28 percent could be expected. The two-man car ordinance was therefore a large step in the wrong direction. LARY not only missed these savings but also incurred substantial costs in converting cars, including PCC cars, to two-man operations.

The Los Angeles two-man ordinance had a profound detrimental effect on transit in the area. Pacific Electric had previously been disposed to continue at least one of its Pasadena-Los Angeles rail lines, until the passage of the ordinance caused the company to take a "position favoring immediate substitution of motor coach operation for rail service." The company's position here is understandable. Whereas plans were made for increased PCC car purchases and the conversion of older cars to one-man operation, the company now, in the words of Steve Easlon, "became infatuated with diesel buses and subsequently abandoned numerous streetcar lines and scrapped many older streetcars."[26] Likewise, LARY became more interested in motor buses, although in 1935 the California Railroad Commission had concluded that a general substitution of motor buses for rail was "unwarranted."[27] In fact, only one line, the "L" line on Olympic Boulevard (discussed below), was a candidate for motorization. This was due to street repairs and widening. In addition, the ordinance was a prime factor in the Los Angeles-Alhambra-San Gabriel-Temple Line rail motorization case.[28]

LARY fought the ordinance all the way to the state supreme court. It finally won in late 1940, although only after incurring the costs of conversion and legal expenses, but the lesson had already been learned.

Chicago: Regulation and Municipal Ownership

The disparity between the popular perception and the reality of regulatory powers and authority, and its consequences, can also be seen in Chicago.[29] Transit had been a city political issue since the turn of the century and remained so until at least 1930. Both regulation and public ownership were often promoted as solutions to the transit problem. Yet, the city's ability to regulate and its ability to acquire the transit system were such as to virtually exclude either of these approaches. The city never had much authority over the elevated railways, since they were classified as railroads, subject to state regulation. With the formation of the Illinois Public Utilities Commission in 1914, however, the city's regulatory authority was preempted in the streetcar field as well. This left the city with only franchise terms as a means of "regulating" transit companies (that is, the same power as the city of Pasadena had in the case above). The city's experience with streetcar regulation prior to 1914 had not been a dazzling success any way. Its attempts at regulating transit with "impartial engineers" had proven impractical, yet the realization of these limitations on the city's ability to regulate was slow in coming. Transit policies continued to be discussed in terms of whether and how the city should regulate transit. A better question would have been: Could the city regulate? The answer was no.

Municipal ownership was another policy that was often discussed and considered, but one that was also becoming increasingly impractical. State legislation in 1907 ostensibly paved the way for a municipal buy-out of transit companies. Yet, court rulings that bonds used to acquire these companies had to be included as part of the city's debt (and therefore subject to the city's debt limitations) made municipal ownership unlikely. In addition, the terms of the city's 1907 transit ordinances actually promoted over-capitalization and stock watering.[30] Municipal ownership thus became increasingly unlikely, as the book value of the properties rose all out of line with their actual value and earning potential.

Both policies were therefore impractical. The harm resulted from not realizing the fact. Valuable time and effort were lost discussing and arguing policies that could not work. Transit suffered as a consequence.

Regulatory Failure: Overcapitalization

Regulation actually promoted overcapitalization and stock watering in Chicago. Yet aside from this twist, overcapitalization and watered stock are themselves evidence of a more fundamental regulatory failure. Regulation has come to mean the submission to public oversight in exchange for a fair rate of return on invested capital. Obviously, watered stock subverts this arrangement, since the base upon which the fair rate applies is inflated. Effective regulation would therefore require the effective handling of this issue. There are indications that watered stock was a serious problem in the transit industry, and one that was not always adequately dealt with by regulatory officials. For example, the California Railroad Commission was challenging the capitalization of the Los Angeles Railway as early as 1913.[31] Because of the discrepancy in valuation, and also because all previous records had been destroyed because company officials believed that they "were of no further value," a LARY request to reorganize the company was denied.[32] In 1937 the California Railroad Commission allowed the company to reduce its road and equipment account from $68,405,611.57 to $45,463,749.59, thus resolving this 24-year-old dispute.[33]

One of the worst problems with overcapitalization was the inability of regulators to deal with it. This is apparent in the case of the Pacific Electric Company in Los Angeles. A California Railroad Commission memorandum, dealing with a 1938 Pacific Electric request for a fare increase, argued that overcapitalization was "one of the most serious ailments of this company."[34] The need for a fare increase (and future increases) was merely a symptom of the more profound problem of overcapitalization and obsolete equipment. But who, the author asked, would invest in a company that was already debt ridden (largely to its parent company) and overcapitalized? No one.

More important, the problem apparently could not be solved by the railroad commission for lack of jurisdiction. The author concluded that "the commission is placed in the peculiar position of being required to protect the interest of the public without the necessary jurisdiction."[35] The only suggestion, the memo concluded, was to persuade the parent company, Southern Pacific Railway, to voluntarily reorganize Pacific Electric, including the writing-off of $43 million in debt owed Southern Pacific, and to completely refinance the remaining debt.[36] The only other alternative was bankruptcy.

It is interesting to note that a similar problem with excessive debt and overcapitalization continued to afflict the Los Angeles Railway. In fact, the survey of LARY done for Chicago Motor Coach, prior to LARY's acquisition by ACL (discussed in Chapter 3), found that the problem of bonded debt was a serious problem, and one that had to be solved if the property was to be motorized. As noted in Chapter 3, this was done in the ACL acquisition, although the details are not clear at this time. Did it, however, require an ACL acquisition to solve this problem? Regulators in both cases, while equipped to deal with rate-base problems, seemed unable to handle the problems of overcapitalization and excessive debt.

Los Angeles was not atypical in this regard. Barrett describes the "gigantic watered investment" on some of the largest Chicago transit companies in 1906.[37] These companies were capitalized at $250,000 per mile, while the U.S. average was $115,000. An earlier study of Chicago transit companies in 1896 had estimated that the actual investment in three major Chicago companies had been $39.5 million.[38] These companies, however, carried combined capital accounts in excess of $63 million. In 1906 Chicago surface companies were claiming $108 million in outstanding securities, while a city engineer had estimated the reproduction value at $46.6 million.[39] For regulatory purposes (in conjunction with the 1907 ordinances) the valuation was set at $50 million.

This adjustment did not, however, resolve the issue. In 1912 the same city engineer estimated that the same Chicago companies were carrying $30 million in watered stock (total capitalization had increased by about $86.3 million between 1908 and 1914).[40] This problem was never fully resolved and, as noted, constituted an insurmountable hurdle to municipal ownership.

Relevant Data

Did regulators seek and obtain the kind of information necessary for adequate regulatory oversight? A review of many cases suggests that they did not. The most common problem in this regard can be seen in a 1941 California Railroad Commission decision. The case involved a request by the Los Angeles Railway to motorize three of its rail lines, to abandon two short rail shuttles and one bus line, and to reroute portions of the newly motorized lines.[41]

In support of the applicant's request for motorization, the company submitted a comparison of the existing two-man car operations with the proposed bus operations. The comparisons cited by the Commission in its decision are shown in Table 4.1.

The problem here is that these data are irrevelant to the real issue. The rail operations in question were characterized as "obsolete, slow, [and] noisy."[42] That being the case, the relevant choice was what to replace them with? The choices were motor buses, trolley coaches, modern PCC streetcars, or some combination of these three. Consequently, the data cited ignored the essential question and stated only the obvious, that is, that the streetcars had to be replaced.

TABLE 4.1. Annual Estimated Results of Motorization, Based on First Six Months of 1940

Present two-man operation	
Estimated revenue	$885,894
Operating expenses	1,020,066
Operating income	(134,172)
Proposed bus operation	
Estimated revenue	$895,949
Estimated operating expenses	857,729
Estimated operating income	38,220
Estimated savings from bus operation	$172,392
Estimated investment required for buses and garage facilities	$1,115,510
Percent savings to investment	15.5

How could an optimal choice be made when the relevant alternatives were not considered? The answer is plain. It must be pointed out that opponents of the motorization seem to have failed to challenge these data. That, however, does not alter the basic point that regulatory officials failed to insist on the relevant data that they would need to fulfill their regulatory responsibilities.

Two other problems with these data ought to be mentioned. First, why was a two-man streetcar compared with a one-man motor bus? The Los Angeles two-man car ordinance may have been the reason, but that would suggest that the relevant issues should have been the ordinance itself. If the commission could not or would not deal with this issue, it should have at least deferred action until the ordinance was challenged (successfully) in court.

Second, the issue under consideration in this case was a package of changes involving not only motorized lines but also abandonments and reroutings as well. To what extent should the savings that were attributed to "bus operations" actually have been attributed to the abandonments and reroutings? This does not appear to have been considered in this case.[43] The figures thus distort the benefits expected from motorization. Once again, it would be impossible to make an optimal regulatory decision on the basis of these data. This case was not unusual in this regard, and to the extent that it was typical, we have another factor contributing to the decline of rail transit.

In addition to these rather glaring examples of inadequate information, a more subtle—yet perhaps more fundamental—problem also existed.

Generally, all of the data comparing bus and rail operations on a line basis suffered from a flaw in the method of assigning costs to the different lines. A true picture of the relative performance of different types of vehicles is therefore not given. Judgments made on the basis of these comparisons must therefore be considered suspect, merely on the basis that the method precluded a correct assessment of the relative costs. Individual line costs were often assigned on the basis of the proportion of traffic handled by the entire rail system or the entire bus system. In other words, if a particular rail line carried 10 percent of the rail traffic, then its share of rail costs was put at 10 percent of total rail costs. A rail carrying 50 percent of motor-bus traffic would be assigned 50 percent of the motor-bus costs.

The problem with this method is that it conceals any economies of scale and ignores the impact of traffic volume on fixed costs. Since we are comparing three transit vehicles with very different levels of fixed costs—that is, streetcars with heavy fixed costs, motor buses with light fixed costs, and trolley coaches in the middle—this method would distort the comparison of relative costs.

The use of this technique would thus also distort the choice of vehicles. Consequently, optimal decisions would be impossible. This criticism covers not only regulatory decisions, but also company decisions, if in fact a company used this kind of data. In any case, regulators should have insisted on data that they would need for their decision making, regardless of company practices.

PUBLIC POLICY AND TRANSIT

Aside from regulation, public policy in general was an important factor in the decline of transit. It is important to emphasize the significance of this part of the story, because we have become more or less accustomed to thinking of transit as a subsidized activity enjoying policy priority. If that was ever true, it was not the case during this earlier time; in fact, we will endeavor to demonstrate that the opposite was generally the case. We will consider many facets of this issue, starting with a basic transportation policy dichotomy.

Private Business versus Public Works

The most profound way in which public policies adversely affected transit arose from the very different way transit was viewed vis-à-vis highways and automobiles. This dichotomy resulted not only in different approaches to policies but also in policies that generally accommodated and promoted automobile ownership on the one hand, but retarded transit on the other hand.

Paul Barrett has done an excellent job in exploring this dichotomy and tracing its consequences in the city of Chicago.[44] Transit, he argues, was always viewed as a business that was expected not only to pay its own way and earn profits for its shareholders, but also to pay the city for the right to use city streets. It was also expected to render many unprofitable services, all in the interest of providing social benefits and paying for its transit monopoly. In addition, many factors kept transit a highly political issue. These included the nature of transit operations; its early monopoly structure; its "traction baron" image; city politics; unrealistic and often contradictory expectations as to what transit could be or do; and a failure of regulation to live up to expectations. These factors not only contributed to keeping transit a highly political issue but also tended to stifle it.

On the other hand, the automobile seldom really suffered from these problems. The automobile was a "democratic" vehicle, that is, everyone seemed to benefit from the efforts at accommodating it. Highway policy remained relatively free of the political controversies that wracked transit policy. Instead of continuous political disputes, planning and consensus (at least on fundamental goals) characterized highway policy.

The most fundamental difference in these two policies derived from the very different ways that each was defined. As noted, transit was viewed as a corporate business that should be taxed, regulated, and run on a business basis. Highways and roads, on the other hand, were publicly provided services that were financed and often subsidized by government. This policy definition was based on the view that highways and roads were a traditional and legitimate responsibility of government (that is, a public good). There was also a political and practical necessity in dealing with and accommodating widespread automobile ownership. This marked difference in fundamental policy definitions was at the root of the differential impact of public policies on transit and the automobile.

Transit's problems in this regard were exacerbated by the fact that, while policies viewed transit as a business, franchise terms often prevented transit companies from acting like private businesses. In other words, transit was expected to provide for public benefits that did not generate corresponding private returns. For example, Chicago's transit companies were expected to "unify" the city through a flat five-cent, citywide fare. This not only saddled the company with an uneconomical fare structure, but also discriminated against the short-haul rider. To the extent that it crippled transit and precluded an effective resolution of transit problems, it contributed to the use of the automobile.

This dilemma can also be seen in Los Angeles. In 1921 the California Railroad Commission ruled that a streetcar line "should not be abandoned or curtailed if there is a real public need for such service, irrespective of whether each individual unit is in itself showing a profit, provided the system as a whole can be put upon a paying basis."[45] The commission did rule that no new extensions should be constructed unless there was a reasonable certainty that they would be self-sustaining. Since the "fair rate of return" doctrine applied to the entire operation, "rationalizing" the system was often precluded or limited by "a real public need." Consequently, the two goals, a fair rate of return and the provision of public service, could be achieved only though general fare increases. That probably hurt transit in its competition with the automobile.

This example points to an even more important criticism of public policies pertaining to transit. If there were "real public needs" that necessitated unprofitable operations, extensions, low fares, and so forth, then why not recognize the "public good" aspect of transit and treat it accordingly? If public benefits did in fact exceed private benefits to the point that the private sector could not provide the necessary service, then the service should have been either publicly provided and/or publicly subsidized. The insistence on "private companies paying their way" was inconsistent with the public-service nature of transit.

This is essentially the conclusion that Barrett reached in his study of Chicago's transit system:

> If ever there was a transit system which, because of the things expected of it, should have been operated as a public benefit under responsible public control, it was mass transit in Chicago. But in Chicago, as in most American cities, transit paid cash returns to local government as well as to stockholders. Between 1907 and 1917, through taxes and the traction fund, the surface lines alone transferred to the city and to other governments nearly $37 million of the straphangers' money. The cost of street paving, sweeping, and plowing must be added to this amount. The companies' share of the annual profits, excluding additional profits received through the effect of overcapitalization on the 5 percent guaranteed return, was, for the same period, $17 million. This rough figure, $54 million, gives some idea of the cost of regulated private ownership to the transit rider in the first ten years of its existence."[46]

In total, about $175 million was paid to government bodies by Chicago transit companies from 1907 to 1931 (the last year of profitability).[47] These monies, Barrett suggested, could have been used to publicly acquire and operate the system, if municipal ownership had been feasible. (It was not, for reasons already suggested.)

The issue here is not so much the pros and cons of public ownership, but rather the inconsistencies of public policy. Instead of subsidizing (in any fashion) transit services where public benefits exceeded private benefits, the typical transit firm was heavily taxed and burdened with franchise charges that were no longer warranted by the value of its "monopoly" franchise. The magnitude of taxes can be seen in Table 4.2, which shows the taxes paid by U.S. transit companies between 1932 and 1947. In addition, Table 3.2 (Chapter 3) shows the taxes paid by the Los Angeles Railway between 1924 and 1939, along with other financial data. Both tables show substantial tax obligations, particularly when one considers the subsidy and accommodation accorded autos and highways.

It is not only the level of taxes that is of interest, but also the manner of taxation. Many taxes were levied on gross income or wages, rather than on some measure of net income. Franchise fees were typically 2 to 3 percent of gross revenues. This posed serious problems for transit companies, because taxes tended to rise relative to net revenue, especially in times of inflation and when fare increases were not quickly granted. This can also be seen in Table 4.2. Taxes calculated on operating revenues, instead of net revenues, tended to rise relative to the latter, because increasing operating expenses were ignored. Consequently, the impact of taxes was often obscured. For example, the American Transit Association (ATA) reported that taxes paid by

TABLE 4.2. Taxes Paid by Transit Operations in the United States, 1932–1947

Year	Taxes (thousands of dollars)	Percent of Revenue	Percent of Net Revenue
1932	51,021	7.33	38.18
1933	47,370	7.37	33.84
1934	49,183	7.29	32.92
1935	50,458	7.41	34.45
1936	56,920	7.82	34.98
1937	63,504	8.66	43.85
1938	65,723	9.38	54.27
1939	67,499	9.37	50.33
1940	62,688	8.51	45.11
1941	66,803	8.35	42.81
1942	128,650	12.37	47.54
1943	186,340	14.40	51.61
1944	189,250	13.89	54.04
1945	164,530	11.92	52.52
1946	129,020	9.23	48.20
1947	104,940	7.54	69.01

Source: Dollar amount of taxes and percentage of revenue figures are from American Transit Association, *Transit Fact Book, 1948* (Washington, DC: ATA, 1948), p. 7. Percentage of net revenue calculated from these data.

U.S. transit companies had fallen 18.7 percent in 1947.[48] Operating revenues, however, had also fallen 0.5 percent, while operating expenses had increased by 9.7 percent. Consequently, *net* revenues had fallen by 43.2 percent, and taxes as a percentage of net revenue had risen from 48.2 to 69.01 percent (Table 4.2). It is important to note that the thrust of the ATA commentary here was to report the reduction in taxes in 1947. The rise in taxes relative to net income was not noted, and in fact, additional calculations were required to uncover this point. (This style of presentation will be further discussed below.)

The same relationship between taxes and net revenue often held when revenues rose, that is, taxes tended to rise faster than net revenue. For example, in a summary of U.S. transit operations from 1936 through 1945, the ATA observed that total revenues had doubled, as had operating expenses. Taxes, however, had tripled, leaving operating income up by only 50 percent.[49]

The impact of these taxes on the bottom line can be seen in Pacific Electric's experience in 1947. In a company newsletter in February 1948, Pacific Electric explained that their $1.76 million loss in 1947 was the result of higher operating costs, combined with a 5 percent reduction in passenger revenue.[50] Taxes had "increased substantially," as had "practically every item of material and supplies." Payroll increases late in the year alone had increased the payroll by $3 million. As a result, the California Public Utilities Commission (the old California Railroad Commission) had granted a fare increase effective February 1948. While there were undoubtedly many factors contributing to the company's loss, the role of taxes was significant. In 1947 the "Taxes Assignable to Railway Operation" came to $2.86 million, that is, about 158 percent of the year's loss.[51] In other words, taxes exceeded the loss to the company. Was this taxation consistent with the provision of public service (to whatever extent)? Was it consistent with highway policy or transportation policy in general?

Another reason for higher taxes was the increasing number of taxes. For example, a study by the Chicago Motor Coach Company in 1938 showed the company's tax experience over the previous 20 years.[52] In 1938 the company was paying 20 separate taxes, including various types of state, city, county, federal, and park district taxes. In 1919 the company had been liable for only 7 of these taxes. As late as 1928, only 10 taxes were being paid. The depression, while reducing patronage, just about doubled the number of taxes that the company was liable for. This resulted in a dramatic increase in taxes paid. The total of all taxes paid by the company out of each dollar of gross revenue received was 3.5 cents in 1919, 7 cents in 1923, 6.5 cents in 1928, and 14.33 cents in 1937.

There is also no doubt that taxes were increasingly seen as a major source of difficulty in the industry. An editorial in *Bus Transportation* in

December 1951 asked city, state, and federal officials to realize that "despite increasing automobile competition which now numbers 40 million registered vehicles, privately operated transit companies are forced to pay 1900 vintage monopoly taxes in order to do business whereas municipally owned systems for the most part are tax-free across the board."[53]

There is nothing that says that public transit should not have been taxed. It is highly unlikely that transit companies would have been granted ex- emptions from income taxes or payroll taxes, and so forth. Taxation per se is therefore not the issue. The issues involve the consistency of this tax policy with overall transportation policy, particularly as compared to highway policy. This heavy taxation of transit was not even consistent with the subsequent subsidy of transit, subsidies that essentially began only after the systems were irreparably damaged. In addition, there is no denying that, despite the good intentions or rationale, the level and manner of taxation certainly weakened transit systems.

Franchises

Transit companies, in addition to being regulated by the state, also had to obtain a franchise from the city. Since these franchises often covered only a line or groups of lines, the typical company generally held many separate franchises.

This franchise system contributed to the decline of urban transit, particularly electric transit, by creating a destructive atmosphere of uncertainty and hostility. For example, in an opinion rendered in 1921, the California Railroad Commission recommended that the City of Los Angeles and the Los Angeles Railway (LARY) take "immediate steps" to arrange for an indeterminate resettlement franchise to cover all of the company's operations in the city.[54] The commission found that "if franchises covering certain units of a street railway system expire within short periods of time, the utility cannot be expected to invest large sums in betterments and improvements to its system unless arrangements are made to protect such investments."

The commission's recommendation was not heeded, and the situation apparently worsened. In the late 1930s and early 1940s, numerous Los Angeles Railway franchises were due to expire. One Railroad Commission document in 1938 referred to the expiration of some 115 LARY franchises "between now and the year 1941."[55] The franchise situation, however, remained "entirely within the hands of the city administration," so the commission still could not act. Chicago, likewise, was never able to resolve its franchise problems during this period.[56]

The importance of this issue must not be underestimated. The expiration of a franchise provided the city with perhaps its only opportunity to "regulate" transit (most regulation having been taken over by the state). In addition, the expiration of a franchise presented the opportunity for opponents of transit (streetcars) to mount an attack. This can perhaps be best illustrated with an example in Los Angeles.

In addition to demonstrating the importance of the franchise issue, the Los Angeles Railway's 1936 request for a renewal of its streetcar franchise on Olympic Boulevard also demonstrates the kind of negative attitudes and policies that often confronted streetcar companies.[57] In conjunction with the franchise hearings, the state of California's director of public works was asked for the state's views on the proposed streetcar franchise. His telegram in response is reproduced in its entirety below.

EXHIBIT 4.1
Postal Telegraph

S112 81-SC SACRAMENTO CALIF 26 437P

JAMES C DOLAN   1936 AUGUST 26 PM5 29
3336 WEST OLYMPIC BLVD

ANSWERING YOUR TELEGRAM OF AUGUST TWENTY SIXTH
RELATING TO REQUEST FOR STREET CAR FRANCHISE ON
OLYMPIC BOULEVARD WILL STATE THAT WE ARE NOT ONLY
OPPOSED AS A MATTER OF GENERAL POLICY TO GRANTING
STREET CAR FRANCHISES ON ARTERIAL STATE HIGHWAYS
ALREADY CONSTRUCTED BUT ALSO URGE THAT SERIOUS
EFFORTS SHOULD BE MADE TO REMOVE EXISTING STREET CAR
TRACKS FROM THOSE STREETS WHICH ARE TO BE DEVELOPED
INTO IMPORTANT TRAFFIC ARTERIES WITH STATE HIGHWAY
FUNDS STOP TRUST THIS WILL GIVE YOU DESIRED
INFORMATION —

EARL LEE KELLY
STATE DIRECTOR OF PUBLIC WORKS

There can be no doubt as to the state's position, and the tone of the response certainly conveys the state's general hostility to streetcars. This hostility had to have posed a formidable and ongoing impediment to streetcar operations, particularly when coupled with local hostility. The franchise renewal provided the opportunity to vent that hostility.

The disposition of the Olympic Boulevard streetcar case demonstrates the impact that these attitudes and the franchise process had on streetcar operations. A memo from Charles Bean, chief engineer and general manager of the city's Board of Public Utilities and Transportation, had requested that any rail franchise be granted for only three years, revocable at any time after 18 months.[58] The opinion of the Board of Public Utilities and Transportation noted that it had even received requests from citizen groups for a one-year franchise that was cancelable upon 30 days' notice.[59] Although the opinion cited considerable public support for the continuation and extension of rail service, and also admitted the impracticality of relying on buses to meet the city's transportation needs, it nonetheless recommended the three-year franchise with the revocation provision.[60] It also called for a provision requiring the "track to be of temporary type," so that LARY could relocate its tracks "when directed to do so by the city." The cost of any relocation was to be borne by LARY.

The city granted the LARY request, but with the three-year franchise term and a revocation clause empowering the city to cancel the franchise at any time after one year (with six-months' notice).[61] LARY never installed the streetcar line, however, and was back in 1939 with a request for the conversion of the existing Olympic rail line to bus operations. This request for conversion is not hard to understand, given the hostility of state and city governments and the rail franchise terms. One must conclude that LARY's request was deliberately killed, unless one seriously believes that city officials actually expected a rail line to be reinstalled under a three-year franchise (street construction necessitated reinstalling the tracks).

LARY had felt that their best interests lay in extending rail operations, but city and state officials, for whatever reason, caused the entire line to be motorized. The occasion for this action was the expiration of the Olympic franchise (and street improvements). Consequently, the uncertainties associated with the expiration of some 115 franchises in Los Angeles can be readily appreciated.

In addition to the franchise fees owed the city, streetcar companies often had to provide for street repairs around their tracks, street sweeping, snow removal, and so on. These expenditures could be substantial. For example, in 1921 the California Railroad Commission put the cost of street paving alone at about 6 percent of the company's gross revenues.[62] The commission held that such franchise provisions were "unduly burdensome," since neither the company nor its patrons secured any benefits. Once again, however, franchise terms were outside the jurisdiction of the commission.

Aside from the cost of these franchise requirements, they also seem to have been a factor in the choice of transit vehicles. They were a legacy of the "traction baron" age, when transit enjoyed a monopoly and the city sought to extract the maximum benefits for granting that monopoly. These requirements often lasted only as long as streetcars were used. In other words, they could be changed or eliminated by changing the vehicle. Cities seem to have been loath to change these franchise requirements, even though they were the product of monopoly conditions that no longer existed, as long as the streetcars were still there. If the streetcars left, however, these franchise terms might be scrapped or renegotiated.

Freeways and Transit: The Pacific Electric's Experience

A sharp contrast between attitudes toward transit policies and highway policies was drawn above. This section will explore the ways in which the promotion of highways contributed to transit's problems. It should be obvious that urban freeways and highways would have contributed to the general dilution of transit patronage. This was an important effect, perhaps even the most important, but the development of freeways appears to have also affected transit companies even prior to their construction or completion. Most of our attention in this regard will be confined to Los Angeles because of the availability of data. Perhaps Los Angeles may have encountered these effects somewhat earlier than other cities, but it is otherwise not atypical.

Company reports and memorandums make it clear that the Pacific Electric had, in the early 1940s, formulated plans to integrate their transit operations with the extensive network of freeways planned for postwar Los Angeles. Occasionally the company took a stand opposing a planned freeway, but seems to have generally acquiesced to the fact that public transportation policy after the war was going to be freeway oriented.[63] For example, Pacific Electric officials met in September 1944 to discuss "post war plans for Pacific Electric Railway in connection with the system of parkways proposed by the state, county and city for post war construction."[64] It was agreed to study the abandonment of eight rail lines and the curtailment of passenger service on six other passenger/freight lines. The stated reason for this position was the anticipation of the construction of 23 different freeway projects in the area, which were scheduled to begin immediately after the war. In addition to the abandonments, the study was to also consider the cost to the company of providing "a large number of grade separations constructed at the points of crossing our lines." These costs were certainly instrumental in some of the decisions to abandon rail lines. In other cases, the freeways were expected to take the rail rights-of-way, since this was generally an inexpensive way of acquiring a freeway right-of-way. Pacific Electric had to consider how it was going to finance the relocation of tracks, the construction of bridges across freeways and grade separations, and so on. There is no indication that the state was going to help with these costs, although the freeways were constructed with state and federal money.

The problems that freeways created for transit companies, as well as the attitude of freeway promoters toward transit, can be seen in another

Los Angeles rail case. The reason given for the motorization of Pacific Electric's Pasadena Short Line and its Sierra Vista Line was a conflict between these rail lines and the Aliso Street access to the Santa Ana Freeway. In the 12-page "Statement of Position" submitted in the motorization request, the California Division of Highways based its entire case for motorization on the fact that the rail lines on Aliso Street interfered with no less than five different freeways in the downtown area.[65] The entire document essentially reviewed the state's highway policy since 1900, emphasizing the state's commitment to freeways as the solution to Los Angeles' transportation problems. This emphasis is illustrated by the state's argument that streetcars *caused* street congestion. The state cited Bureau of Public Roads studies that indicated "that streetcars operating in the center lane of a city street system reduce the traffic carrying capacity of that lane by 50 percent, making it in effect equivalent to half a lane." This being the case, the *only* way that Aliso Street could carry the traffic that would be generated by the freeway was to remove the streetcars so as to provide an *unimpeded* flow of traffic (emphasis in original). In other words, streetcars were not compatible with freeways, either on them or around them.

The report did not consider the relationship between buses and road congestion. The attitude of the California Railroad Commission, however, at least until the late 1930s, was that motor buses were impractical in the downtown area. Buses were smaller, thus requiring more vehicles and creating more congestion. Unless it was only the tracks that were considered to be the cause of the congestion, and there was no indication that that was the case, then the motor bus would have been equally (or more) congestive. The argument for buses and freeways does not appear consistent in this regard.

The Aliso Street case is of interest for one additional reason. The entire matter before the Public Utilities Commission was apparently a moot point, since the city of Los Angeles had already, in its renewal of Pacific Electric's Aliso Street franchise on April 1, 1946, inserted a clause specifically providing for the termination of Pacific Electric's operations on Aliso Street. The termination could be ordered by either the city or by the Division of Highways on 90 days' notice. The state had served notice prior to the filing of its statement with the PUC.

The point here is not the merit of the Los Angeles freeways or the specific rail lines in question. The point is that a public policy that promoted freeways made electric transit a less viable option, regardless of the economic merits. One might respond with a "so what?" What was wrong with deciding that freeways were better than streetcars? Nothing, provided one recognizes the nature of the choice and recognizes especially that a choice was being made. Unfortunately, discussions of the decline of transit and the promotion of freeways often miss this policy connection.

The Aliso case was not unusual. In fact, freeways, even when they did not directly or permanently take a streetcar or trolley-coach right-of-way or facilities, could still make the lines nonviable. For example, a Los Angeles street traffic engineer's report in April 1948 had recommended that buses replace rail on the Watts-Sierra Vista Line, because freeway overpass construction was creating a traffic jam. Buses could be rerouted around the construction zone.[66] In another case, rail lines were removed from a major downtown Los Angeles street, because the streets were made one-way in order to facilitate access and egress from the freeway.[67]

It is clear from Pacific Electric papers that the company fully intended to integrate many of its rail and bus lines with the new freeways. Rail was to be operated on median strips and freeways were to be equipped with bus turn-outs. Putting rail lines on median strips would have reduced the rail's right-of-way costs, as well as increased the carrying capacity of the freeway. Such a system would also have created the nucleus of a rapid transit system.

Most of these plans were never realized. Buses did operate on freeways, but they, too, were stuck in the same rush-hour traffic. Rail was operated on the Hollywood Freeway median strip (the freeway took part of its right-of-way) until 1952, but was eventually abandoned and replaced by another lane of traffic.

That these plans were hardly ever realized raises an important question. Were they ever seriously considered, or were they convenient arguments designed to make freeways appear to be in everyone's best interest, including transit companies and transit patrons? The company's plans seem to have been genuine, but beyond that, it would be difficult to hazard a guess.

Finally, the question of flexibility must be reconsidered in view of the effects of freeways on transit. The bus was more flexible in that it did not conflict with freeways and freeway development. Converting to motor buses could save the company the substantial costs of renovating transit to fit the freeways. Since little financial help in this regard could be expected, and since there was little doubt as to policy priorities, this was no small consideration.

In addition, that old standy-by argument—that the buses could be used on the freeways—allowed one to sidestep the issue of choosing a transportation system. One could argue that buses, and therefore transit, benefited from the same road improvements that benefited the automobile. The fact that freeways seldom lived up to their advance billing in this regard did not seem to negate this you-can-have-your-cake-and-eat-it-too argument. A de facto choice was being made, however, and one must wonder to what extent the public and public officials were aware of the dimensions of their actions.

Planners and Transit

The freeway-orientation of urban transportation policy also raises a question as to the role of planners in these developments. It is difficult to generalize about the views and policies of planners as a whole, since there was a considerable diversity of opinion and emphasis. It is a fair generalization, however, that most planners tended to see the automobile as not only the solution to urban transportation problems but also as a solution to a whole myriad of social and economic problems as well.[68] It would be hard to argue that planners were responsible (either in a positive or negative sense) for transportation policies that promoted the automobile or retarded public transit. Planners simply never had that kind of power. They did, however, have an impact, particularly a legitimizing impact. That is, they were the "impartial experts" who imparted an aura of science and objectivity to what were essentially political issues.

In addition, planners contributed to the general hostility toward transit noted above. Streetcar companies in Los Angeles often had to contend with city officials bent on promoting freeways. For example, Lloyd Aldrich was appointed city engineer for Los Angeles in 1933. Aldrich was an active freeway partisan, described by one author as the "principal champion of the L.A. freeway."[69] A city official with an opinion or even a strong position on a controversial matter is not unusual. But Aldrich seems to have embraced the cause with vigor, even persuading P. G. Winnett, president of Bullock's department store, to raise $100,000 from the business community to fund a private study of trunk-line roads to serve the downtown area. The report, in late 1939, proposed an initial 300 miles of urban freeways and eventually a 600-mile freeway network. A city official who went to such extraordinary lengths must certainly have contributed to the city's decidedly profreeway policies.

The Public Holding Company Act of 1935

It is perhaps ironic that one of the first federal policies to have had an effect on transit was an antimonopoly measure. The Public Holding Company Act of 1935, and the interpretations given it by the Securities and Exchange Commission, must be considered as one of the factors having contributed to the decline of urban transit.[70] There is evidence to suggest that Congress did not have transit in mind when it passed this act, and it may not even have considered its impact on transit in its deliberations,[71] but the law was enacted and it was interpreted as applying to transit companies. It appears to have had an impact on as many as 50 percent of transit companies, which had generated 80 percent of total revenue passengers in 1931.[72]

The act basically required that electric utilities limit their activities to a single, integrated utility system. This was interpreted to mean that utility companies had to choose between their electricity-generating activities and their transit activities. Many utilities gladly took the opportunity to divest themselves of unwanted transit operations. Others, however, were forced to choose, with most deciding to dispose of their transit operations.

This forced divestiture after 1938 (the law became effective on January 1, 1938) seriously weakened those transit companies affected by it. Management was depleted, since the best managers generally went with the utility rather than transit. Investment, which had often been channeled into transit through the utility, was disrupted. Consequently, numerous opportunities for acquisition and motorization were created by this act. It was often a definite factor in the NCL campaign.

The Key System and Bay Bridge Rail

One final insight into the role of policy and policy makers in transit's decline can be seen in the fate of the Key System's rail service on the San Francisco Bay Bridge.[73] This has often been cited as an example of how NCL dismantled a transit system and irrevocably disposed of its valuable right-of-way. After acquiring the Key System in 1946, NCL did cancel financial authorizations to buy two experimental bridge trains as a first step toward a modernization of the transbay line. This cancellation, along with the cancellation of the trolley-coach orders (discussed in Chapter 3) are often cited as good examples of National City Lines' modus operandi and the impact that it had on transit.

But there is more to the story. Public policy at many levels must take part of the blame or responsibility for the elimination of rail service on the Bay Bridge. For example, a decision was made at a Key System meeting in December 1946 to delay an amortization schedule that was to be part of the modernization program for the bridge rail. It was also decided to reconsider the use of motor buses on the span. This represented "a substantial shift from the previous management's emphasis on bridge rail use rather than buses."[74] The fact that National City Lines had just acquired the Key System was definitely a factor in this change, but the minutes of the meeting also cite concerns over "studies now being made regarding additional transbay bridge facilities."[75]

The most important of these studies was a joint army-navy report on the future of the San Francisco Bay area, which was to be released in 1947. (The results were anticipated at the December 1946 Key System meeting.) The army-navy report proposed an underwater tube for rapid-transit trains, as well as a new bridge crossing several miles to the south of the existing Bay Bridge. The idea of a rapid-transit tube also found favor with the

San Francisco Bay Area Rapid Transit Commission in the mid-1950s. It was also favored by the commission's successor, the San Francisco Bay Area Rapid Transit District. California's Toll Bridge Authority had also discussed the prospects for a second bridge. It later decided in favor of a $35 million Bay Bridge renovation program that eliminated the tracks in favor of more freeway lanes. In addition, the authority dramatically reduced auto tolls on the bridge from the 65-cent toll set in 1936 to a 25-cent toll in 1940. There was therefore little doubt as to the authority's priorities. The bridge rail was allowed to slip into a regulatory twilight zone. Requests to motorize the line were denied, but improving the rail would have taken a strong commitment, a commitment that was not forthcoming from the NCL-owned Key System, or from state or regional transit authorities. Apparently, only the Alameda-Contra Costa Transit District had expressed an interest in running the bridge trains, but the trains were gone by 1958, well before the district actually acquired the Key System in 1960.

The prospects of another bridge and/or an underwater tube created uncertainties about the future of bridge rail. There also seems to have been a lack of interest in or even a hostility to rail on the part of public officials. National City Lines was a factor, yet public officials certainly did not fight to keep the rail. We do not know how a company that had not been controlled by National City Lines would have dealt with these policies, but one would certainly not expect National City Lines to promote rail or to try to counter public bodies on this issue.

PROMOTIONAL COMPETITION

There is one final factor that must be considered in any review of factors contributing to the decline of transit. Simply put, the promoters of motor buses may have simply beat their competition; that is, they beat those who promoted or should have promoted trolley coaches and PCC streetcars. For example, although it is not widely known, there was an industry group called the "Trolley Coach Consultant Committee," which had been formed in 1943 in order to promote the trolley coach.[76] In fact, a transit trade journal had claimed in 1954 that this group had "given the transit industry its only consistent, continuous public relations campaign it has had during the past decade."[77] Even after spending $1 million dollars on this campaign, however, and with the backing of such members as General Electric, Westinghouse, Pullman-Standard, St. Louis Car, and Marmon-Herrington, its promotion of the trolley coach never came close to the success of bus promotion. The obscurity of this group attests to its impact. I discovered it by accident in a *Mass Transportation* article that presented two awards to people in the transit industry for their promotional efforts.

The second recipient was a member of the Trolley Coach Consultant Committee. The first recipient, however, was the public relations officer at National City Lines.

We must not overlook the possibility, even the likelihood, that those who promoted the bus, including National City Lines and General Motors, did a better job at it. Certainly in one area, financing bus sales, this appears to have definitely been the case.[78] The true measure of the success of the bus promoters, however, is to be found in the degree to which they virtually equated "modern transit" with "bus transit." This can be seen in the degree to which bus promoters' claims for lower costs, greater comfort, greater flexibility, and so forth, were generally accepted without supporting data.[79] The ease with which these same claims are repeated today, with the same or even less supporting data, is a further mark of their success.

Recognition of the competitive prowess of motor-bus promoters must, however, be tempered by two considerations. First, this entire discussion of NCL has been essentially an attempt to determine if this type of promotion was "unfair" (not necessarily in a legal sense, but in a broader sense). The fact that they "won" may be more a reflection of their recourse to unfair tactics. Second, bus promoters may have beaten the trolley-coach promoters, but they certainly lost to the auto promoters. Then again, were the bus promoters and the auto promoters really separate parties? That has also been part of the question at hand. In any case, there can be little doubt that auto promoters fared better than transit promoters.

While there may be many reasons for transit promoters' lack of success, we must not simply assume that auto promoters had the contest locked up. Transit promoters seem to have often failed to convey their message to the public and public officials. A good example of this failure can be seen in the tax issue already considered. The data used in our discussion of taxes relative to net income was drawn from an American Transit Association *Transit Fact Book*. As noted, the transit industry was complaining about excessive taxation, but while it was doing so, the ATA was talking about a reduction in taxes as a percentage of gross revenue in 1947. Presenting the data in this manner tended to obscure rather than explain the industry's complaints about taxes. Why weren't taxes compared with net revenues? Why talk about a tax reduction in 1947 when, as we have shown, the tax problem worsened that year? This was not the way to make a case.[80]

CONCLUSIONS ON THE MOTORIZATION CAMPAIGN

These first four chapters have sought to investigate the allegations that a motorization campaign had foreclosed the market to efficient transit vehicles (trolley coaches and modern streetcars), and thus contributed significantly to the decline of urban transit. While the record is unclear on certain points, some conclusions, based on a total assessment of the question, can be drawn.

First, there was something to "conspire" about in the sense that there had been more economical alternatives to motor buses. A good economic case for trolley-coach and streetcar operations was made. That is not to say that there was no place for the motor bus in transit systems (indeed a mixed system would appear to have been optimal). A wholesale motorization of transit systems, however, such as occurred on those systems that had been acquired by National City Lines (or one of the others), does appear suspicious on economic grounds.

Second, a review of the available evidence purporting to show a "conspiracy" at work reveals a strong case for the existence of such a "conspiracy" (again the term is used in its broadest sense). While one must admit that a "smoking gun" has not been found, one continually trips over spent cartridges in this field.

Third, the question of relative significance was raised. How important was this campaign or conspiracy? Here we are on weaker ground, simply because of the nature of the question; that is, we are essentially inquiring in a counterfactual fashion. What would have happened if this campaign had not taken place? This is certainly the correct question, but it is immune to frontal assault. A second line of attack sought to enumerate and explore the other factors contributing to the decline, to shed some light on how important these other factors might have been. I would conclude in this regard (although still tentatively in some cases) that the competition from the automobile was probably a far less important factor than has been generally accepted; that policies that promoted the automobile, especially urban freeways and highways, have received far too little attention; that the flexibility argument is grossly overrated, since the buses' potential flexibility was never utilized; and that regulatory failure was a significant factor in the decline, and one that has received too little attention. Regulation not only allowed the motorization campaign, it also facilitated it.

I find that regulation and antagonistic public policies were significant factors that ought to receive more attention in discussions of the decline of transit. This being the case, it would seem that the motorization campaign must to be accorded considerable importance, as well. Dealing with public authorities and regulatory bodies is never easy, but that is precisely why the elimination of independent transit companies in this manner was of critical importance.

One would be hard pressed to argue, as some have, that transit declined solely because of this campaign. Such a position assumes, implicitly or explicitly, that transit was in good shape, except for the campaign. That was not the case. One would be equally incorrect in arguing, in view of the total picture sketched above, that the motorization campaign was inconsequential. That was not the case, either.

We will return to this question in Chapter 7. The next two chapters will explore federal road policies. We have already seen some examples of how road policy affected transit. We will look at developments in this area and then return to a final assessment of developments in both transit and highway policy.

NOTES

1. Mark Foster, *From Streetcar to Superhighway* (Philadelphia: Temple University Press, 1981), p. 219.

2. See, for example, Paul Sweezy, "Cars and Cities," *Monthly Review* 24 (April 1973); 1–18.

3. For an excellent discussion of how public policies affected transit and automobile use in Chicago, see Paul Barrett, *The Automobile and Urban Transit* (Philadelphia: Temple University Press, 1983).

4. John Rae, *The Road and Car in American Life* (Cambridge, MA: M.I.T. Press, 1971), p. 277.

5. See, for example, Richard J. Solomon et al., *History of Transit and Innovative Systems* (Washington, DC: U.S. Department of Commerce, 1971).

6. This observation can be found in David Brodsly, *L.A. Freeway* (Los Angeles: University of California Press, 1981), pp. 2–4.

7. On the continuity of traffic patterns (and problems) in Chicago, see Barrett, *The Automobile and Urban Transit.* Chicago's transportation patterns have revolved around the Loop since the nineteenth century.

8. See, for example, Lyndon Henry, *A New Perspective on the Decline of Regional Public Transportation Services* (Austin, TX: Texas Association for Public Transportation, 1974), p. 5. Henry cites Wilfred Owens, *The Accessible City* (Washington, DC: Brookings Institution, 1972) as a source.

9. One should not assume that motor-bus fixed investment was not significant. Aside from the vehicle costs, maintenance and storage facilities often had to be constructed. (For example, cold climates almost always required indoor storage of diesel buses.)

10. This discussion of foreclosure was originally presented in David J. St. Clair, "The Motorization and Decline of Urban Public Transit, 1935–1950," *Journal of Economic History* 41 (September 1981): 579–600. Reprinted by permission.

11. *U.S.* v. *National City Lines, Inc., et al.*, 186 F. 2d 562, January 3, 1951.

12. Joseph J. Spengler, "Vertical Integration and Antitrust Policy," *Journal of Political Economy* 58 (August 1950): 347–52.

13. See Chapter 3, especially note 65.

14. A test of Spengler's argument is difficult for a number of reasons. First, the level of service, routing, frequency of service, and so forth were often changed after NCL acquired properties. Can fares be compared, then? Second, even if fares were reduced, can the reduction be attributable to overcoming oligopolistic restrictions? This seems doubtful. Any modernization program that replaced antiquated streetcars should have lowered costs and, conceivably, prices. It is likewise hard to see where in transit operations the oligopolistic restrictions existed. General Motors has been the largest bus producer since the 1920s and was the largest trolley-coach producer in the late 1930s. Its growth does not appear to have been curtailed by oligopoly in transit operations.

15. See Robert H. Bork, "Vertical Integration and Competitive Processes," Willard F. Mueller, "Public Policy Toward Vertical Mergers," and Sam Peltzman, "Issues in Vertical Integration Policy," in *Public Policy Toward Mergers*, ed. J. Fred Weston and Sam Peltzman (Pacific Palisades, CA: Goodyear, 1969), pp. 139–76. Also, see Robert H. Bork and Ward S. Bowman, Jr., "The Crisis in Antitrust," *Columbia Law Review* 65 (March 1965): 363–76; and the reply of Harlan M. Blake and William K. Jones, "In Defense of Antitrust," *Columbia Law Review* 65 (March 1965): 377–400. For a criticism of the Yellow Cab case, see Edmund W. Kitch, "The Yellow Cab Case," *Journal of Law and Economics* 15 (October 1972): 327–36.

16. The costs incurred by the foreclosing firm resulted from (a) the nonoptimal product mix engendered by foreclosure; or (b) the nonoptimal production levels engendered by foreclosure; or (c) the price effects from the expansion of market output, again engendered by foreclosure.

17. Bradford Snell, *American Ground Transport* (1973), reproduced as an appendix to U.S., Congress, Senate, Committee on the Judiciary, *The Industrial Reorganization Act, Hearings before a Subcommittee on the Judiciary on S. 1167, Part 4A*, 93rd Cong., 2d sess., 1974, p. A–38.

18. See, for example, Ross D. Eckert and George W. Hilton, "The Jitneys," *Journal of Law and Economics* 15 (October 1972): 293–325.

19. The description of both cases is drawn from California Railroad Commission Decisions, Decision No. 33088, In the matter of Application No. 21656. Decided May 14, 1940, especially pp. 638–44. Further citations will be deleted. While technically an interurban or suburban line, the Los Angeles-Pasadena case was essentially an urban issue. Pasadena was actually closer to downtown Los Angeles than were many parts of Los Angeles itself—for example, the San Fernando Valley sections of the city.

20. The commission's engineers surveyed and studied the Pasadena Local System as part of an extensive, ten-volume report on Pacific Electric operations in the Los Angeles area. The Pasadena report is found in Volume 6, introduced as Exhibit No. 54, November 29, 1938, in this case.

21. Today called the Pasadena Freeway (Harbor Freeway).

22. California Railroad Commission, *Report on the Local Public Transportation Requirements of Los Angeles, Case No. 4002*, Los Angeles, California, December 16, 1935, pp. 248, 268.

23. California Railroad Commission, Transportation Department, Research Division, *Report on Urban Mass Passenger Transportation Facilities and Requirements of Los Angeles*, vol. 2, *Case No. 4461*, 1940, p. 14.

24. Steven L. Easlon, *The Los Angeles Railway Through the Years*, (Anaheim, CA: Easlon Publications, 1973), p. 35.

25. Exhibit No. 14 in Application Case No. 4002, California Railroad Commission. Filed April 15, 1936. The figures are from this source.

26. Easlon, *The Los Angeles Railway Through the Years*, p. 35.

27. California Railroad Commission, *Report on the Local Public Transportation Requirements of Los Angeles*, 1935, p. 261.

28. See Pacific Electric, *Revised Study of Los Angeles-Alhambra-San Gabriel-Temple Line*, May 2, 1938. PE File 340–301. Prepared by O. A. Smith. Three plans for renovating the line were considered here, including complete motor-bus substitution, new one-man streetcars, and partial bus substitution. The streetcars looked to be the most practical. One reason why streetcars were considered was the one-man operating features of PCC cars (p. 6). The viability of rail was dependent to a large degree, however, on whether the two-man ordinance was successfully challenged in court. See letter of O. A. Smith to A. D. McDonald, dated December 13, 1940, included in this study.

29. This discussion is based essentially on Paul Barrett's study of Chicago transit policy. Paul Barrett, *The Automobile and Urban Transit*.

30. Ibid., pp. 86, 120–122.

31. The company estimated its reproduction costs as of December 31, 1913 at $26,030,865, and a current value of $24,288,406. The commission's engineers submitted estimates of $22,332,430 and $19,747,767, respectively. See California Railroad Commission, *Report on Urban Passenger Transportation Facilities and Requirements of Los Angeles Case No. 4461, vol. 2,* submitted October 17, 1940. Figures are from p. 2.

32. Ibid., p. 180. The commission rejected the company's excuse that the books had been burned by mistake.

33. Ibid., p. 181.

34. Memorandum from Arthur C. Jenkins, engineer, Transportation Department, to J. S. Hunter, chief engineer, Transportation Department, San Francisco, August 1, 1938. Re: Application No. 21656. Copy in possession of author. Quote is from p. 2.

35. Ibid., p. 4.

36. Ibid., p. 6.

37. Barrett, *The Automobile and Urban Transit,* p. 19. The figures are from this source.

38. Ibid., p. 40–41.

39. Ibid., p. 41.

40. Ibid., p. 85–86.

41. *California Railroad Commission Decisions,* Decision No. 33984, decided March 11, 1941, pp. 372–86. The discussion is based on this source.

42. Ibid., p. 379.

43. The record is not completely clear here. The comparison was between present and "proposed operations as applying only to those lines under consideration" (p. 377). I take this to mean a before-and-after comparison. The comments made in the text are based on this interpretation.

44. Barrett, *The Automobile and Urban Transit.* Barrett's treatment of this theme is excellent. The phenomenon was ubiquitous, but this discussion will be based primarily on Barrett's treatment.

45. California Railroad Commission, Application No. 4238, Decision No. 9029, May 31, 1921. Quote is from Case No. 4461, p. 6 (in a review of the 1921 case).

46. Barrett, *The Automobile and Urban Transit,* p. 127.

47. Ibid.

48. These figures are from the ATA source cited in Table 3.1.

49. American Transit Association, *Transit Fact Book, 1946,* Chart 1.

50. Pacific Electric, "Monthly Information Letter (For Staff Officers)," February 6, 1948, p. 1. Figures and quotes are from this source.

51. Ibid., p. 9. This figure, ($2.86 million) in taxes, does not match a figure of $1.38 million cited in the July 1, 1948 Pacific Electric Newsletter. p. 9. No explanation is given for the difference. While less dramatic, the second figure does not negate the point here.

52. Letter of B. Weintraub, president of Chicago Motor Coach Company, to Allen Box, City Coach Lines, January 30, 1940. These figures were in an attachment to the letter, which was itself a transmittal letter for the Sherwood, Isaacsen, and Lorentzen survey of the Los Angeles Railway. This is the study that was originally transmitted to J. A. Ritchee of Fifth Avenue Coach (and earlier Omnibus and General Motors). All of the figures are from this source.

53. Editorial, "This Is 1951, Not 1900," *Bus Transportation* 30 (December 1951).

54. California Railroad Commission, Application No. 4238, Decision No. 9029, May 31, 1921. Quote is from case No. 4461, p. 7 (in review of the 1921 case). The quote is also from this source.

55. California Railroad Commission, interdepartment correspondence, Letter from Arthur F. Agar to Ward Hall, December 6, 1938. Case No. 4002, File 125-19-64.

56. For example, see Barrett, *The Automobile and Urban Transit,* pp. 180–81.

57. This discussion of the Olympic Line request is based on Application Nos. 22994, 18820, and 23030. Board of Public Utilities and Transportation, city of Los Angeles. The telegram reproduced here is from Exhibit No. 15, December 18, 1939, Olympic Line Case, p. 2.

58. Excerpt from a report of K. Charles Bean, chief engineer and general manager of Board of Public Utilities and Transportation, dated September 4, 1936. Placed in Exhibit No. 15, Olympic Line Case, p. 3.

59. Opinion of Board of Public Utilities and Transportation, dated September 10, 1936. Placed in Exhibit No. 15, Olympic Line Case, p. 8.

60. Ibid., p. 9.

61. City of Los Angeles, Ordinance No. 77,226, Section 2. Approved November 19, 1936.

62. California Railroad Commission, Application No. 4238, Decision No. 9029. Cited in Case No. 4461, p. 7. The quote is from this source.

63. See, for example, Pacific Electric's intention to "resist . . . in every way possible" a Los Angeles Council resolution calling for a freeway on Long Beach Boulevard that would have taken out PE tracks. Pacific Electric Railway Company, Memorandum of Staff Meeting, Los Angeles, California, April 21, 1948, p. 3.

64. Pacific Electric Memo, September 22, 1944. The discussion and quotes are from this source.

65. California Public Utilities Commission, Application No. 32137, Statement of Position of the State of California Department of Public Works, Division of Highways, April 11, 1951. The quotes and discussion are from this source.

66. Pacific Electric Railway, Memorandum of Staff Meeting, Los Angeles, May 12, 1948, p. 3.

67. California Railroad Commission, reporter's transcript in Application No. 27,975 (and Supplemental Application No. 19,179).

68. For a discussion of the view of planners, see Mark S. Foster, *From Streetcar to Superhighway*. Also see this source for a discussion of the limitations of planners' influence.

69. Rae, *Road and Car*, p. 82. The discussion of Aldrich is from this source.

70. 15 U.S. Code, Section 79 (August 26, 1935). This discussion is based primarily on Solomon et al., *History of Transit and Innovative Systems*, pp. 1–13 through 1–18.

71. Ibid., pp. 1–13 through 1–14. Solomon notes that the FTC's 95-volume, 150,000-word investigation of the power and gas industry does not even mention electric railways or urban transit in its 1,000-page index.

72. Ibid., p. 1–15.

73. This discussion of the Key System is based on Harre W. Demoro, "The Conversion of the Key System," *National Railway Bulletin* 44, No. 6 (1979): 4–42.

74. Ibid., p. 23.

75. The discussion is based on ibid., pp. 21–27.

76. This group was headed by Jay Palmer of Ohio Brass. In 1952, members included General Electric, Westinghouse, Westinghouse Air Brake, Bridgeport Brass, Union Metal, Pullman-Standard, St. Louis Car, and Marmon-Herrington. See "PR Men of the Year," *Mass Transportation* 48 (September 1952): 60–62. The start-up date of 1943 is inferred from this article.

77. Ibid., p. 62.

78. Financing terms, often no money down, and so on, were often mentioned in Los Angeles motorization requests. See, for example, California Railroad Commission, Decision No. 33984, pp. 381–82.

79. Even regulatory officials were guilty of this. As discussed above, they often did not even request supporting data. Often a view of motorization as a cost-reducing program was merely accepted as an established fact. See, for example, the Pasadena case cited above, C.R.C. decision No. 33088, p. 632, where the commission refers to motorization as a logical source of cost reduction, but without any supporting documentation, and that in a case where

it recommends the trolley coach! General Motors cited the commission on this point in its rebuttal of Bradford Snell's *American Ground Transport*. See General Motors, *The Truth About "American Ground Transport"—A Reply by General Motors*, reproduced as an appendix to *The Industrial Reorganization Act* (1974), p. A–115.

80. Yago suggests that the ATA was heavily influenced by NCL. NCL was the nation's largest transit operator, and ATA voting was based upon operating revenue. Yago, *Decline of Transit*, p. 63.

5

Federal Highway Policy and the Automobile Industry

Chapter 1 sketched developments in highway policy up to 1930. The significant trends during that period included the increasing role of the federal government in highways, the successful completion of the original federal highway program that had begun in 1916, and the beginnings of the break-up of the highway coalition that had been successful in 1916. In this chapter, we will return to the break-up of this coalition, emphasizing the interests and goals of the automobile industry in redirecting federal highway policy.[1]

It must be emphasized at the outset that the automobile industry was not the only group interested in this redirectioning, nor was it the only group that was increasingly interested in urban highways after 1930. Many others, including planners and city officials, were also involved. The goal here is not to argue that these other groups were not important, but rather to identify the automobile industry's interests in these issues. We cannot appreciate their efforts at redirecting highway policy unless we have an idea of what motivated their actions.

In trying to determine the automobile industry's interests in this area, the logical starting point is Paul Hoffman's 1939 article cited in Chapter 1.[2] This was one of the most articulate and visible statements of the industry's interest in urban highways. Hoffman was president of Studebaker Corporation, as well as the president of the Automobile Safety Foundation (or ASF, an industry lobbying group, discussed below). In addition, he later served on the Automobile Council for War Production during World War II and was appointed to head the Economic Cooperation Administration (the organization that administered the Marshall Plan). Hoffman's article, entitled "American Goes to Town," was published in the *Saturday Evening Post* and was subsequently reprinted and distributed by the ASF in their promotional efforts for an urban-oriented federal highway policy.

120

Since the early 1930s, Hoffman had argued for making cities more compatible with the auto,[3] but the stated occasion for this 1939 article was the publication of a series of road and traffic surveys by the Bureau of Public Roads. Completed in 1939, this was the first detailed nationwide survey of the nation's roads ever taken (46 of the 48 states cooperated in the survey.) The traffic surveys clarified traffic patterns and also revealed a number of interesting and "unexpected" patterns. The most important finding in the study, at least from Hoffman's perspective, was that transcontinental traffic was rather unimportant. As Hoffman put it, "Long-distance motoring does not play nearly as big a part in our traffic as most of us imagine."[4] Survey data indicated that coast-to-coast traffic was less than 1 percent of total traffic along coast-to-coast routes. Only 30 percent of the out-of-state passenger cars surveyed on western through-roads were bound for destinations east of the Mississippi River. The same pattern emerged in the north-south transcontinental traffic survey.

Trip-mileage surveys revealed a similar pattern. As Hoffman concluded, a large proportion of all oneway passenger-car trips made outside city limits actually covered distances of only 5 miles or less. In addition, 90 percent of all trips made by car were 30 miles or less in length, and only 2.3 percent of the trips were 100 miles or longer. Hoffman summarized the implications of the survey data in these terms: "We use highways, then, chiefly for short trips. And where do we go? We go to town."[5]

Furthermore, this traffic was concentrated on a few principal roads. Nearly 60 percent of motor-vehicle traffic was on main rural highways and on those transcity streets with which they connected. An additional 30 percent of travel took place on city streets. Therefore, it was determined that about 90 percent of the nation's travel took place on only 11 percent of the nation's roads! This left about 10 percent of the total traffic on the remaining 89 percent of the roads.

The other important point brought out by the survey data concerned the destination of traffic. Hoffman noted that "a significant thing is that most of this traffic is going to or coming from the center of town. It doesn't want to by-pass the city. The city is the objective."[6] From studies of two moderate-sized cities located on "main through highways," it was found that only 12 percent of the traffic wanted to miss the cities.

What did it all mean? What did all of these new survey data imply for the automobile industry? Hoffman felt that the results "indicate inescapably that our next great highway adventure is not to be in the big open spaces, but in and near the cities. . . . The great changes during the next twenty years will come, not in the country, but in the cities."[7] More specifically, Hoffman was explicit as to what this meant for the automobile industry:

> Many of our cities are almost as antiquated, trafficwise, as if they had medieval walls, moats, drawbridges. . . . If we are to have full use

of automobiles, *cities must be remade.* The greatest automobile market today, the greatest untapped field of potential customers, is the large number of city people who refuse to own cars, or use the cars they have very little, because it's such a nuisance to take them out. A waiting industry that will do wonders for prosperity will spring up when we revamp our cities and make it safe, convenient, pleasant and easy to use a car on city streets.[8] (emphasis added)

Hoffman effectively presented most of the arguments that the industry would later use during its lobbying campaigns—economic growth and prosperity issues, slum clearance, safety, and the high opportunity costs of poor highways. The essential point and purpose of urban highways, as far as the auto industry was concerned, were clear. As Hoffman pointed out, it was the potential market for automobiles, "locked up" in cities that were not conducive to automobile use and ownership, that was the main concern of the automobile industry. What would remedy this problem? According to Hoffman, tapping the market required the use of the federal government to completely transform and remake cities, in order to make them accessible to automobile use and conducive to automobile ownership. Hoffman was candid and explicit on just what this would mean:

Chief MacDonald [Bureau of Public Roads] insists that we must dream of gashing our way ruthlessly through built-up sections of overcrowded cities, in order to create traffic ways capable of carrying the traffic with safety, facility, [and] reasonable speed. The city of the future, in a word, is going to be vastly different from the city of today, swamped in the "mud" of congestion.[9]

The cities were to be "ruthlessly gashed" in order to tap what the automobile industry considered "the greatest automobile market today, the greatest untapped field of potential customers."[10] This argument was to be repeated many times in the future, with more sophisticated market data, more attention to promoting the social benefits to be derived from highways, and usually with much less candor, but the industry's basic interest in urban highways remained essentially as Hoffman stated it in 1939.

Hoffman never explicitly referred to the proposed Interregional Highway System, although he did make reference to General Motors' scale model of a transcontinental highway system, presented at the 1939 New York World's Fair. But if highways were to have their greatest use (for the industry) in urban centers, then why consider transcontinental systems? Likewise, why promote a 40,000-mile Interstate System that would contain only 6,000 miles of urban routes? The answer lay in the local nature of highway traffic. Hoffman emphasized this with a quote from Thomas MacDonald, Chief of the Bureau of Public Roads, and a leading proponent of urban highways:

It is essential to remember that a highway is intrinsically a local facility. It is not necessary or desirable to think of highways in terms of long-distance express routes built far out in the country at a maximum cost. We do connect one road with another and so build up a transcontinental, Lakes-to-Gulf, Mexico-to-Canada system. *But the principal function isn't long distance.* The great number of movements that constitute the traffic stream are individually minute; they occur in large part on main rural highways and in their trans-city connections. The highways that need most attention are those with the most traffic.[11] (emphasis in original)

The reason for advocating a transcontinental system to serve local traffic was simply due to the fact that federal participation could not be justified on the grounds of local traffic. It could however be justified on the grounds that traffic was "interstate." There was no inherent contradiction in advocating a "transcontinental" or Interstate System, which, in reality, would serve essentially local traffic. The long-distance connotations of the system made it politically feasible, but it was obvious that this was the extent of the industry's interest in a long-distance system.

Two tactical problems were also raised by Hoffman, problems that would stand in the way of his proposed changes in federal highway policy. First, as was mentioned above, the original system of designating mileage in the federal aid system was on the basis of the percentage of rural roads in the state. Only rural roads were eligible, since it was the expressed purpose of the program to get the U.S. farmer out of the mud. This rural system, however, would obviously be unable to handle the task of providing urban highways. Hoffman noted this problem and provided a rationale for a city-oriented program:

Motor traffic is where people are, that is around cities; so we have come full-circle from our starting thirty years ago. When Federal Aid roads were first proposed, Congress stipulated that money must be spent on highways outside cities; it was assumed that city streets were all right. Now we're back to something not unlike the old mud age. Only the "mud" today is congestion. And it is not in the country, but in the cities and on roads approaching them.[12]

Hoffman stressed the point that with this new "mud" problem, a different system for designating federal aid mileage was necessary. The new survey data provided the basis for the new designation. Attempts to put the designation system on a "need basis" became the principal point that was taken up in the lobbying campaign after the war.

The second problem was not rectified until 1956. Under existing policies, the government had to acquire all property and settle all questions as to purchase price prior to construction. Needless to say, this created a nearly impossible situation in urban areas. The problem was recognized by Hoffman in 1939 and subsequently became an issue in the ensuing lobbying campaign.

CHANGES IN THE AUTOMOBILE MARKET

Hoffman articulated both the auto industry's need to exploit the urban market and the changes in federal highway policy that were necesary to bring it about. His analysis was based on an appreciation of a basic change in the automobile market that had occurred since the late 1920s—a change from a new-owner's market to a replacement market. The dimensions of this transformation can be seen in Table 5.1, where domestic automobile sales for 1921–1941 are shown, along with a breakdown of these sales into new-owner versus replacement-demand sales. The change to a replacement market meant the exhaustion of that virgin territory whose exploitation had fueled the industry's earlier vigorous expansion.

The change is now widely recognized and appreciated, but almost all analysts have missed a very important point. Growth in the auto industry still depended on the growth of the new-owner market, even after the change to a replacement market. Growth in the new-owner market could take the form of either growth in the multiple-car-owner market, or further growth in the first-time-owner market. The point is that a growing auto industry required a growing new-owner market. Replacement demand was a "floor," a stable market, but not a growth market. To my knowledge, no one has noted or explored this rather important fact.

Table 5.2 illustrates this relationship by showing the increase in new-owner sales as a percent of the increase in total domestic sales. It is clear that when sales increased significantly, it was due to a strong increase in the new-owner market, not the replacement market. This is not to say that the replacement market was not important, or that it did not grow over this period. Rather, replacement demand appears to have been rather stable in comparison to the new-owner market. There were years when "postponed" replacement demand "caught up," and sizable gains in production were recorded. The basic proposition remains, however: An increase in the size of the auto market depended primarily on an increase in the new-owner market.

THE SATURATED MARKET

Expansion of automobile sales was thus dependent on expanding new-owner sales, but these sales were getting harder to come by. The

TABLE 5.1. Domestic Automobile Sales: New Owner
versus Replacement Demand (in millions)

Year	Domestic Sales	Replacements	New Owners	New Owners as Percent of Domestic Sales
1921	1.55	0.48	1.07	68.8
1922	2.42	0.79	1.62	67.1
1923	3.80	0.88	2.92	76.9
1924	3.31	1.15	2.16	65.2
1925	3.84	1.67	2.17	56.4
1926	3.91	1.82	2.08	53.3
1927	2.93	2.11	0.82	28.1
1928	3.78	2.52	1.26	33.3
1929	4.62	2.83	1.79	38.7
1930	2.95	2.95	0.00	—
1931	2.15	2.15	0.00	—
1932	1.25	1.25	0.00	—
1933	1.74	1.65	0.09	5.1
1934	2.44	1.71	0.73	29.8
1935	3.61	2.18	1.43	39.5
1936	4.11	2.42	1.69	41.1
1937	4.33	2.59	1.74	40.2
1938	2.16	2.16	0.00	—
1939	3.26	2.40	0.86	26.3
1940	4.21	2.35	1.86	44.1
1941	4.43	2.09	2.34	52.7

Source: Automobile Manufacturers Association, Automobile Facts and Figures, 1947
(Washington, DC: Automobile Manufacturers Association,1947), p. 14.

automobile industry's recognition of the limitations on the continued expansion of the new-owner market is found in their discussion of "saturation,"
which began in the 1920s. [13] The basic notion of saturation generally involved
the idea of chronic, institutional limitations on new demand. Saturation in
the automobile industry arose when the existing stock of automobiles was
able to meet the demand for automobile services, given the existing pattern of
automobile usage. To increase demand, in the context of a saturated
automobile market, often required that new uses for automobiles be found.
This then required that institutional or structural changes be made in the role
played by the automobile in society (for example, multiple-car ownership, increased reliance on the automobile for transportation, and so on). Barring
such changes, a chronic condition of demand limitation would persist. The
automobile market would be saturated in relation to the existing structure of
demand and the existing pattern of automobile use.

TABLE 5.2. Increase in New-Owner Sales as a Percentage of the Increase in Domestic Sales, 1922–1941

Year	Percent	Year	Percent
1921	—	1932	—
1922	64.0	1933	18.0
1923	94.0	1934	91.7
1924	—	1935	59.6
1925	1.7	1936	52.6
1926	—	1937	24.5
1927	129.3	1938	—
1928	51.6	1939	78.4
1929	62.8	1940	105.3
1930	—	1941	214.6
1931	—		

Source: Compiled by the author from Table 5.1.

Saturation is an interesting concept, because it was in efforts at overcoming it that many notable changes in the automobile industry were made. For example, annual model changes, the decline of price competition in the industry, planned obsolescence, "trading-up" strategies, and increasing barriers to entry were all the result, to one degree or another, of efforts at counteracting saturation.

The role of saturation in bringing about these developments has been generally recognized,[14] but it is my contention that these same changes in market conditions in the late 1920s, and the problem of saturation, were also factors in the automobile industry's promotion of urban freeways. Beginning in the 1930s, the industry sought to overcome saturation in the automobile market by seeking to remove the limitations that prevented an expansion of automobile use and ownership in urban areas. This actually required that U.S. cities be restructured in order to make them more compatible with the automobile. The key to this restructuring was the creation of an *urban-oriented* Interstate Highway System and the elimination of viable, electric urban transit systems (discussed above). An analysis of the urban automobile market can shed further light on the rationale behind this strategy.

THE IMPORTANCE OF THE URBAN MARKET

The urban auto market was important for two reasons. First, we were becoming increasingly urbanized. Second, urban residents owned fewer cars per capita. The first factor will be considered here, and the second in the following section.

The auto industry expected rapid urbanization to continue and accelerate. For example, a study commissioned by the Automobile Manufacturers Assocation (AMA)[15] noted that all urban areas held 67 percent of the population in 1960.[16] The percentage of the population living in urban areas had grown steadily through the twentieth century: 39.7 in 1900, 45.7 in 1910, 51.2 in 1920, 56.2 in 1930, 56.5 in 1940, 59.0 in 1950, and 63.1 in 1956.

Not only was urbanization increasing, but so was the concentration of the urban population in major metropolitan areas. In 1960 there were 78 major metropolitan areas, which held 48.3 percent of the population. By 1980 the study projected 117 major metropolitan areas, holding 59.4 percent of the population. By 2000, 145 major areas were expected to hold 65.9 percent of the population.

The growth of urban areas was also broken down into the growth of "central cities" versus the growth of the urban "rings," that is, suburban areas. The study concluded that growth was strongest in the suburban areas. In fact, the percentage of the U.S. population living in the central city had remained roughly constant, at about 28.9 to 32.3 percent, between 1920 and 1950. Rapid growth in the central cities had occurred earlier, between 1900 and 1920. The percentage living in the rings, however, had grown steadily over the entire 1900–1950 period. More important, by 1940 the rings were growing faster than the central cities. In 1940, 34.9 percent of the total U. S. population growth was occurring in the rings, while only 22.8 percent was occurring in the central city. By 1950 the respective figures were 48.6 and 30.7 percent.

All of these demographic trends indicated the increasing urbanization of the population, its concentration in major metropolitan areas, and the increasing importance of suburban growth in those major metropolitan areas. These trends were of interest to the automobile industry, since they would influence the demand for automobiles. The indication was that demand would increasingly depend on the travel and car-ownership patterns of the growing urban population.

THE POTENTIAL OF THE URBAN MARKET

A growing urban population was one reason for emphasizing the potential market in the larger cities. The second reason stemmed from the lower car-ownership levels (per person and per family) in the larger cities. In other words, a very large potential market for aubomobiles existed in large cities, provided that city car-per-person levels could be brought up to noncity levels.

In addition to Hoffman's article, interest in this potential market in the larger cities can be seen in auto-industry trade publication in the late 1930s.

For example, during this time *Automobile Facts and Figures* (an auto industry trade journal) began reporting population-to-car-ownership ratios and families-to-car-ownership ratios for the largest urban areas in the country. All of the larger cities had higher person-per-car and family-per-car ratios than smaller cities or rural areas. With the trend toward increasing urbanization, a clear threat to future auto sales was readily apparent, unless urban auto-ownership patterns were altered. At the same time, the higher urban ratios clearly indicated a large potential market, *if* urban car-ownership patterns could be increased. This would require changes in urban travel patterns, but the rewards would be great.

The potential of the urban market can be seen in the case of the city of Los Angeles. Los Angeles had become the auto industry's prime example of how a city could develop. George Hilton has argued that by 1914 it already had a reputation as an auto-oriented city.[17] In addition, an extensive freeway system was begun in the late 1930s and the city became the object of one of the largest motorization campaigns after the war. The Pacific Electric system, including the Los Angeles Railway, had comprised one of the world's largest public transit systems.

Los Angeles stood out as an exception to the usual pattern of urban auto ownership. For example, in 1949 Los Angeles had 2.9 persons per car and 1.0 families per car. In the same year New York had 8.7 persons per car; Chicago (Cook Country) had 5.1 person per car.[18] New York also had 2.5 families per car, while Chicago had 1.5 families per car.

A rough gauge of the potential market can be seen in these figures. For example, if New York, Chicago, and other major cities could be made over in the image of Los Angeles, what effect could this have on auto sales? Ignoring future population growth, we can get a rough idea of the potential market in 1949 in these two cities by applying the Los Angeles ratios to the populations of New York and Chicago. If the Los Angeles persons-per-car ratio had been characteristic of New York, then 1,871,682 *more* cars would have been owned by New Yorkers. This increase alone was almost twice the 943,283 cars that actually had been owned in New York city in 1949. On the basis of the Los Angeles families-per-car ratio, the increased car ownership in New York would have amounted to 1,445,717 more cars, again a substantial increase. No account is taken here of the increase in the replacement market that would develop in these areas as car ownership increased. For Chicago, the increased ownership indicated by the Los Angeles person-per-car ratio would have been 669,031 cars, or a 76 percent increase. The increase based on the families-per-car ratio would have been 461,814 cars, or an increase of 52.5 percent.

If we go one step further and apply the Los Angeles ratios to all urban areas surveyed in *Automobile Facts and Figures* in 1949, the resulting estimates of the potential market are rather astounding. When the Los

Angeles persons-per-car ratio was applied to the population of the 95 largest counties in the United States, we get an estimate of 8,198,256 *additional* vehicles that would have been owned in these 95 most-populated counties. This would represent an increase of about 59 percent over the actual level of ownership in these counties (the actual 1949 ownership figure was 13,161,275 cars). If the Los Angeles families-per-car ratio is applied, car ownership in the 95 counties would have increased by 5,002,881, that is, a 35.8 percent increase. Once again this does not take into account the increased replacement demand from this increased car ownership.

Clearly these calculations are only crude estimates and should not be pushed too far. They do, however, clearly indicate the potential size of urban markets, if urban areas could be made compatible with increased car ownership. In addition, similar estimates of this sort can be found in industry publications.[19] Los Angeles not only indicated the potential, but also the strategy, that is, more urban freeways and the elimination of electric urban transit systems.

THE EFFECTS OF URBAN FREEWAYS

The reasons for urban freeways being considered the key to tapping this urban market can be found in the anticipated effects of urban freeways. A number of these effects were elaborated on in the AMA study. For example, on the subject of trip length, the study noted that freeway users tended to travel almost three times as far as other urban drivers. And the role of freeways in contributing to longer trips was not lost: "New urban freeway systems constructed during the next 20 years will also encourage the production of long trips. . . . The combined effect [of freeways] . . . will increase average trip length in urban areas by 10 to 15 percent."[20] Reduced travel times, the dispersion of employment, and suburbanization, all encouraged by urban freeways, were the main reasons that urban freeways tended to increase trip length.

In addition to increasing trip length, urban freeways were expected to carry a significant proportion of urban travel, especially in the larger cities. Freeways were expected to carry from 30 percent to over 50 percent of traffic in larger cities.[21] It is important to note, however, that urban freeways were expected to generate a significant portion of the traffic that they were expected to carry.[22] Regarding the anticipated impact of additional urban freeways on existing travel, the study concluded that "present 1960 travel in the nation has been estimated to aggregate 728 billion vehicle-miles, of which half takes place in urban areas. With all needed freeways in operation, annual 1960 travel would be approximately 811 billion miles—an increase of about 11 percent over actual experience."[23]

If anything, these figures appear too low,[24] but in any case, freeways were seen as the key to increased travel. In each case the relationship was the same: More freeways meant more traffic. More traffic and a more accessible city, in turn, meant more car sales and ownership. And this relationship was strongest in the larger urban areas, since the "potential use of freeway systems increases as urban areas get larger."[25]

TURNING THE ARGUMENT AROUND

At this point it would be wise to consider an often-used lobbying tactic. After determining that urban freeways would increase suburbanization, car ownership, trip frequency, trip length, and auto travel and traffic, freeway proponents—including auto-industry lobbyists—often turned the argument around. More freeways were necessary, even required, by the expected increases in traffic, travel, car ownership, suburbanization, trip frequency, and trip length. In other words, the argument was circular. Legislators were asked to approve freeways to meet increased traffic, but the estimates of increased travel were often themselves based upon the availability of these same urban freeways.

There was nothing circular about this from the auto industry's vantage point. Freeways were the key to increased traffic, travel, and therefore sales. This was the goal. The circular argument was a lobbying maneuver that enabled industry lobbyists to express the need for more urban freeways in a more acceptable public form.

This circularity can be seen in the AMA-commissioned study. The need for urban freeways was based on the expected volume of travel and traffic. This, in turn was estimated under the assumption that urban freeways, particularly the urban portions of the Interstate Highway System, would be available. "Analyses of travel characteristics and freeway use in the study cities . . . provide the bases for appraising total future travel within the country's urban and rural areas, and the expected use of the Interstate highway system and other urban freeways."[26] The 15 study cities were all located on the Interstate System. Future traffic and travel were therefore estimated assuming the completion of the interstate and all other proposed urban freeways in those cities. It is important to remember that all 15 study cities were on the interstate, since "in most cities, Interstate highways . . . have determined the general structure of the urban freeway network."[27]

The same circular argument was presented by auto-industry lobbyists during congressional hearings. For example, James J. Nance, president of the Automobile Manufacturers Association and president of Studebaker-Packard Corporation, testified before the House Public Works Committee in 1955. Nance based his argument for the interstate, in part, on the expected increase in motor vehicle registrations. His estimates clearly showed, however, how the industry saw the future growth of registrations to be dependent on adequate freeways. As Nance testified,

> The President's Highway Advisory Committee had predicted that motor vehicle registrations in the Nation will rise from 58 million for 1954 to 81 million by 1965—an increase of 40 percent. The automobile industry's own market studies support this prediction, indicating a net gain of about 23 million vehicles in use by 1965. *We assume here, of course, substantial improvement of our highway system during the next 10 years.*[28] (emphasis added)

Mr. Nance was testifying before Congress on the need for the rapid completion of the Interstate System over the next ten years.

URBAN FREEWAY REQUIREMENTS

There is a consistency in Hoffman's 1939 argument for urban highways and the AMA-commissioned study in 1960. The latter study is far more complete, detailed, and documented, but the argument remained essentially the same on key points. Hoffman called for the reorientation of the federal highway program to emphasize urban highways. The AMA study called for the rapid completion of the National System of Interstate Highways, which was to be "the backbone of an urgently needed urban freeway network."[29] Only about 5,000 miles of the 41,000-mile interstate were "urban" in 1960. By 1980 this urban mileage was expected to rise to 9,600 miles, as suburbanization brought new areas (and interstate routes) into the city. The study, however, cited a need for about 16,000 miles of urban freeways by 1980. (One mile per 10,000 urbanites was the suggested formula.) Consequently, the interstate was only the critical first step in developing urban freeways.

Hoffman talked about the need to gash through cities, and the AMA study emphasized the same point, although in different terms. "It would appear from analysis of urban growth and structure, that freeways should be developed progressively *outward* from the key focal points such as downtown"[30] (emphasis in original). With this requirement in mind, highest priority was to be given to downtown distributor loops and selected radial routes. Second preference was to go to intermediate circumferential routes *through* (rather than around) the city itself. Third priority was for the remaining radial routes, and last priority was for the outer circumferential routes. Again the rationale was to open up the city to the automobile. The priority system would best accomplish that. As we will see later, this priority was diametrically opposed to the priorities of the Department of Defense, which were based on their determination of defense highway needs. Their priorities called for circumferential routes, especially those outer routes, to be given first priority. This was not, however, compatible with the automobile industry's requirements.

TOLL ROADS: UNACCEPTABLE

Insight into the auto industry's desire to use urban freeways to tap the urban auto market can be found in their opposition to toll roads. The early 1950s saw the rapid growth of toll roads undertaken by state governments (with federal aid in many cases).[31] At the time of the inauguration of the Interstate System in 1956, there was an extensive and generally profitable toll-road system in operation. In addition, significant new toll roads were being planned by various states, plans that were scrapped with the start of the Interstate System.

The purpose here is not to review these roads per se, but rather to note the automobile industry's opposition. This was typified by the testimony of James Cope, vice-president of Chrysler and representing the Automobile Manufacturers Association in congressional hearings in 1953. With respect to the toll-road boom in the early 1950s, Cope testified that "it is a development that offers no important answer to our major rural roads problems—and no answer at all to the critical urban traffic problem in most jurisdictions, for no method has ever been devised to adapt the toll principle to urban highway needs."[32]

Why were toll roads "no answer at all" to urban freeway needs? The successful toll roads were primarily found in the eastern part of the country and were financially sound because they served this urbanized part of the country. What was lacking for the automobile industry? Cope suggested part of the answer in his testimony, when he argued that the toll road could not be adapted to the urban setting. Since, however, toll roads were found in cities (Chicago, for example), it must have been the way toll roads functioned in the urban setting that bothered the auto industry.

This was, in fact, the difficulty. Collecting tolls posed no problem, provided it was not done too often, but this required limited access and egress and long driving stretches between toll points. Less access reduced the traffic-generating capacity of urban toll freeways. This was why the automobile industry opposed them. Toll roads could serve urban traffic, but they could not generate traffic the way a tax-supported freeway could. In addition, toll roads had to be limited, so as not to "dilute" traffic and therefore revenues.

The AMA-commissioned study made the same point about the inability of toll roads to generate traffic: "Throughout the country, "free" express highways have been found to generate as much as 60 percent new traffic, whereas toll roads have usually generated as much as 30 percent."[33] Toll roads were therefore unacceptable, because they could not adequately do what the auto industry wanted urban freeways to do, that is, open up the city and generate increased traffic and auto ownership.

LOBBYING AND LEGISLATION

Analyzing the impact of lobbying on legislation is a difficult undertaking. This is especially true if we do not have a clear grasp of the interests or motivations of the lobbying groups. We can often determine who favored a piece of legislation and who opposed it. If it was passed, then we can perhaps identify the supporters as the "winners" and the most powerful. If the legislative proposal failed, then the opposite must have been the case. The analysis becomes much more difficult, however, when we try to assess the relative strengths of the winning coalition. Questions as to the relative strengths and impacts of the various lobbying groups arise. Which group of supporters were most influential, which led, which followed, and, most importantly, which groups were able to shape critical aspects of the legislation to their liking or requirements? All of these questions go beyond the question of who supported and who opposed legislation.

Interstate highway politics from the 1930s onward clearly demonstrate this problem. It should be obvious that the automobile industry supported the Interstate Highway System. So did a number of other groups and individuals. Should we then assign equal weight to the influence of the various supporters of the interstate? Were they all equally successful in 1956? Our ability to answer these questions may be limited; they are, nonetheless, the relevant and significant questions.

It is hoped that this effort to identify the autombile industry's interests in the interstate, particularly the urban portions of the interstate, will better enable us to interpret and evaluate the industry's lobbying efforts. It may also contribute to an assessment of the industry's success or failure in this promotion. We will turn to these activities in the following chapter. Again, the goal is not to argue that the auto industry unilaterally manipulated policy to its ends, or that it alone was somehow responsible for the highway policy that emerged. The goal is to understand its efforts, to follow its strategies and lobbying efforts, and perhaps to gauge the extent of its success.

NOTES

1. Many of the ideas expressed in this chapter were presented earlier in: David J. St. Clair, "The Automobile Industry's Interest in Interstate Highway Legislation, 1930–1956,"

in, *Essays in Economic and Business History*, ed. Edwin J. Perkins (Los Angeles: Economic And Business Historical Society; and History Department, University of Southern California, 1984), pp. 160–75.

2. Paul G. Hoffman, "America Goes to Town," *Saturday Evening Post*, April 29, 1939. Citations and page numbers refer to the Automobile Safety Foundation reprint of the article.

3. For example, in 1934 Hoffman argued that "sales resistance to further absorption comes from inability to use automobiles effectively rather than from inability to buy them. Many well-to-do people do not own automobiles, not because they cannot afford to own them, but because as they will tell you, the ownership lacks advantage. They can use mass transportation more conveniently for many of their movements." *New York Times*, January 7, 1934. Quoted in Mark Foster, *From Streetcar to Superhighway* (Philadelphia: Temple University Press, 1981), p. 230. Also, in the same source, see the 1930 Hoffman quote regarding the automobile industry's interests in city planning and its impact on auto sales: Paul G. Hoffman, "Why the Automobile Industry Should Believe in City Planning," *City Planning* 6, No. 2 (April 1930): 96. Cited in Foster, *From Streetcar*, p. 111.

4. Hoffman, "America Goes to Town," p. 4. The statistics below, on travel patterns revealed in the 1939 study, are all from this source. In general, citations of Hoffman's article will be confined to quotes.

5. Ibid.

6. Ibid., p. 5.

7. Ibid., pp. 5, 2.

8. Ibid., p. 5.

9. Ibid., p. 6.

10. Ibid.

11. Ibid.

12. Ibid., p. 5.

13. One cannot appreciate how the industry perceived its problems, or even how various industry analysts have viewed them, without considering this idea of saturation. Economists, however, have tended to avoid the term, because they find it somewhat ambiguous. It has a connotation of "finality" or "absoluteness" which does not seem theoretically justifiable or historically accurate. Indeed, on a theoretical level, the economic term "satiation" refers to the rather extreme case where a consumer has a zero or negative marginal utility for a commodity. Of course, a good saturated in this sense would not command a positive price. Since automobiles did command a positive price, this could not have been what was meant by the term. At the same time, a casual glance at auto sales figures will dispel any idea of an absolute limitation or ceiling on automobile sales. Saturation in that sense would indeed be historically inaccurate and uninteresting.

14. For a review and discussion of how various automobile-industry analysts have dealt with saturation in the automobile industry, see David J. St. Clair, "Entrepreneurship and the American Automobile Industry" (Ph.D. diss., University of Utah, 1979), pp. 153–65.

15. Wilbur Smith and Associates, *Future Highways and Urban Growth* (New Haven, CT: Wilbur Smith and Associates, 1961). Referred to below as Smith, *Future Highways*. The following statistics on anticipated urbanization trends are from this source at page 193. In addition to being commissioned by the AMA, the trade association reproduced and circulated a part of the Smith study as an AMA position paper on freeways. This pamphlet, entitled *Highways for the Future*, was a verbatim copy of the Summary (pp. i–x.) of the Smith study. I treat this study as an invaluable collection, compilation, and articulation of the industry's views and positions on freeway issues. I do not wish to imply that Smith and Associates were "hacks" for the auto industry. They were not. They just did a job that the industry trade association requested, and they did it well enough to have the industry embrace their results. We will simply treat the study the way the industry did. The AMA did not attempt to conceal the nature of the study, and often referred to it as their own. For example, L. L. Colbert of Chrysler

Corporation, and president of the AMA, was referring to the 1961 Smith study when he noted that "our recent published studies of highway economics helped to shape the legislation now moving through Congress and aimed at keeping the Interstate Highway on schedule and soundly financed." Quoted in Helen Leavitt, *Superhighway—Super Hoax* (Garden City, NY: Doubleday, 1970) p. 151. As will be noted in Chapter 6, the urban freeway issue was still very much alive in the early 1960s. In any case, there appears to be no doubt that the Smith study was essentially a good presentation of the industry's views and positions and I treat it as such.

16. Ibid., pp. 332–33. The statistics on urbanization and suburbanization are all from this source.

17. Testimony of George W. Hilton in U. S., Congress, Senate, Committee on the Judiciary, *The Industrial Reorganization Act, Hearings before a Subcommittee on Antitrust and Monopoly*, 93rd Cong., 2d sess., 1974, p. 2231.

18. Automobile Manufacturers Association, *Automobile Facts and Figures*, 1950 edition, pp. 26–27. The discussion is based on figures from this source.

19. For example, see Leavitt, *Superhighway—Super Hoax*, p. 148, for a description of this kind of analysis in an ASF publication entitled "Urban Freeway Development in Twenty Major Cities."

20. Smith, *Future Highways*, p. 197. On the subject of trip lengths and urban freeways, see p. 181.

21. Ibid., p. 172.

22. "By 1980 up to 16 percent more vehicle miles of travel will result from use of urban freeways than if there were no freeway systems. In the study cities, this additional travel ranged from four percent in Miami to sixteen percent in Kansas City." Smith, *Future Highways*, p. 175.

23. Ibid., p. 187.

24. The question is clearly counterfactual, so it cannot be totally resolved; but there are reasons for thinking them too low. For example, in the study, Detroit's freeway carried 53.1 percent of the city's traffic in 1960, but freeways were credited with generating only 9 percent more traffic (p. 173). This implies that most traffic would have reverted back to city streets, if freeways had not been available. It is unlikely that city streets could have handled the congestion. These estimates, therefore, probably underestimate the traffic-generating potential of urban freeways.

25. Ibid., p. 172.

26. Ibid., p. 192.

27. Ibid., p. 160.

28. Testimony of James J. Nance, in U. S., Congress, House, Committee on Public Works, *National Highway Program. Hearings before the House Committee on Public Works on H. R. 4260, Part 1*, 84th Cong., 1st sess., 1955, p. 766.

29. Smith, *Future Highways*, p. 188. All of the figures are from this source at page 191.

30. Ibid., pp. 228–9.

31. For a discussion of these toll-road developments, see John B. Rae, *The American Automobile, A Brief History* (Chicago: University of Chicago Press, 1965).

32. Testimony of James Cope, in U. S., Congress, House Committee on Public Roads, *National Highway Study, Hearings before a Subcommittee on Roads of the House Committee on Public Roads*, 83rd Cong., 1st sess., 1953, p. 422.

33. Smith, *Future Highways*, p. 244.

6

Promoting An Urban Interstate

Realizing the potential that urban freeways held for expanding automobile sales required a high degree of perception on the part of the autombile industry. The industry recognized this potential in the 1930s, while many people, including many Interstate-Highway supporters, never realized the dramatic implications of these urban freeways until well after construction had begun. Perception, however, was only half the battle. The other half entailed the mobilization of energy and assets in order to bring about the required changes. This second step involved both strategies and tactics. We have already sketched the strategy: Develop an urban-oriented Interstate System. This chapter will consider the tactics developed and employed by the automobile industry in the program.

Once again, we are not simply arguing that the industry alone was the force behind the interstate legislation, but as will be shown, the industry was successful in promoting its views in a variety of ways. One must probably also conclude that the legislation that did emerge in 1956 (and its implementation after 1956) was consistent with what the auto industry had sought.

THE LOBBYISTS

The automobile industry's lobbying activities were carried out at all levels, from personal contacts with government officials to mass-media campaigns. Both individual and group efforts were involved. This section will consider two aspects of this lobbying effort. We will first endeavor to trace the formation of numerous auto-industry lobbying organizations. Second, we will look at the interchange of personnel between the automobile industry, the government, and the various lobbying organizations. The personnel interchanges and interlocks with the federal government were extremely important, because they allowed the industry to participate directly in the formation of highway policy. It must be admitted that human beings are complex entities and mere association does not necessarily constitute "proof" of their motives. These interlocks were very extensive, however, and this aspect of lobbying ought to be considered.

Lobbying Organizations

Automobile trade associations were organized in the first decade of this century for the purpose of promoting federal automobile laws, and in response to a rift in the industry over the Seldon patent. Most of these early organizations lasted only as long as the patent issue, which was adjudicated in 1911. Of more concern to us was the formation of the National Automobile Chamber of Commerce (NACC) in 1914. This organization became and has remained the industry's primary trade association. It has, however, changed its name twice—to the Automobile Manufacturers Association (AMA) in 1932, and to the Motor Vehicle Manufacturers Association (MVMA) in 1972. The AMA and later the MVMA have always been exclusively automobile-industry organizations. For this reason they traditionally sought to lobby away from the public spotlight, lest their motives appear self-serving. Exceptions were made in 1953 and 1955 when the industry's critical need for the interstate brought the AMA out to testify before the Clay committee and in congressional hearings. It also testified in 1968 against a bill calling for two public hearings on urban interstate routes. The industry seems, however, to have generally preferred less visible organizations from which to lobby.

The most interesting of these organizations was the Automobile Safety Foundation (ASF), which was organized in 1937, when the AMA simply decided to reorganize its own safety division into an "independent" organization. So, from its inception, the ASF was essentially an extension of the AMA. It was still mostly financed by the auto manufacturers, and its officers remained automobile-industry personnel. It was, however, an invaluable creation, because, with its name, it fit the requirements of a lobbying organization perfectly; that is, it sounded nonpolitical and impartial. Although its name implied a safety orientation, "safety" was always secondary. The ASF never really supported vehicle safety legislation at either the state or federal level. In fact, it did not testify during the congressional hearings on automobile safety in the 1960s. The ASF never missed an opportunity to promote highways, however. As we will see, it was in the forefront of the automobile industry's campaign for urban highways after 1939, and it boasted that it gave a "high priority to urban transportation matters."[1] While it did not participate in the hearings on automobile safety, it did find time to make numerous pleas for highways before Congress. For example, the ASF testified in 1968 that "current levels of highway expenditures do not meet present highway needs. . . . Additional sources of revenue [for the Trust Fund] must be considered."[2]

Although the ASF usually tried to relate its highway proposals to safety, the relationship was often tenuous, at best. Certainly some of its activities, such as its active oppositon to the Los Angeles rapid transit proposal in 1968, could not possibly have been related to safety.[3] In any case, the ASF has been one of the automobile industry's most active lobbying organizations.

Another important lobbying group was formed in 1932, when Alfred P. Sloan, Jr., of General Motors, organized the National Highway Users Conference (NHUC). This organization was originally established to bring together highway users to resist the diversion of user taxes during the depression. Beginning in 1946, however, NHUC began devoting its energies toward highway lobbying. In 1946 the first Highway Transportation Congress was held in Washington, D. C., under the chairmanship of Sloan. These "congresses" would continue until the passage of the interstate legislation in 1956. Sloan remained the chairman of the NHUC from 1932 until 1948. He was then replaced by Albert Bradley, chairman of the board of General Motors, who served until 1956. Although NHUC boasted some 3,000 member groups, the automobile industry was always dominant.

NHUC, largely through the activities of Bradley, organized the Project Adequate Roads (PAR) publicity campaign in 1951. This was intended to be a huge publicity campaign for the Interstate Highway System. Dissension racked PAR from the start, however, and NHUC had to continue the publicity campaign on its own. The experience with PAR served to reenforce NHUC's role as a unifying force among highway lobbyists. Consequently, NHUC never testified at congressional hearings, in order to avoid getting involved in any disagreements among its member organizations.

In 1969, ASF and NHUC merged to form the Highway Users Federation for Safety and Mobility (HUFSAM). Grant Mickle, newly appointed president of HUFSAM, said the merger would soften the "image of political lobbying" that ASF and NHUC had acquired.[4] The new organization did not, however, shed its automobile-industry ties. For example, in 1972 almost one-half of the HUFSAM budget came from that industry.[5]

Although there were other industry groups and organizations, AMA, ASF, and NHUC were the primary participants in the lobbying effort.[6] We shall have occasion to follow their activities in the lobbying campaign.

Personnel Interlocks

The problem inherent in evaluating the consequences of personnel interlocks was noted above. We will try here to show the extent of this phenomenon and to suggest its implication. A rather extensive and pervasive pattern of personnel interlocks will be evident, which can hardly be explained as coincidence, and which afforded ample opportunity for the industry to express its views.

The initial personnel interchanges between the automobile industry and the government began, significantly enough, during World War I. This initiated a long association between the automobile industry and the War Department (later the Department of Defense). In 1915 Howard E. Coffin, vice-president and chief engineer at Hudson Motor Car Company, along with five members of the Society of Automotive Engineers, volunteered for the Navy Department's Advisory Committee.[7] This lead to Coffin's subsequent appointment as chairman of the Council for National Defense (CND), formed in 1916 to mobilize our industrial system for war. At the same time Alfred E. Reeves, head of the NACC was appointed chairman of the Motor Transport Committee by Coffin. This committee of the CND was responsible for formulating plans for the mobilization of motor vehicles in the event of war. Reeves then brought Roy D. Chapin, president of Hudson and an early highway advocate, into the CND to chair the Highway Transport Committee. This committee reported to Reeves and sought to coordinate all highway transport.

This was only the beginning of the "defense connection," which continued in the next war. Prior to the Second World War, William S. Knudsen, president of General Motors, was appointed by Roosevelt to cochair the Advisory Commission to the Council of National Defense (comprised of cabinet members). In January 1941 this loosely knit organization was superseded by the Office of Production Management (OPM) with Knudsen as director. Knudsen then oversaw the country's massive industrial war-mobilization campaign. His auto-industry orientation was explicit, and not too tactfully hidden. As Knudsen told Roosevelt, "What I think we should do . . . is to bury the automobile manufacturers under defense orders—three times as much stuff as they can make with their present facilities."[8]

This did not go over well with most of the small firms involved in the mobilization effort. They complained that the auto industry got all the contracts, and also criticized Knudsen's tactless way of handling their complaints. Consequently, in late 1941 Donald Nelson from Sears, Roebuck Company was brought in as Knudsen's superior. In 1945 Knudsen went back to the board of directors at GM.

The Automobile Council for War Production (ACWP), which played an important role in the mobilization, brought a number of automobile executives and future lobbyists into government service. The list of participants included Alfred P. Sloan, Jr. of GM; I. B. Babcock, who had figured so prominently in the National City Lines operation; C. E. Wilson, president of GM and a future secretary of defense; Pyke Johnson of the ASF; Alfred Reeves from the AMA (and the CND in the First World War); Paul Hoffman of the ASF; and Alvan Macauley, head of the AMA and the Packard Motor Company. Macauley served as chairman of both the AMA and the ACWP. George Romney, a future secretary of housing and urban development, served as the managing director of the AMA and also as the chief executive officer of the ACWP. James Cope, after serving with Roosevelt's NRA, came to the AMA in 1935 and subsequently served with the ACWP. He joined Chrysler as a vice-president in 1944 and later became one of the industry's leading lobbyists in the early 1950s. The war effort provided invaluable exposure, contacts, and training for future lobbying.

The case of C. E. Wilson is of special interest. In 1953 he left his position as president of GM to become secretary of defense in the Eisenhower administration. This is the same Charles "Engine" Wilson whose purported statement, "What is good for General Motors is good for the United States," has now become famous.[9] We will have occasion to consider the impact of his appointment on highway matters below, but it should be noted here that Wilson was not alone at the Defense Department. Harold Talbott, who served as air force secretary, was formerly a member of the Chrysler Corporation's Finance Committee. At the same time, the undersecretary of defense was Roger Kyes, from GM, who earlier had sold all those buses to the Minneapolis–St. Paul Transit System (referred to above). After Wilson, the "defense connection" continued with Robert McNamara, from Ford Motor Company, who took over as secretary of defense in the Kennedy administration. Defense and the automobile industry seem to have had a long association.

Automobile executives also served in other government positions. Roy D. Chapin had become one of the indutry's most active lobbyists prior to the Second World War. He had been involved in the Lincoln Highway project in 1913 and had lobbied vigorously for a federal highway program. His efforts were rewarded when he was invited to dedicate the "Zero Milestone" of the new federal aid highway system in Washington, D. C., in 1922. This dedication kicked off the entire federal aid system, set up in the Federal Highway Act of 1921. Chapin remained active in the lobbying field and was called upon in 1932 to serve as Hoover's secretary of commerce. The Hoover administration, in 1932, made the first break in the rural domination of the federal highway program by allowing federal funds for use on urban highways (discussed below).[10] Chapin also made J. Walter Drake, chairman of the board at Hupp Motor Car Company, his undersecretary of commerce.

Special attention must also be accorded another Eisenhower appointment. Francis Du Pont, of the Du Pont family that controlled GM, was appointed to succeed the retiring director of the Bureau of Public Roads

(BPR), Thomas MacDonald, in 1953. The Eisenhower administration already had in inordinate number of automobile people in its ranks, including Wilson, but Du Pont appears to have exerted a very large influence on Eisenhower himself.[11] This may be a very plausible explanation for why Eisenhower, never noted for his bold domestic policy innovations, took the lead in getting the interstate underway.

The Du Pont family had been in the forefront of highway developments since the early 1920s. The five-mile Du Pont Highway was constructed in 1924 over land owned by the family in Delaware. Prior to his appointment as commissioner of the BPR, Francis Du Pont had served as a member of the Delaware State Highway Commission from 1922 through 1949. He resigned as commissioner of the Bureau of Public Roads on January 1, 1956, in order to become a special consultant to the secretary of commerce, the department in which the BPR was then housed. He is generally credited with being an ardent and effective lobbyist for the interstate. He had also argued at one time for 100 percent federal funding of the interstate, based in large part on the defense argument.[12] The significance of the appointments of C. E. Wilson and Francis Du Pont will be discussed below, in connection with the designation of urban interstate routes in 1955.

We should consider not only the personnel interlocks between the industry and government, but also the interlocks between the automobile industry and other lobbying organizations. They were too numerous to account for completely, but a few examples will suffice. Within the "automobile lobby," personnel movement between organizations was common. For example, Paul Hoffman of the Studebaker Packard Corporation and the author of the 1939 article discussed in the previous chapter, left as president of the ASF in 1942 to participate in the Automobile Council for War Production (ACWP). He was replaced by Pyke Johnson, who left his position as general manager of the AMA to go to the ASF. Johnson also participated in the ACWP. Johnson's position at the AMA was then taken by George Romney, who was simultaneously serving as managing director of ACWP. Such periodic shuffling of personnel was commonplace, especially between the AMA, the ASF, the ACWP, and the NHUC.

Perhaps more important was the influence with other organizations that the automobile industry gained through this same practice of personnel interlocks. For example, the Chamber of Commerce of the United States had, on highway matters, generally deferred to auto-industry members and other highway lobbying groups in setting its highway policies. Automobile-industry personnel, as members of the Chamber of Commerce, were in the forefront of drafting the Chamber of Commerce's highway policy positions. For example, on December 10 and 11, 1953 the Chamber of Commerce held a national conference on highway financing. The first day's panel was chaired by George Romney from Nash-Kelvinator Corporation and the AMA. He was also serving simultaneously as the director of the Chamber of Commerce of the United States. Romney was also a member of the chamber's Construction and Civic Development Committee. His first task at the conference was to introduce James Cope, of Chrysler and the AMA, to give the automobile industry's positon.

The Highway Research Board (HRB) is another example. This organization brought together state highway departments, BPR officials, the American Society of Civil Engineers, and other highway-oriented organizations to promote and stimulate highway research. Here again we find auto-industry personnel in high positions in the organization. For example, in 1964–1966 we find D. Grant Mickle, an 18-year veteran in the ASF, as director of the HRB. While still with the ASF, he served as the federal highway administrator at the BPR between 1961 and 1964. After his tenure as HRB director, he became vice-chairman of the HRB. In addition, many HRB activities relating to urban freeways were funded by the ASF.[13] The HRB was a valuable lobbying ally because it brought lobbyists together with officials from all levels of government, and because of its reputation for being primarily a research organization.

The special presidential committees charged with formulating highway policy have also had substantial automobile-industry representation. For example, on Roosevelt's important Interregional Highway Committee (discussed below) we find George D. Kennedy from the ASF. In addition, when the Special Committee on Post-War Economic Policy and Planning was preparing an extensive, economy-wide survey of postwar policies and planning in 1943, the highway section of the report was based, in large part, on a study by Kennedy, entitled "The Role of the Federal Government in Highway Development."[14] The report was passed on to the committee by Representative Carl Hayden, one of the auto industry's strongest allies and sponser of depression highway legislation. Hayden was also the industry's source of input into the important 1944 highway legislation (discussed below). Hayden received the report through Paul G. Hoffman, chairman of the ASF. Participating in the preparation of Kennedy's report was Grant Mickle of the ASF.

This extensive network of personnel interchanges demonstrates how active auto-industry people were in securing positions of influence in government, other lobbying groups, and business and professional groups. One could treat this as an "infiltration," but the sinister connotation of this term seems unwarranted and really obscures the necessity of this type of action. In highway lobbying, as in probably any other endeavor, one has to work to be heard, to get access to policy making, and to get one's views accorded due consideration. Those who think that simply stating one's position will suffice in this regard are doomed to failure. For example, transit lobbying organizations failed even to get heard at the Clay committee hearings (discussed below).[15] They had not developed the capacity to make sure that their views were heard and considered. The stakes in this matter were high for both transit and the auto industry, but the auto industry was much more successful in developing policy-access channels. Personnel interchanges were an important part of that strategy. We will now look at how the auto industry sought to influence the formation of highway policy.

EARLY LOBBYING ACTIVITIES

The first policy issue to confront auto-industry lobbyists in the early 1930s was the problem of user-tax diversion. The depression hit state and local government revenues very hard, and their first reaction was to find new revenue sources and to cut highway expenditures. One new source of revenue came from the introduction of state sales taxes. More significant for the subject at hand, however, was the increased diversion of state highway-road-user taxes for nonhighway projects. Highway-user taxes had been initiated in Oregon in 1919 and had quickly spread to other states. The rationale for these taxes had been to finance highway construction and maintenance, but these taxes had generally not been explicitly reserved for highway projects, and the amount of diversion had varied from state to state. Some states, like Minnesota in 1920 and Kansas in 1928, had enacted antidiversion laws before the depression. Most, however, had not. Diversion of highway-user taxes had occurred during the 1920s, but the diversion was generally kept at tolerable levels. At the onset of the depression, however, diversion became epidemic and critical as far as the auto industry and all others interested in the continuation of the highway program were concerned. The auto industry referred to diversion as "raids on user taxes" and saw them as the greatest threat to the road program.

It was around this critical problem of "raids" on user taxes and the threat that they posed to the highway program that Alfred D. Sloan, Jr., of General Motors, organized the National Highway Users Conference (NHUC) in 1932. This organization sought to limit diversion through the promotion of antidiversion laws in the various states. NHUC kept a running commentary on state legislation and lobbying activities and supplied a steady stream of information and statistics to its local chapters and to state officials for use in lobbying campaigns. It was also instrumental in putting an antidiversion provision in federal highway legislation in 1934, which provided for a curtailment of federal aid to states that "excessively" diverted.[16] The "excessive" provision was interpreted, however, in such a manner as to prevent it from ever being invoked. The antidiversion campaign therefore focused on state antidiversion laws and managed to get such laws passed in a majority of states in the 1930s. A federal excise tax was placed on gasoline in 1932 and was also subject to diversion. This was generally considered at the time to have been a temporary depression revenue measure, but it was never repealed.

Depression Highway Policy

In addition to the diversion problem, the federal highway program itself underwent some important changes in the depression. The regular federal aid highway program was essentially suspended in favor of emergency road programs that emphasized depression relief. This view of federal highway expenditures as an ideal macroeconomic stabilization tool seems to have had a strong following through the mid-1950s.[17] In any case, the depression relief expenditures were responsible for the bulk of the highway expenditures during the early years of depression.

A major change in federal highway policy was included in the Emergency Relief and Construction Act in 1932. This was a product of the Hoover administration, and as noted above, Hoover's secretary of commerce was Roy D. Chapin, president of Hudson Motor Car Company and a long-time highway advocate. Although his tenure was short, it is unlikely that the major changes in highway policy in the act were unrelated to his presence in the Hoover administration.

In any case, the 1932 act suspended the requirement for 50-50 matching funds and provided for 100 percent federal financing. At the same time, aid was made available for urban as well as for rural road projects. Hoover apparently balked at the urban provision, but bowed to the urban unemployment-relief argument.[18] To the auto industry, this first break in the exclusively rural program was a step in the right direction. Aid was also made available for "farm-to-market" (or secondary) roads.

Roosevelt's New Deal highway policies basically continued, albeit on a larger scale, the policy of the Hoover administration. George Smerk has noted that in Roosevelt's New Deal employment programs, "highway construction was among the first items on the list—especially those highways going into and out of our great cities."[19] In 1933 the National Industrial Recovery Act again made emergency highway-construction funds available to cities. The most important piece of New Deal legislation, however, was the Hayden-Cartwright act of 1934. This legislation was the first to explicitly extend federal highway aid to urban areas. The bill's cosponsor was Congressman Hayden from Arizona, who often worked with highway lobbyists. By 1934 the anti-urban provisions had been formally purged from the federal highway program. It would take a lot more, however, to actually get the urban highways under way.

Regular grant in aid through the federal aid program were restored in 1936. Federal funds were now available for both rural areas and for extensions of the federal aid system into and through urban areas. Funding for urban projects was *not* explicitly provided, however, and the decision to undertake urban projects was left to the states. In addition, the entire issue was clouded by the "temporary relief" nature of the 1934 enabling legislation. States generally ignored the urban provisions, so the victory was rather hollow. The failure of New Deal legislation to permanently change the rural domination demonstrated that such a change was not going to be an easy matter. When the regular highway program was resumed, this foray into urban construction remained largely symbolic.

Depression highway programs fell short, at least from the automobile industry's perspective, in another important way. It was generally dissatisfied with the kind of urban highway projects undertaken. For example, in 1943 NHUC had made clear its objections to a return to the New Deal policies, calling them "a grandiose, money spending unemployment relief program which would fail to give a dollar return for a dollar spent."[20] What was lacking here was a program designed to change the structure of cities. Roosevelt's programs were unacceptable to the auto industry because they generally provided for the construction of city streets, with too little emphasis on a radical reorganization of urban transportation. Programs for dramatically altering the accessibility of the city to auto traffic and auto ownership were lacking. Given its interests in urban freeways, the auto industry's displeasure with depression highway programs is understandable. Something more was required.

Toward the end of the 1930s the industry found that something: the Interregional Highway System (later changed to the Interstate System). In 1939, *Automobile Facts and Figures* published six maps, including various "Interregional Highway" proposals and the "Strategic Defense Highway Map."[21] In 1945 the journal published a map showing the National System of Interstate Highways, along with the expected increase in traffic from the system, with this observation: "The peaks [indicating higher traffic densities] at principal cities picture the greatest increases of traffic to be expected on sections of the routes traversing the cities."[22] The Interstate System, with an emphasis on its urban portions, had became the focal point for industry lobbying by the end of the 1930s.

Promoting an Urban Interstate

One of the earliest efforts at planning an interstate-type system led to a congressional report, *Toll Roads and Free Roads*, in 1939.[23] This report was initially undertaken at the direct request of President Roosevelt in 1937.[24] He reportedly gave Commissioner MacDonald a map on which he had sketched six transcontinental routes, and asked the bureau for a study of the proposal. Congress asked for the same study in the 1938 Federal Aid Highway Act, specifically requesting a feasibility study of a toll-road system of about 14,000 miles, to be comprised of three north-south and three east-west arteries. The report, however, argured against the idea of a toll system and, in place of the 14,000-mile network, proposed a 27,000-mile "Master Plan of Free Highway Development." The rejection of toll roads and the three-corridor transcontinental system brought federal highway policy back into line with planning in the Bureau of Public Roads that had been under way from at least the mid 1930s.[25] The BPR plan centered around the type of system that was advocated by Paul Hoffman in his 1939 article, and was similar to the plan advocated by General Motors in its popular exhibit at the 1939 New York World's Fair.[26] *Toll Roads and Free Roads* also emphasized the urban orientation of the proposed system, suggesting that the system go through and/or closely around major urban areas.[27] This reflected not only the bureau's sentiments but also the growing interest in urban freeways among urban planners and others, including the auto industry.

This emphasis on urban freeways was certainly an accomplishment, given prevailing anti-urban sentiments, particularly in state highway departments. The victory was more symbolic than substantive, however, since very few specific recommendations were made. Indeed, the greatest impact of the 1939 report was that it led to Roosevelt's appointment of the National Interregional Highway Committee in April 1941.[28] In contrast to the *Toll Road and Free Road* report, *Interregional Highways,* the committee's report, made specific recommendations and essentially gave the Interstate System its present form. The report was submitted to Roosevelt on January 1, 1944, and transmitted to Congress on January 12, 1944. A "National System of Interstate Highways" was designated in *Interregional Highways.* This system was then directly incorporated into legislation in 1944 (and subsequent route designations in 1947 and 1955).

The Interregional Highway Committee had considered five proposed freeway systems of different lengths: 14,200 miles, 26,700 miles, 33,920 miles, 36,000 miles, and 48,400 miles. The 33,920-mile system, containing 4,400 miles of urban route, was the committee's choice. It also, however, recommended 5,000 miles of additional urban routes to supplement the original 33,920 miles. The total 38,920 miles served as the basis for the 40,000 mile Interstate System set up in 1944. In August 1947, 37,800 miles of interstate route were officially designated, including 3,900 miles of urban routes. The designations in 1947 were substantially the same as had been recommended by the committee. The 2,200 miles left undesignated in 1947 were generally to be based on the additional urban miles suggested by the committee in 1944. They were designated in September 1955.

Interregional Highways was therefore a crucial juncture in highway policy and the Interregional Highway Committee played a very large role in shaping the Interstate System.[29] The composition of this important committee is of interest: Commissioner Thomas MacDonald of the BPR; George D. Kennedy, incoming president of the American Association of State Highway Officials (AASHO), a Michigan highway commissioner, and member (and soon to be president) of the ASF; Charles H. Purcell, state highway engineer from California; Harland Bartholemew, a prominent city planner from St. Louis; Rexford Tugwell, chairman of the New York City Planning Commission and member of the president's "Brain Trust"; Fredric A. Delano, chairman of the National Resources Planning Board; and Bibb Graves, former governor of Alabama. Herbert S. Fairbanks, from the BPR, was named committee secretary. He had been instrumental in including the call for urban routes in *Toll Roads and Free Roads*, even using his home town of Baltimore as an example of how the sytem would traverse cities.[30]

The composition of this important committee reveals a very strong urban orientation. In addition, the Kennedy and Purcell appointments are particularly noteworthy. Kennedy, as a member of the ASF lobbying organization, was in a position to directly represent industry views in committee deliberations. The committee's report certainly did strongly support the kind of interstate system that the industry had sought. Whether it would have done so even without Kennedy's participation is a question that cannot be answered. It was, however, an important appointment and an invaluable opportunity to directly influence highway policy.

Purcell's appointment was also significant. We have already had occasion to gauge the sentiments of the California Highway Department in the Olympic Line rail case and later in the Aliso Street rail case. Antirail and prohighway seems to sum it up in both cases. California's Highway Department was also somewhat atypical of state highway departments, in that it appears to have shed its rural bias in the early 1930s. In 1933 and 1935 the state legislature had doubled the state's highway mileage and included routes through incorporated urban areas.[31] In addition, one-fourth of a cent of the state's two-cent gas tax was reserved for extensions of the highway system through incorporated urban areas. About 71 percent of the state's population was urbanized by 1940, and the state's first urban freeway was opened in January 1941 (the first, or one of the first, urban freeways in the country). In addition, California had also rejected the toll-road concept. Consequently, Purcell was experienced in the kind of highway policy that the automobile industry favored. Without impugning his loyalties in any way, his appointment had to have been welcomed by the industry.

After the war the ASF became intimately involved in formulating California highway policy. In 1945 a joint interim committee of the California Senate and Assembly was established to study and report on street and highway problems. Between 1945 and 1947 extensive surveys of traffic and highway problems were made. This resulted in the publication of the first California highway "needs study" in 1946, the first in the nation. These studies also served as the basis for the Collier-Burns act of 1947, the legislation that launched California's ambitious postwar freeway program. The impact of the Collier-Burns act went far beyond California's borders. A U.S. Department of Transportation publication in 1977 concluded that "The Act laid down conditions perceived as needed for a successful survey of highway deficiences and which became virtually "principles" that were generally adopted by other States as they followed California's lead."[32] Nineteen states had followed California's lead by 1956, and 35 had undertaken needs studies by 1959.[33]

In California, as in the other 35 states, the needs studies were carried out by, or in conjunction with, the Automobile Safety Foundation.[34] Indeed one of the "principles" laid down in the Collier-Burns act was that the surveys should be carried out by outside traffic consultants and engineers. The ASF provided just such a service. In this endeavor the ASF received the strong endorsement of the Public Roads Administration. The actual studies were carried out by the ASF's engineering division, which was organized under George D. Kennedy, the Interregional Highways Committee member. The ASF's survey work was not peripheral, either in California or in the other 35 states. The ASF was, in the words of Fairbanks at the BPR the "principal support" behind the postwar highway-needs studies.[35] Consequently, the auto industry's lobbying group, the ASF, was thus able to participate directly in the preparation of highway policy through the need studies. Kennedy was involved in the preparation of both the Interregional Highways report and the need studies. In both instances there had to have been great benefit in being able to directly participate in the formation of highway policy.

This successful tactic of providing technical, engineering, and administrative support to government agencies was later employed with city governments. In 1954 the National Committee on Urban Transportation (NCUT), which was "initiated and sponsored by the Automobile Safety Foundation," was created in order to help cities with urban transportation planning.[36] In the words of the Department of Transportation, NCUT "not only exemplified the ability of the Foundation to marshall resources to bear on a specific problem, but also marked the beginning of the cooperative approach to urban transportation problems."[37] In 1958 NCUT had its book, *Better Transportation for Your City*, along with 17 procedural manuals, published by the Public Administration Service. They went through several printings and became "best sellers" for the Public Administration Service.[38] These publications later became the basis for the "Action Programs" in the early 1960s (discussed below).

HIGHWAYS, NATIONAL DEFENSE, AND WARTIME LEGISLATION

During the Second World War, highways were regarded as comparatively expendable and were, in fact, generally neglected in favor of higher-priority production. Nevertheless, highway legislation and highway planning during the war years were quite significant. In addition, the war clearly demonstrated the value of the defense argument in promoting an expanded federal participation in highway policy. Indeed, in 1956 the Interstate System officially became the National System of Interstate and Defense Highways.

The issue of highways and national defense has many facets. For example, what were the origins of the various defense road networks? What role did highways play in World War II? Did the German *Autobahn* stimulate interest in the interstate? Was the defense argument legitimate, or was it merely political window dressing in the interstate issue? And finally, what type of interstate would best serve defense highway needs? Space does not permit a treatment of all of these issues. Consequently, only those that directly relate to the topic at hand will be considered here.[39]

Wartime Legislation

The Defense Highway Act of 1941 was a wartime measure that designated certain highways for troop, war materiel, and supply movement. The act incorporated the "Strategic Defense Highway Map" into the highway system. Nothing was really done, however, beyond the designation stage. More important, the 1941 act provided for a 75-25 funding ratio. This was indeed significant, because it was the first departure from the 50-50 matching-funds ratio established in 1916 (depression legislation excepted). Military necessity was the rationale for the increased federal funding, and the strength of the defense argument in bringing about this change was not lost on supporters of the Interstate System after the war.

The really critical and significant change in federal highway policy occurred in 1944 with the passage of the Federal Aid Highway Act of 1944. This legislation radically altered the emphasis of the federal highway program. Although the act had only limited success in actually bringing the Interstate System about, it still laid the groundwork.

Federal highway funding for the entire federal program was increased to $1.5 billion, available over three years, which was a sizable increase over past funding. Funds were also specifically provided for extensions of the federal aid system within muncipalities and urban areas with a population of over 5,000. Funds had previously been available for these urban areas at the discretion of the states. With only a few exceptions, however, the states, with their rural-oriented highway departments, had not chosen to use their highway funds in urban areas. The ABC system was also established in the 1944 legislation. The A system was to be the primary system, that is, the regular, established federal aid program. The B system was to be the rural secondary system, comprised of bus routes, mail routes, and farm-to-market routes in rural areas and in municipalities of 5,000 population or less. The C system was the newly established urban system, comprised of urban arterials. Each of these systems received specific funding under the 1944 legislation, and this was to be the future method of appropriation as well. This would guarantee resources and expenditures for each of the systems, especially for the long-neglected urban routes that were now in the C system. The states were allowed, however, to shift up to 20 percent of the funds earmarked for one system to another. Actual funding under the 1944 legislation called for $500 million to be spent each year, divided as follows: $225 million or 45 percent for the primary system; $150 million or 30 percent for the secondary system; and $125 million or 25 percent for the C system. The funding of the C system was to be in addition to any urban mileage the states had already included in the primary system. This however, was inconsequential, since few states had taken advantage of the earlier provisions.

The funding ratio reverted back to the prewar 50–50 matching-funds scheme. The lobbying efforts surrounding this reversion will be described below. There was, however, a positive development for urban freeway proponents in a new provision for federal funding of up to 33 percent of right-of-way acquisition. Given the prohibitive cost of urban right-of-way, this was significant.

The most momentous provision of the 1944 legislature was the creation of an Interstate System, not to exceed 40,000 miles, based on the *Interregional Highways* report. Separate funding for this system, however, was not provided. States could, if they chose, fund the interstate with primary funds, since it was still formally a part of the primary system. Few states exercised this option, but the freeway program was inaugurated in 1944, so attention in subsequent years was focused on route designations and financing.

As can be seen, clear progress was made in emphasizing urban road construction in the 1944 legislation. It is equally clear that effective control of the program remained with rural interests. Twenty-five percent of the funds were designated for urban roads, but the Interstate System was not funded. Equally important, the anti-urban sentiments in the states remained intact. Consequently, the part of the roads program that was of most interest to the automobile industry was left drastically underfunded and never really got under way. In addition, the 75–25 funding ratio that had been won in 1941 and that was considered crucial to meeting the high costs of urban construction, was lost in 1944.

While automobile interests did not testify in congressional hearings in 1944, they did lobby to keep the higher funding ratio. Congressional hearings records state only that "during closing hours of the hearings, five highway-user organizations submitted a joint statement emphasizing the need to keep "special user levies on a sound basis and within reasonable and justifiable needs."[40] The industry, however, in this case apparantly chose to avoid high visibility lobbying, such as testifying before Congress. Instead, the industry's inputs and views were channeled through Senator Hayden of the Senate Committee on the Post Office and Post Roads. It is extremely difficult to trace this kind of lobbying, but we are fortunate to have an account in this case. Mark Rose describes "confidential" meetings in August 1944 between Hayden and representatives of the ASF, the Chamber of Commerce of the United States, and the American Automobile Association (AAA).[41] At these meetings a strategy for achieving a 60-40 funding ratio was discussed. While Hayden got the Senate Committee on the Post Office and Post Roads to approve the 60-40 ratio, the 50-50 ratio was restored, due to rural opposition in the House and from Senator Byrd in the Senate. This episode illustrates the industry's lobbying tactics in 1944, as well as its interest in this issue. It may also have demonstrated to the auto industry the need for a more visible profile on such issues, which it did adopt in the early 1950s.

The Defense Issue and Promoting the Interstate

The victory on the funding issue in 1941 and the reversal in 1944 showed the power of the defense argument in securing increased federal funding, but also demonstrated that this issue had to be cultivated in order to last beyond periods of national emergency.

Discussion of the defense aspects of roads and highways can be traced back to the First World War, although the suggestion that this was a direct antecedent of the Interstate System is a rather shaky argument. In any case, the military's defense-road needs remained essentially unchanged from 1919 to 1957, and were often presented at public hearings. For example, in various congressional hearings before 1956, General Paul F. Yount, chief of transportation, United States Army and Department of Defense, expressed the same viewpoint that had been put forth by the military in 1919 in conjunction with the Pershing Map—that is, any highway system that satisfied civilian needs would generally satisfy military needs, provided that access roads to military installations were available.[42] General Yount also called for orderly completion of the interstate, uniform design standards, and limited access on the highway system. He expressed the military's continued interest in circumferential routes around cities. Regarding consultations between the Department of Defense and the Bureau of Public Roads over highway matters, Yount testified:

The area in which we have done the most consultation in recent years with the Bureau of Public Roads has been on the problem of circumferential routes around cities. The question of circumferential routes, as you gentlemen know, is not totally resolved. It is certainly a matter of great concern to the Bureau and the Department, because with the possibility of blocking of the radial spoke type of urban highway which we currently have, we should have the circumferential routes as an alternative.[43]

General Yount's testimony indicated the military's desire to avoid built-up urban areas. This position was further attested to in congressional testimony given by the army's assistant chief of transportation engineering, Mr. D. K. Chacey, in 1960:

For some time the Department of Defense has felt that highways would be of greatest potential value in urban areas if they were circumferential in character. We are not talking about circles, but we are talking about roads that go around the highly developed urban areas, with their tall buildings, and congestion, and such as that, rather than a plunge route that goes through the center of the city. I think it is rather obvious under some conditions of national emergency, especially in the days of guided missiles, that there is more potential in the use of the highway if it is in suburban areas where buildings are lower, and it could be cleared, and such as that, than if it is downtown and it is not available.[44]

The automobile industry's position, on the other hand, was almost directly opposed to this reasoning. It was not against circumferential routes per se, but it was clearly opposed to keeping the Interstate System out of urban areas or to emphasizing circumferential routes. In other words, circumferential routes were acceptable, if they were in addition to radial routes through the cities, but not acceptable as a replacement for these urban radial routes. One of the clearest expressions of the need for radial routes through the cities, that is, the view shared by the auto industry, was voiced by Robert Moses, city construction coordinator of New York City and the 1953 recipient of a $25,000 General Motors award for an essay on adequate highways.[45] In a speech addressing NHUC in 1964, Moses summed up the need for radical action rather bluntly: "You can draw any kind of pictures you like on a clean slate and indulge your every whim in the wilderness in laying out a New Delhi, Canberra or Brasilia, but when you operate in an overbuilt metropolis you have to hack your way with a meat ax."[46] Where was the "hacking" to be done? Eleven years earlier, before the Clay committee, Moses had been explicit.[47] He stated that freeways, expressways, and so forth had to go directly through cities rather than around them, as was usually planned. His justification was traffic-volume requirements.

The actual disagreement over radial versus circumferential routes centered on the urban interstate routes left unassigned in 1947. The intercity mileage designated in 1947 totaled about 37,700 miles, while the remaining 2,300 miles, constituting additional urban portions of the system, were left undesignated until 1955. As General Yount had indicated, this had been the issue on which the Defense Department had consulted most extensively with the Bureau of Public Roads. General Yount was emphatic as to the designation of the remaining 2,300 miles, when he stated that "improvement of the 2,300 miles recently added to the Interstate System should mostly take the form of circumferential routes around population centers."[48] Consequently, the defense issue, while useful in promoting increased federal participation in highway construction, could, if military requests were taken seriously, promote an Interstate System that avoided or minimized going through the cities. To the auto industry, the defense argument was thus a double-edged sword—useful on the one hand, but threatening on the other. Consequently, to avoid the unpalatable implications of the defense argument, another defense issue, one that would justify the radial routes, was employed—civil defense.

This issue was addressed by the President's Advisory Committee on a National Highway Program, otherwise known as the Clay committee. The committee was established by President Eisenhower in 1954 and reported to the president in *A Ten-Year National Highway Program* in 1955. Its purpose was to study the nation's highway needs and suggest necessary legislation. The committee made the following one-paragraph reference to the civil-defense aspects of the Interstate System:

> From the standpoint of civil defense, the capacity of the interstate highways to transport urban populations in an emergency is of utmost importance. Large scale evacuations of cities would be needed in the event of A-bomb or H-bomb attack. The Federal Civil Defense Administrator has said the withdrawal task is the biggest problem ever faced in the world. It has been determined as a matter of Federal policy that at least 70 million people would have to be evacuated from target areas in case of threatened or actual enemy attack. No urban area in the country today has highway facilities equal to this task. The rapid improvement of the complete 40,000-mile interstate system, including the necessary urban connections thereto, is therefore vital as a civil defense measure. Responsibility for selecting the highway facilities needed for this defensive action has been delegated by executive order to the Bureau of Public Roads.[49]

This is not the place to consider the merits of this rather dubious argument, but General Clay himself was apparently aware of the serious limitations in relying on highways to evacuate civilians in a crisis. Although it was his committee that had included the civil-defense role of the Interstate System in its report, he testified before the Senate Committee on Public Works in 1955 that "he certainly would not want to be an advocate that you could possibly protect the people of the United States with any program of mass evacuation."[50]

Nevertheless, the argument was taken seriously by some, perhaps in large part due to the atmosphere of fear and insecurity during the cold war. In other words, we might simply conclude that the same hysteria that gave rise to the promotion of backyard bomb shelters was responsible for this thinking as well. There can be no doubt that the general hysteria of the times did play a role in allowing this type of suggestion be taken seriously. We should not, however, overlook one of the major sources and proponents of this argument—the National Highway Users Conference and other groups in the automobile lobby. For example, a NHUC pamphlet, after extolling the virtues of urban highways in providing for civil defense, went on to show additional uses of the automobile during times of attack.[51] During an attack, the pamphlet noted, your car would become a "rolling home. . . . Persons can eat and sleep in it, keep warm and dry, receive vital instruction by radio, drive out of danger areas and even be afforded some protection against nuclear fallout."[52]

The ease with which the evacuation argument could be dovetailed with more reasonable arguments—though less dramatic—is best illustrated by the comments of Francis Du Pont during his tenure in the Commerce Department. On the subject of evacuation routes, he noted: "By the same token, roads are escape routes for all of us when we go home every night and come to work in the morning. In other words, if we consider the civilian defense needs, then again they serve the daily needs of all of us. So that there is no difference."[53]

No difference; perhaps this was the real value of the issue. That is, the civil-defense issue was important because it was consistent with other, more important considerations. It was good window dressing for the real "escape" that was needed. The civil-defense aspect of the Interstate System, if given serious heed, would necessitate emphasizing the urban radial routes of the system. U.S. cities would have to be opened up to the automobile, if the automobile was to play this vital role in civil defense. The civil-defense argument therefore provided a good counterargument to the military's suggestion that the Interstate System avoid built-up urban areas through circumferential routes. By arguing in this way, the automobile lobby could argue for the interstate on defense grounds, and at the same time it could argue against the type of system the military was saying it needed. On balance, this appears to have been a fairly innovative and effective tactic in dealing with this delicate issue.

As noted, the actual interstate routes were designated on two separate occasions. In 1947, 37,700 miles of route were designated, including 3,900 miles of urban route. This 3,900 miles of urban route comprised the core of the 4,400 miles that had been proposed in *Interregional Highways* to carry traffic through cities. The remaining 2,300 miles of the 40,000 miles provided for in 1944 were left undesignated to allow for further study and consideration of their location. They were all urban routes.

The issue of locating the interstate in cities was resolved when the remaining urban routes were designated in September 1955. In addition, all of the 3,900 miles of urban route that had been designated in 1947 were reviewed. All of the urban interstate routes were subsequently published in the Bureau of Public Road's *General Location of National Systems of Interstate Highways* (known as the *Yellow Book*).[54] This publication contained a map of the entire Interstate System, as well as 100 individual maps displaying the routes in urban areas. Typically a major metropolitan area contained an "inner belt" route that encircled all or part of the downtown areas, with radial routes extending outwards.[55] An outer belt then encircles all or part of the entire metropolitan area. This outer belt often ran through suburban areas. Medium-sized cities typically had the interstate splitting as it approached the city, one route going through the city, while the other went around it. A smaller city was generlly given a "spur" connecting it with the system. The Interstate System, as designated in 1947 and 1955, was essentially the type of Interstate System that the automobile industry had advocated since the late 1930s. The basic principle of putting the interstate into and through cities was upheld.

The issue was resolved in 1955, for a variety of reasons. One reason was to muster congressional support for the interstate legislation, especially from urban congressmen. The designations were successful in generating interest in the system and in giving politicians something substantive to rally behind. Equally important, though, was the strategy of designating the entire system before Congress enacted legislation in 1956. This tended to keep the Interstate System a "package deal"; that is, it tended to lock the routes in as designated. It could be (and was later) argued that passage of the interstate legislation in 1956 had been a ratification of the system *as designed* in 1947 and 1955. As we will see, this was an important factor after 1956, and a farsighted tactic in 1955.

Another likely reason for the designation in 1955 stems from the fact that both the Defense Department and the Bureau of Public Roads were then headed by people with strong ties to the automobile industry (as noted, Wilson and Du Pont). The significance of this fact is hard to determine. We really do not know how controversial the circumferential-versus-radial-routes issue was, because we do not really know how seriously the defense issue, and the military's suggestions, were taken. In addition, there does not seem to have been a specific meeting or correspondence on the subject between Du Pont and Wilson or their representatives, although such contact may have been made.

That, however, may not be the point upon which the importance of this development turns. Timing the decision so that the desired outcome is most likely is a significant tactic. In addition, the placement of reserves and contingency planning are just as much a part of battle strategy as is the actual engagement of forces. While not as dramatic, they are nonetheless of great consequence. That was no doubt the case here. There may have been no occasion to use either Wilson or Du Pont in this issue, but if there had been, if the need had arisen, would there have been much doubt as to what a meeting between Wilson and Du Pont would have produced?

LOBBYING TO 1956

Between 1944 and 1956 the Interstate System stalled. Part of the reason was the rural-urban conflict that was present until the early 1950s. For example, in 1948 the definition of a rural principal road was broadened to encompass virtually every rural road in the United States.[56] In 1952 rural interests were even able to pass legislation that required that all future urban grants be limited to the municipal links of the rural primary system. The BPR interpreted this to mean the abandonment of all urban arterials not directly serving the rural primary system. This salvo was actually part of a controversy that had arisen over the interpretation to be given the C system in the 1944 legislation.[57] One view held that the funds were to be used to serve the highway needs of the individual urban area. An opposite interpretation held that the intent of the C system was only to extend the primary system into urban areas. The first interpretation was favored by the Bureau of Public Roads, which tried to require states to plan urban freeway systems rather than merely urban extensions. Most states, however, insisted on a strict adherence to the extensions interpretation. After encountering resistance from the states and Congress, the bureau accepted the restrictive interpretation in 1955. In additon, many states allocated urban highway funds in a manner that discriminated against the larger cities. Consequently, by 1956 there were only 480 miles of urban freeways in the nation's 25 largest cities.[58] In contrast, the 1956 legislation would ultimately lead to the construction of about 8,600 miles of urban interstate freeways.

Only limited progress was achieved before 1956 in correcting some of the deficiencies of the 1944 legislation. The Federal Aid Highway Act of 1952 provided explicit funding for the Interstate System for the first time. The amount was only $25 million, however—a small sum in comparison to the cost of the system. In 1954 funding was increased to $175 million and the funding ratio changed to 60–40, but even these changes, which were largely inspired by the toll-road boom, were inadequate. Consequently, the Interstate System never got off the ground, due to inadequate funding and continued restrictions on federal aid.

By the mid 1950s, success in getting the interstate under way appears to have become more dependent on the ability of highway promoters to mobilize public opinion and to establish a working agreement among the diverse interests working for the Interstate System. This became more important as rural opposition to urban construction and the interstate became less determined and less formidable. In any case, the drive up to 1956 focused on public opinion and consensus building. It was, in fact, disagreements over financing, among the supporters of the interstate, that held up the legislation until 1956, and actually killed legislation in 1955.

Project Adequate Roads

A massive publicity campaign for the interstate was initiated with the formation of Project Adequate Roads (PAR) in 1951. As noted earlier, PAR was created by NHUC. The publicity campaign was initiated with PAR, but strife among members, largely over differences in financing arrangements for the interstate, quickly arose. PAR soon became ineffective, due to this in-fighting, but the publicity campaign was salvaged and put under the direct supervision of NHUC. It carried on the campaign through its own publication, *Highway Highlights*, and by working closely with the Hearst newspaper chain. In 1956, William Randolph Hearst, Jr., received the American Road Builders Association's Bartlett Award for his "forceful and inspiring public interest campaign for adequate roads since 1952."[59] The award was presented by L. L. Colbert, president of Chrysler, who referred to Hearst's 3 million lines of print on the highway problem, enough print to fill 1,229 newspapers, or enought to fill a metropolitan city newspaper for 26 consecutive days.

NHUC was able to maintain the publicity campaign, where PAR had failed, due to its insistence on staying neutral on issues on which highway users were not in full agreement. For the same reason, NHUC did not testify before congressional hearings for fear of damaging the unity that remained among highway proponents. Their stated purpose was not to mediate disputes between members, but to keep the vital publicity campaign going.

Congressional Testimony

The automobile industry began testifying in 1953 at congressional hearings on the need for an Interstate System. James Cope, vice-president of Chrysler Corporation, appeared before the House Subcommittee on Public Works in 1953 as a representative of the AMA.[60] His arguments for an expanded federal aid highway program were based on the industry's claim of a need for more highways due to increasing vehicle registrations, the decline of road construction activities since 1931, and the loss of life and wasted resources from unsafe and inefficient highways. These arguments for the interstate were largely based on AMA data that showed the concentration of traffic on a small percentage of the nation's roads. The arguments were essentially the ones Hoffman had promoted in 1939.

Cope argued, on the basis of the AMA data, that 19 percent of our roads carried about 81 percent of the nation's traffic, with urban arterial streets carrying 39 percent of the nation's traffic.[61] He argued that the Interstate System would reduce congestion on these overcrowded roads, especially in urban areas. Cope added that the roads would also improve the automobile market, but was quick to disclaim self-serving motives.[62]

The next appearance by an automobile industry representative before a government body was before the Clay committee. President Eisenhower had made known his administration's support of a massive highway program, at the Governors' Conference at Bolton Landing, New York, in July 1954. Vice-president Nixon had presented the administration's proposal for a highway network that would serve the domestic economy, national defense, and, following a 1954 report by the Council of Economic Advisors, be a public works project that would help stabilize the economy. Following the Governors' Conference, a special presidential committee to study the Eisenhower proposal was formed. General Lucius Clay, retired, was appointed to chair the committee. The Clay committee held hearings on October 7–8, 1954. The immediate subject of the hearings was Eisenhower's proposal for a $50 billion self-liquidating highway system, which was to utilize toll financing wherever possible. At the opening of the hearings, Clay announced that the cost estimate had been raised to $101 billion.

The AMA representative before the Clay committee, William J. Cronin, did not mince words on the industry's interests in the road project. In response to a question by Chairman Clay as to whether there was a point where the availability of adequate highways affected the increased use and ownership of the automobile, Cronin answered: "I think very definitely it does, Mr. Chairman. I think that is particularly true in the large cities where you have the extreme congestion that you find in New York for example. I think it definitely discourages the ownership and use of both passenger cars and motor trucks."[63]

During the Clay committee hearings the split between trucking and oil interests on the one hand, and automobile interests on the other became apparent. For example, the Private Truck Council of America and the American Petroleum Institute both criticized the revised cost estimate, claiming that it reflected the high costs of urban construction in the large cities. [64] Long-haul truckers would receive only limited benefits from an urban-oriented system, but they would end up paying much higher taxes to finance it. Many truckers therefore threatened to oppose the entire project, if urban freeways were included in the system. The main opposition to the kind of interstate that the auto industry sought was coming from truck-ing interests and other groups that balked at the user-tax burden that would be imposed by an urban-oriented interstate.

The Clay committee reported its findings in 1955, and its recommenda-tions became the administration's proposed legislation that year. The commit-tee recommended that the interstate be constructed over the next ten years at a cost of $27 billion. Eleven billion dollars would be allocated to the urban routes designated in 1947, while another $4 billion was available for the urban routes left undesignated until 1955. Financing was to be through bond issues.

When congressional hearings on interstate legislation began in 1955, the automobile industry was an active participant. An extensive and well-received presentaton was made in 1955, before the House Committee on Public Works, by James J. Nance, president of Studebaker-Packard Cor-poration; William F. Hufstader, vice-president of General Motors Corpora-tion; and William J. Cronin of the AMA. The three appeared as represen-tatives of the AMA and presented the auto industry's views and proposals. Their four-point program called for the following:

• The Interstate Highway System should be modernized over the next 10 years, *because it holds the key to future expansion of traffic in the United States.* (emphasis added)
• The Federal Government should assume most of the cost of the In-terstate System improvement, because of its paramount national importance.
• The Congress should grant some increases in other federal aid road funds, to help the states step up improvement of routes outside the In-terstate System.
• To the extent that this federal road program could be met from current federal tax revenues, Congress should authorize the use of long-term securities, to be serviced by schedule appropriations from the federal Treasury.[65]

Nance, the chief spokesman, emphasized the critical need for the interstate and the key role it was to play in augmenting traffic, testifying that "if the interstate is fully modernized over the next 10 years, highway authorities estimate that growth in traffic on this system will account for one-half of the total increase in all United States traffic during the coming decade."[66] He also presented a traffic analysis, reminiscent of both Cope and Hoffman, which showed that the greatest increases in traffic were expected on the In-terstate System in the larger cities.[67] At the same time, Nance was explicit in claiming that both increased traffic and increased vehicle sales depended on getting the highway program off the ground.[68] With regard to financing, Nance was noncommittal. Any financing was acceptable as long as a com-plete Interstate System was provided for, including the urban portions.

Nance then went on to break with lobbying tradition by explicitly iden-tifying the industry's interests in the highway program. His comments were very forthright:

Obviously we have a selfish interest in this program, because our products are not good except on the road. Unless we know that there is going to be an expansion of the roads of this country and an expansion to take care of the saturation which we are rapidly approaching on our present highway system, it is very difficult for us to plan over the next 10 years as to what our expansion is going to have to be. Just looking at the population growth is not the answer, because we have to have the roads if we are going to make wage earners and car buyers out of these people. . . .

Of course our product, I say again, is no good unless it is used. So that is not only our problem but it is the problem of all the basic industries that are linked in together in the total of about 20 percent of the national economy that is directly tied to the automobile industry.[69]

Earlier Nance had summed up his basic position with these two comments: "We are for good roads, and lots of them," and "obviously, we have a direct interest in safer, more free-flowing highways, [since] the future of our industry depends on them."[70]

Such candor had not been common in the past and was always considered potentially damaging or embarrassing. In this case it appears to have been the product of a new lobbying approach. His basic position was that the auto industry would benefit from the interstate, and to the extent that it did, so would the country. Interestingly, this was also the thrust of C. E. Wilson's famous comment of a few years earlier.

The Federal Aid Highway Act of 1956

The Federal Aid Highway Act of 1956, also known as the Interstate Highway Act of 1956, was a milestone in highway legislation. It essentially made possible the actual construction of the Interstate System, the largest single construction project in history. It began by changing the name of the Interstate System to the National System of Interstate and Defense Highways. This was done primarily to bring in national defense as the rationale for the increased federal participation. In addition, the size of the system was increased to 41,000 miles, and most important, the funding ratio was changed from the existing 60–40 to a 90–10 ratio (95–5 in some western states). These financial changes effectively launched the interstate, and were especially significant in enabling the costly urban construction to proceed.

Funds were authorized to begin in 1957 and were provided through 1972, the original scheduled completion date.[71] This long-term financing was supposed to have removed the hassle of legislating periodic appropriations, thereby preventing continuing attacks on the system after 1956. Cost overruns, however, did pose problems in this regard after 1958. Funding was provided through user taxes on automobile parts and accessories, motor trucks, motor truck parts and accessories, and petroleum fuels. Automobiles were not taxed.[72] All of these highway-user tax revenues were placed in a Highway Trust Fund which was to used exclusively for highway construction. Later, in 1958, the interstate was increased to 42,500 miles.

Interstate politics in 1955 and 1956 is a story in itself, and one that cannot be recounted here.[73] The legislative success in 1956 culminated a protracted lobbying campaign in which the automobile industry participated vigorously to promote the type of Interstate System that would best serve its interest. Again, the industry was not the only group lobbying, but it was a significant factor.

The passage of the Interstae Highway act in 1956 followed the defeat of similar legislation in 1955, when truckers, tire producers, petroleum interests, and other highway groups had balked at the high user taxes. In 1956 these disagreements among interstate supporters over financing were resolved. The need for periodic appropriations was also supposed to be resolved once and for all. And until about 1958, it did look as if the entire issue had finally been settled. In the closing years of the decade, however, new threats to the urban interstate arose, and the auto industry again had to mobilize in response. We will turn to those events now.

AFTER 1956—CHALLENGES TO THE URBAN INTERSTATE

Between 1956 and at least the early 1960s, two additional hurdles arose. First, serious reservations about the urban portions of the interstate were expressed, and efforts were made to reconsider and eliminate at least part of the urban routes. Second, planning disputes and problems threatened progress on the urban interstate. Each of these issues had to be, and was, vigorously dealt with. We will begin with the second thoughts about the urban interstate expressed by some important figures in the Eisenhower administration.[74]

Second Thoughts

The first occasion for second thoughts about the interstate arose over funding the system. The mechanism for funding was established in 1956 and was supposed to have settled all of the funding issues. It was determined early on, however, that the level of funding for the interstate was very inadequate. In 1958 the Bureau of Public Roads had raised the estimate for the interstate from the 1956 figure of $27 billion to $41 billion. The Interstate System was scheduled for termination in 1972, and the user taxes that fed the Highway Trust Fund were set to expire at that time. With the higher cost estimate, the only two options open were to extend the taxes beyond 1972 or cut the interstate back, that is, reduce the size of the system from 41,000 miles to a level that could be constructed with the original $27 billion.

The latter course found a strong supporter in General John S. Bragdon. He was a former West point classmate of Eisenhower and served on the Council of Economic Advisors after 1954, specializing in federal highway policy. He was later appointed to the White House staff as a special assistant for public works. Bragdon generally opposed an extensive urban interstate and supported the idea of a toll-road system. His solution to the funding problem was to delineate a high priority "first stage" for the interstate that could be constructed within the $27 billion limit.

In his 1960 "Interim Report," Bragdon recommended that the inner belts be eliminated; that preference be given to circumferential routes over either arterials or spurs; that preference also be given to spurs, as opposed to arterial routes going all the way through cities; and that the length of spurs be kept to a minimum. About 1,700 miles of urban interstate could have been eliminated in this manner. This suggestion, if followed, would have gutted the urban interstate of the features that the automobile industry had worked hard for since the late 1930s. Bragdon even broached the issue of toll roads once again.

Aside from the fact that Bragdon was an influential member of the Eisenhower administration, there were other reasons for according his views considerable attention. First, the inadequate funding meant that the system was not attainable as projected. Something had to be done since the 1956 decision could not simply be left to follow its prescribed course. But reopening the issue presented the opportunity for second thoughts. Second, Bragdon claimed to have discovered the legal means to implement his suggestions. In 1958 Congress included in the highway act general language that authorized the secretary of commerce to modify any part of the federal aid highway system. In early 1960 Bragdon requested and recieved an opinion from an assistant attorney general to the effect that this provision did apply to the interstate. The secretary of commerce told Eisenhower that he disagreed with this opinion (he also opposed Bragdon's suggestions). Furthermore, the secretary did not transmit the legal opinion to Congress, nor was it made public. Since neither the Commerce Department or, later, the Department of Transportation has ever sought to exercise this implied authority, it has never been tested, but it could have served in 1959–60 as the basis for action on Bragdon's proposals.

Further grounds for modifying the interstate arose from the controversy as to whether the Interstate System was meant to serve both intracity and intercity traffic needs equally. This controversey centered around differing interpretations of Section 116(b) of the 1956 Interstate Highway Act,[75] which required that "equal consideration" be given both local traffic needs and the needs of interstate commerce. Depending on how one interprets the section's punctuation and context, it could be argued that the "equal consideration" applied only to the integration of existing highways into the Interstate System, not to new construction. The Bureau of Public Roads took the broad interpretation, giving "equal consideration" to the entire system. As a consequence, the bureau dramatically increased the number of urban interstate lanes, interchanges, grade separations, and frontage roads.[76] This was one of the reasons for the higher cost estimate in 1958.

The narrow interpretation was embraced by Bragdon, the Bureau of the Budget, and others.[77] By this interpretation, the increase in urban lanes, interchanges, and so forth was unwarranted. In fact, with a strict adherence to this interpretation, much of the urban interstate could have been eliminated because it did not primarily serve interstate traffic. To make matters worse, the disagreement between the BPR and Bragdon over Section 116(b) was determined by the Justice Department to be essentially a policy matter, rather than a legal issue. Consequently, the door was left open for revising the interstate, if Bragdon's views held sway in the administration. Bragdon's recommendation for deleting the 1,700 urban miles from the system was acutally based on this interpretation. In fact, even without securing a full reevaluation of the urban interstate, Bragdon was nonetheless able to pare down the urban system by getting the BPR to agree to limitations on the number of lanes, interchanges, and so on.[78]

Finally, Bragdon's challenge must be accorded considerable weight, because his reservations seem to have been shared by Eisenhower himself.[79] The president claimed to have opposed the idea of running the interstate through congested urban areas. He was apparently unaware of the urban orientation of the system, assuming that it generally bypassed heavily populated urban areas. Eisenhower purportedly became aware of the extent of urban involvement in 1959, when he noticed construction in the Washington, D.C. area. It will be recalled that many urban routes were only designated in 1955, but this would still have been a serious oversight. In any case, Eisenhower's serious reservations about the urban interstate were real in 1959 and 1960 and lent considerable weight to Bragdon's efforts.

In addition to the reservations being expressed in Washington, local complaints were arising elsewhere.[80] In 1958 controversy in Reno, Nevada, erupted over the interstate in that community. In 1965 opposition to the interstate in San Francisco led to the deletion of the Embarcadero Freeway from the system. Controversies developed in 13 other urban areas, and this urban opposition threatened the urban interstate.

To deal with these threats, the auto industry geared up for lobbying. The 1961 study commissioned by the AMA and cited extensively above was part of this effort and was used in the lobbying effort.[81] Fortuitously (from the industry's vantage), events greatly contributed to a quick resolution of the problem to the industry's satisfaction. First, Eisenhower apparently decided against challenging the urban portions of the system, concluding that it "had reached the point where his hands were virtually tied."[82] Apparently he took the bureau's view that it lacked the power to drop interstate routes without congressional approval. Congress could act, but Eisenhower rejected this approach, noting the role that the 1955 route designations had played in garnering support for the interstate. In addition, time was running out for the Eisenhower administration. Bragdon's "Interim Report" was presented at a meeting in April 1960, but a few weeks later, Bragdon was appointed to the Civil Aeronautics Board.[83] With the principal proponent of an interstate review gone, and Eisenhower deciding against a reevaluation, the "Interim Report" shrank to a perfunctory 12-page final report that was submitted a few days before President Kennedy was inaugurated. Kennedy then put the entire issue to rest by providing for a continuation of user taxes past 1972. This has subsequently been the method employed for dealing with the large cost overruns and delays that have held up the completion of the interstate. Kennedy strongly favored completing the entire system.[84]

Problems with Urban Freeway Planning

Second thoughts about the urban interstate were only part of the problems after 1956. An additional problem arose over integrating and coordinating the activities of urban planners and state highway officials. Traditionally, state highway departments had been rural bastions, which only grudgingly admitted the necessity of including their urban areas in the highway program. On the other hand, cities were generally less accustomed to freeway planning. In any case, cooperation between these two groups was not very good, and this, on top of the other problems discussed above, posed serious problems for implementing the urban interstate.

The auto industry, through the ASF, quickly addressed this problem. A U.S. Department of Transportation publication in 1977 described the ASF activities in this area in the following manner:

> Sensing well the problems that would arise, Pyke Johnson, President of the Automotive Safety Foundation, following the role it often played of getting people with common interests together, arranged to meet with the Executive Secretary of the American Association of State Highway Officials, Alfred E. Johnson, and Patrick Healy, Executive Director of the American Municipal Association, in the Office of the Commissioner of Public Roads, C. D. Curtis.[85]

This meeting in early 1957 confirmed the problem, but also resulted in the formation of a joint AMA-AASHO Committee on Highways (AMA here refers here to American Muncipal Association). The Public Roads Administration participated by providing the committee secretary.

One of the committee's first efforts at rectifying urban planning problems was to cosponsor the first National Conference on Highways and Urban Development in October 1958. The conference was held at Sagamore and was cosponsored by the Highway Research Board, a quasi-public research and lobbying group (discussed above). At the time, the ASF was supporting the staff activity of the Highway Research Board's Committee on Urban Research. This was later changed to the Urban Reseach Department of the Board, and was chaired by Pyke Johnson after he retired from the ASF. The ASF was therefore intimately involved with both of the sponsors of the Sagamore conference. In addition, it provided the financial and technical support for the conference.

The conference was apparently beneficial in helping to resolve some, but not all, of the problems. After the conference, the ASF printed and distributed a pamphlet convering the Sagamore conference, entitled *Guidelines for Action*. It purportedly received "wide distribution and general acclaim."[86] The AMA-AASHO Committee on Highways then continued in its efforts to resolve urban highway disputes by adopting the "Action Program" at its January 1962 meeting. These Action Programs had their origins in work done earlier by the NCUT (an ASF affiliate) in conjunction with city planning officials (discussed above). Through a series of Action Program conferences held through June 1963, over 1,500 state and local officials were brought into urban freeway planning, many for the first time.[87]

Two more national conferences followed the Sagamore conference. The Hershey Conference on Freeways in the Urban Setting was held in Hershey, Pennsylvania, in 1962. It was sponsored by the Bureau of Public Roads, the Housing and Home Finance Agency, and the Automotive Safety Foundation. The ASF again provided the financial and staff support for the conference as well as handling the reporting on the conference. The Hershey conference was able to address specific problems that had grown out of the construction of the urban interstate. In general, though, it sought to continue and extend the cooperative approach to urban freeway planning that had begun in 1955 with NCUT and had continued at the Sagamore conference.

The Second National Conference on Highways and Urban Development was held in Williamsburg, Virginia, in December 1965. The AMA-AASHO committee and the federal highway administrator were primary sponsors of the Williamsburg conference, while the ASF provided half of the financial support for it. In addition to financial aid, the ASF also provided most of the staff support, and handled the conference report. Like the Sagamore and Hershey conferences, the Williamsburg conference sought to extend the cooperative approach to urban freeway planning so important to keeping the urban interstate program on track.

At all of these conferences, and in the creation of organizations like NCUT and the AMA-AASHO Committee on Highways, we find the ASF as the financial backer, organizer, and coordinator. It was, if you will, the "entrepreneur" in the push to get the urban interstate implemented. The growing urban resistance to the urban interstate, the Eisenhower administration's review of the urban interstate, and the friction generated in early urban freeway planning all threatened the urban interstate. Through the efforts of the ASF, as well as the efforts of the Automobile Manufacturers Association, the automobile industry was able to prevent the gutting of their victory won in 1956.

It would be silly to argue that all who participated in these conferences, meetings, and so on, were brainwashed into sponsoring the ASF line. Supporting and financing meetings and conferences does not buy that kind of power; in fact, probably nothing does—but that is precisely what makes these efforts important and noteworthy. The process of building support for one's positions is an arduous as well as an innovative task. Money alone won't do. That task was undertaken through these efforts and, it appears, carried through quite successfully.

CONCLUSIONS

This chapter has sought to show how the automobile industry went about influencing highway policy to best serve its interests. This involved the formation of such lobbying groups such as the AMA, NHUC, ASF, and NCUT; the acquisition of positions of influence in government, other lobbying groups, and business and professional groups; congressional lobbying, both formal and informal; organizing policy conferences for government officials, such as the Sagamore conference; funding publicity campaigns such as PAR, and consensus building through the activities of NHUC; and the deft handling of such issues as the national defense aspects of the interstate. On balance, it appears that one must conclude that the automobile industry's promotional activities were quite successful. Again, it was not alone in the promotional effort, but that in no way should detract from its efforts.

NOTES

1. Quoted in Ben Kelley, *The Pavers and the Paved* (New York: D. W. Brown, 1971), p. 46. For a description of the extent of the automobile manufacturers' financing of the ASF, see the same source at p. 48.

2. Quoted in ibid.

3. For a description of the ASF's opposition to the ballot measure, see Kelley, *The Pavers and the Paved*, p. 47.

4. Ibid., p. 150.

5. This figure is from Snell, *American Ground Transport* (1973), reproduced as an appendix to U.S., Congress, Senate, Committee on the Judiciary, *The Industrial Reorganization Act, Hearings before the Committee on the Judiciary on S. 1167, Part 4A,* 93rd Cong., 2d sess., 1974, p. A–95.

6. Two other organizations deserve attention here. During the Second World War the automobile industry and various auto executives did a truly remarkable job in organizing a large part of this country's war-production effort. The industry set up the Automobile Council for War Production (ACWP) to coordinate and oversee the mobilization effort. What impact this organization had on subsequent industry lobbying is still unclear at this time. In any case, the war effort certainly brought a lot of auto executives to the seat of power at a time when critical highway planning and legislation was being formulated. War-time lobbying can be seen in the activities of a group known as the "Road Gang." The Road Gang was an informal group, formed in 1942, which was quite publicity-shy. It met every Tuesday at lunch, but its activities were rather low-profile and secretive. Leavitt described the organization as follows: "The group describes itself as a very informal group of business and government executives, highway engineers and consultants, press and public relations specialists, company representatives and trade association officials from highway transportation and its allied fields located in the District of Columbia." Leavitt characterized one of the group's chief activities as holding "round table" discussions on highway legislation. The group consisted of about 240 members, with virtually all the automobile lobby organizations represented as well as other highway groups. In 1962 the Road Gang began giving awards for outstanding service in the highway field. The first award went to Pyke Johnson of the ASF. The activities of the Road Gang were secretive, and outsiders were not allowed at meetings. Requests for information about the group were usually denied, so little else is known about it. The time at which the Road Gang started meeting, however—that is, during the war—does suggest a link between the auto-industry-dominated war-mobilization effort and lobbying for highways. See Helen Leavitt, *Superhighways—Super Hoax* (Garden City, NY: Doubleday, 1970) pp. 151–53.

7. This discussion of positions held by auto-industry executives during World War I is based on James J. Flink, *The Car Culture* (Cambridge, MA: M.I.T. Press, 1975), pp. 92–93.

8. Quoted in Thomas C. Cochran, *American Business in the Twentieth Century* (Cambridge, MA: Harvard University Press, 1972), p. 142.

9. This famous quote, generally atributed to Wilson, was probably a misquote. The correct statement appears to have been, "What was good for our country was good for General Motors and vice versa." The popular version still persists, however. For a discussion of this and other issues relating to allegations of a conflict of interst in Wilson's appointment, see E. Bruce Geelhoed, "What Was Good For Our Country Was Good For General Motors, Charles E. Wilson and the U.S. Senate, " *The Changing Challenge* (General Motors, 1981), pp. 26–31. This was a reprint from an article that appeared in *Michigan History* (September / October 1980).

10. John Rae, commenting on Chapin's short tenure as secretary of commerce, noted: "It is unfortunate that his term in office was so short, since few men have had such a comprehensive grasp of the potentialities of highway transportation." John B. Rae, *American Automobile Manufacturers,* (Philadelphia: Chilton, 1959) p. 193. Chapin resigned in order to resume the presidency at financially troubled Hudson.

11. Regarding the numerous automobile executives in the Eisenhower administration, New York Governor Harriman went so far as to charge that Eisenhower's highway policy was simply an expression of the proliferation of automobile interests in his administration. In addition to Wilson and Talbott at the Defense Department and Du Pont at the BPR, Harriman noted that the secretary of the interior and the postmaster general (a position with an input on road matters) were both former automobile dealers. See *New York Times,* January 13, 1955, p. 21. On Du Pont's influence with Eisenhower, see Gary T. Schwartz, "Urban Freeways and

the Interstate System," *Southern California Law Review* 49 (March 1976): 427–28, and note 156. Schwartz bases this observation, in part, on interviews with A. E. Johnson and Francis Turner in the early 1970s (see p. 407).

12. See, for example, Mark Rose, "Express Highway Politics, 1939–1956" (Ph.D. Diss. Ohio State University, 1973), p. 218. Suggestions that part of the Interstate System's cost be charged against the Defense Department's budget have always been vigorously opposed by the Defense Department.

13. U. S. Department of Transportation, Federal Highway Administration, *America's Highways, 1776–1976* (Washington, DC: U. S. Government Printing Office, 1977), p. 307.

14. U.S., Senate, Special Committee on Post-War Economic Policy and Planning, *The Role of the Federal Government in Highway Development*. 78th Cong., 2d sess., 1944. See especially pp. iii–iv.

15. For a description of the ATA's problems in getting the Clay committee to listen to their views, see Richard O. Davies, *The Age of Asphalt: The Automobile, the Freeway, and the Condition of Metropolitan America* (Philadelphia: Lippincott, 1975), pp. 60–63.

16. For a discussion of the diversion issue, see Schwartz, "Urban Freeways," pp. 420–22.

17. For a discussion of the macroeconomic argument for the interstate, as well as a good discussion of the political events leading up to 1956, see Mark Rose, *Interstate: Express Highway Politics, 1941–1956* (Lawrence, KS: Regents Press of Kansas, 1979).

18. See Schwartz, "Urban Freeways," p. 415, note 50.

19. George M. Smerk, ed., *Readings in Urban Transportation* (Bloomington: Indiana University Press, 1968), p. 124.

20. Quoted in Rose, "Expressway Highway Politics," 1973, p. 70.

21. Automobile Manufacturer's Association, *Automobile Facts and Figures*, 1939, pp. 32–33.

22. Automobile Manufacturer's Association, *Automobile Facts and Figures*, 1945, p. 32.

23. U.S., Bureau of Public Roads, *Toll Roads and Free Roads*, 76th Cong., 1st sess., 1939, House Document 272.

24. Department of Transportation, *America's Highways.*, p. 271.

25. Ibid., pp. 268–74.

26. For a description of the GM exhibit, see Rose, *Interstate*, 1979, p. 1.

27. BPR, *Toll Roads and Free Roads*, pp. 90–102.

28. This is also the view of the primary impact of *Toll Roads and Free Roads* expressed in Department of Transportation, *America's Highways*, p. 273.

29. This assessment is also shared by the Department of Transportation: "Without doubt *Interregional Highways* was and remains the most significant document in the history of highways in the United States." Department of Transportation, *America's Highways*, p. 274.

30. Ibid., p. 272.

31. This discussion draws heavily on the review of California highway policy presented in California Public Utilities Commission Application No. 32137, Statement of Position of the State of California Department of Public Works, Division of Highways, April 11, 1951.

32. Department of Transportation, *America's Highways*, p. 278.

33. Ibid., p. 279.

34. Ibid., p. 278–79.

35. H. S. Fairbanks, "What is This Thing Called Planning?" Address before the Sixth Annual Meeting of the Southeastern Association of State Highway Officials, Miami, December 8, 1947, pp. 6–7. Reproduced, in part, in Department of Transportaion, *America's Highways*, p. 279.

36. Department of Transportaiton, *America's Highways*, p. 281.

37. Ibid.

38. Ibid., p. 282. Also, see pp. 372–75 for a discussion of the "Action Programs."

39. For a discussion of defense and highways, see David J. St. Clair, "Entrepreneurship and the American Automobile Industry" (Ph.D. diss., University of Utah, 1979),

pp. 220–63; Department of Transportation, *America's Highways*, pp. 142–53; Schwartz, "Urban Freeways," pp. 466–68; Paul F. Royster, "Highways for Peace and War," *National Defense Transportation Journal* 18 (May-June 1962): p. 21 passim.

40. U.S., Congress, House, Committee on Roads, *Federal Aid for Post-War Highway Construction, Hearings before the House Committee on Roads on H.R. 2426*, 78th Cong., 1st sess., 1944, p. 9.

41. See Rose, "Express Highway Politics," pp. 80–81.

42. See, for example, the testimony of General Yount in U.S., Congress, House, *Hearings on S. 1048, Before a Subcommittee of the Senate Committee on Public Works*, 84th Cong., 1st sess., 1955; and U.S., Congress, House, *Hearings on H.R. 4260 Before a House Committee on Public Works, National Highway Program*, 84th Cong., 1st sess., 1955. Also see St. Clair, "Entrepreneurship," pp. 220–28, regarding the military's defense highway needs prior to 1957. After October 1957 (following Sputnik and our own Atlas program) military needs changed dramatically. See, in the same source, pages 228–40.

43. Cited in Royster, "Highways for Peace and War," p. 22.

44. U.S., Congress, House, Committee on Public Works, *Defense Highway Needs, Hearings before a House Special Subcommittee on the Federal Aid Highway Program*, 86th Cong., 2d sess., 1960, p. 12.

45. While Robert Moses was the 1953 winner of a $25,000 prize from General Motors for an essay on adequate highways, this probably means very little except to indicate how the automobile industry agreed with his position. Suggestions that GM "bought" Robert Moses, for $25,000, are ludicrous. For a biography of Moses, see Robert A. Caro, *The Power Broker* (New York: Knopf, 1974).

46. Quoted in Leavitt, *Superhighway—Super Hoax*, pp. 57–58.

47. Ibid., p. 30.

48. Quoted in Jay Dugan, "Highways in National Defense," in Poyintz Tyler, ed. *American Highways Today*, (New York: Wildon, 1957), p. 131.

49. U.S., President's Advisory Committee on a National Highway Program, *A Ten-Year National Highway Program* (Washington, DC: U.S. Government Printing Office, 1955), p. 5.

50. Testimony of General Lucius Clay (Ret.) in U.S., Congress, Senate, Committee on Public Works, *A National Highway Program, Hearings before the Senate Committee on Public Works*, 84th Cong., 1st sess., 1955, p. 407. For a different view of how Clay evaluated the civil-defense argument, as well as a different view of the validity of the argument, see Schwartz, "Urban Freeways," p. 468.

51. National Highway Users Conference, *The Highway Transportation Story in Facts* (Washington, DC: National Highway Users Conference, 1969).

52. Ibid., p. 10.

53. Quoted in Ronald Kahn, "The Politics of Roads: National Highway Legislation in 1955–56" (M.S. thesis, University of Chicago, 1967), p. 43.

54. U.S., Bureau of Public Roads, *General Location of National System of Interstate Highways* (Washington, DC: U.S. Government Printing Office, 1955).

55. This "typical" description is drawn from Schwartz, "Urban Freeways," pp. 425–26.

56. See Philip H. Burch, Jr., *Highway Revenue and Expenditure Policy in the United States* (New Brunswick, NJ: Rutgers University Press, 1962), pp. 226–27.

57. For a good discussion of this issue, see Schwartz, "Urban Freeways," pp. 415–17.

58. Ibid., pp. 419, 443.

59. "For public Service: Hearst Newspapers Receive Citation for Adequate Roads," *Highway Highlights*, June-July 1956, p. 26. For an example of Hearst's views, see William Randolph Hearst Jr., "A Newspaperman's Views on Highways," *Highway Highlights*, February 1956, p. 24. Colbert's comments can be found in L. L. Colbert, "Presentation of Award to William Randolph Hearst, Jr.," *American Highways* 25 (January 1956): 13, cited in Kahn, "Politics of Roads," p. 47.

60. Testimony of James Cope in U.S., Congress, House, Committee on Public Roads, *National Highway Study, Hearings before a Subcommittee on Roads of the House Committee on Public Roads*, 83rd Cong., 1st sess., 1953, pp. 413–431.

61. Ibid., p. 419.

62. Ibid., p. 413.

63. Quoted in Leavitt, *Superhighway*, p. 31. The ASF also testified in favor of the $101 billion system at the hearings.

64. See the testimony of A. B. Gorman, representing the Private Truck Council of America, and that of Joseph P. Walsh, representing the Sinclair Oil Company and the American Petroleum Institute. Both are described in Leavitt, *Superhighway*, pp. 33–35.

65. Testimony of James J. Nance in U.S., Congress, House Committee on Public Works, *National Highway Program, Hearings before the House Committee on Public Works on H.R. 4260, Part 1*, 84th Cong., 1st sess., 1955, pp. 760–61.

66. Ibid., p. 769.

67. Ibid.

68. Ibid., p. 766.

69. Ibid., pp. 785–86.

70. Ibid., pp. 783, 778.

71. For a description of the time and funding extensions, see Schwartz, "Urban Freeways," especially p. 451.

72. See Schwartz, "Urban Freeways," p. 458.

73. For a discussion of the political events culminating in the 1956 legislation, see Rose, *Interstate*; Rose, "Express Highway Politics;" Department of Transportation, *America's Highways*, especially pp. 154–97; Schwartz, "Urban Freeways," especially pp. 427–39.

74. This discussion is drawn from Schwartz, "Urban Freeways," p. 477.

75. Ibid., p. 470–71. The section in dispute was Federal Aid Highway Act of 1956, ch. 462, section 116 (b), 70 Stat. 385 (codified at 23 U.S.C. section 101 (b) 1970).

76. Ibid., p. 474.

77. Ibid., pp. 471, 472.

78. Ibid., pp. 476–77.

79. Ibid., pp. 444–45.

80. Ibid., p. 444. Also, the increasing number of books critical of the Interstate System, and highway policy in general, is indicative of the change in the popular mood. For example, see Leavitt, *Superhighway*; Kenneth R. Schneider, *Autokind vs. Mankind* (New York: Schocken, 1974); A. Q. Mowbry, *Road to Ruin* (Philadelphia: Lippincott, 1969); Kelley, *The Pavers and the Paved*.

81. See Note 12 in Chapter 5, above.

82. Schwartz, "Urban Freeways," pp. 466–67.

83. Schwartz argues that Bragdon's appointment was considered by both the president and Bragdon as a promotion. See Schwartz, "Urban Freeways," p. 447, note 284.

84. For example, see President Kennedy's statement to Congress, H.R. Doc. No. 96, 87th Cong., 1st sess. (1961).

85. Department of Transportation, *America's Highways*, p. 306. This section draws heavily from this source. Subsequent citations will be confined to quotes and specific points.

86. Ibid., p. 308.

87. Ibid.

7

Social Entrepreneurship

This study has sought to trace the activities of members of the U.S. automobile industry in two areas: motorizing urban public transit systems, and influencing federal highway policy after 1930. By motorizing urban transit systems, the industry sought to remove an impediment to expanding the use and ownership of automobiles in U.S. cities. The rationale for the industry's activities in this area can be found in the way in which motor buses could be fitted into the larger goal of restructuring urban transportation around urban freeways. Buses were compatible with this transportation reorganization. Streetcars and trolley coaches were not compatible with the new urban freeways, and electric transit tended to solidify neighborhoods and existing transportation patterns. Electric transit systems were therefore inconsistent with this desired restructuring of cities.

Motor buses were generally less popular with the public than trolley coaches and PCC streetcars, and wholesale motorizations were uneconomical.[1] Motorizations, therefore, not only facilitated the restructuring of cities but also seriously contributed to transit's financial problems and demise. Transit as an alternative to the auto declined, and the necessity of further accommodating the auto in cities increased.

This interpretation explains not only the motorization campaign but also the auto industry's (and National City Lines') vehement opposition to any type of rapid transit system other than motor buses on freeways.[2] Advocating buses on freeways as a rapid transit system allowed the industry to mount a you-can-have-your-cake-and-eat-it-too argument. Highway policy, unlike transit policy, generally benefited from the widely held view that road improvements, freeways, expressways, and so forth benefited everyone. The bus-on-the-freeway argument brought transit, at least in the eyes of the freeway promoters, into the happy family of freeway beneficiaries.

We really cannot tell at this point whether it was the bus compatibility with urban freeways, or the uneconomical nature of all-bus transit, or both, that originally attracted the auto industry to promoting the bus. Whichever the case, it was an innovative and effective strategy.

In its support of urban freeways, the auto industry had to enter the political arena to promote the kind of Interstate System that would best serve its interests. The industry required an Interstate System with an urban orientation, or more precisely, an Interstate System that would go into and through urban areas, so as to open up the city to the automobile. Toward this end, the industry mobilized its resources and directed its efforts. It had to contend with rural interests that were satisfied with the prevailing exclusion of urban highways in the federal highway program. They had to counter the threat posed by the burgeoning toll-roads movement, which threatened to put the wrong kind of freeway system in the wrong places. They had recourse to the defense issue to support a dramatic increase in federal highway aid, but skillfully sidestepped its unsavory implications (that is, as a rationale for bypassing urban areas). The industry also had to contend with other interstate supporters who nonetheless balked at the high cost of the urban portions of the interstate.

As emphasized, the auto industry was not alone in promoting the interstate, but that does not detract from their efforts. Unlike most of the other interstate supporters (such as road construction interests and many city planners and officials), the auto industry had more or less specific requirements for the system. This, coupled with their perceptive strategy, their organizational abilities, and their lobbying expertise, made them an important force in the lobbying effort.

In both of these developments, we must emphasize that the real issue for the motorizers and the auto industry's freeway promoters was the restructuring of cities, not narrow transportation issues. And, in the end, one must conclude that they were right! That was indeed the issue and the battle went to those who correctly perceived this issue, its consequences, and the successful strategies for dealing with it. Motorization was one of those strategies; promoting freeways was another. Both contributed to the decline of transit and to a fundamental restructuring of city transportation around the automobile.

URBAN TRANSPORTATION POLICY

Some observations regarding the conduct of public policy in these events are in order. First, one must conclude that the policy of treating transit as a regulated private monopoly, while roads and highways were treated as public works, was unsound. These policies should have been integrated and dealt with as part of an inclusive transportation policy. The historical roots of this policy dichotomy can be appreciated, but that does not negate the fact that the two types of policy were in fact interwined and inseparable. This dichotomy, coupled with the very different attitude regarding transit policy (vis-à-vis highway policy) debilitated transit. By the time a more balanced federal transportation policy was being considered, in the late 1950s (one that would extend aid to transit), the fundamental issues had already been settled and the essential structure of urban transportation determined.

Second, one cannot help but question our ability to provide adequate regulation in this type of situation. The efficiency of regulation in this case should be seriously questioned. I suspect that this experience is not atypical, and that poses a serious problem. Most academic and political discussions of regulation proceed in terms of, Should we or should we not regulate? The regulation of transit suggests that a more relevant and interesting question might be, Can we regulate? The record is not encouraging in this regard, and part of transit's problems can be traced to this source.

UNECONOMICAL TRANSIT

When one thinks of transit today, red ink and public subsidy immediately come to mind. The decline of transit to this sorry condition is generally attributed to its diseconomy. This, in turn, has been attributed to the public's preference for the car. And while there is a degree of truth in that scenario, this study has sought to demonstrate that the motorization of transit, through activities such as the NCL campaign, was also a factor. So was public policy, in two ways: in the failure of regulation to prevent the motorization (it in fact facilitated the motorizations); and in the promotion of urban freeways, and the dichotomous treatment of transit.

The image of transit as a losing enterprise ought to be tempered by these considerations. What would transit be now, if the motorizations had not taken place, if trolley coaches (along with streetcars, as well as buses where appropriate) had been used more? What would it be now if urban highway policy had not set out to restructure cities to accommodate the auto to the extent that it did? Or if transit had been viewed in the same terms as highways, that is, as a public work?

The diseconomy of transit and the decline of transit should not be viewed apart from these considerations. Perhaps more important, future consideration of transit, particularly electric transit, should not be unfairly prejudiced by its current diseconomy.

SPECIAL-INTEREST INFLUENCE

Questions regarding the safeguards in our political, regulatory, and economic systems arise in both the NCL case and the freeway and lobbying episode. The failure of regulation in the transit case has been discussed, but what about the freeway lobbying? Petitioning government, lobbying government officials, advocating government policies, and so forth are open to all individuals and businesses alike. In cases like this, however, concerns arise about the integrity of the system. Was our highway policy the result of special-interest lobbying or, worse, the capture of public institutions by special interests? If one looks at any of the public hearings on the interstate, one encounters a virtual parade of interest groups. Does this prove the case against interest groups?

It does not appear that the preponderance of special-interest groups in the formulation of highway policy, or any public policy for that matter, need necessarily alter our fundamental view of the propriety of such activities. It should, however, serve to warn us of a danger. It is hard to imagine how we could expect special-interest groups not to strive to promote their interests. Could we expect the auto industry not to have tried to influence highway policy? We might not have expected them to do so well in this regard, but we ought to expect the effort. On the other hand, should we, or could we, have prevented the auto industry or any other interest group from lobbying, acquiring positions of influence, and so on? It is hard to see how that could have been done in a manner that would not have created more problems than it would have solved.

Because the benefits from public projects tend to be concentrated, there will always be a large incentive for beneficiaries to vigorously pursue these benefits. The costs of doing so can be justified by the potential reward. In other words, an Interstate System offered tremendous rewards to the auto industry, as well as to other industries. It was to their advantage to strive for them.

The costs of public projects, the interstate included, were spread out over numerous taxpayers and were, therefore, relatively small per individual. It would not have been worth the costs of opposing the program, if the cost of opposition exceeded the expected savings from stopping the system. In addition, many people may have not perceived the changes that the interstate would eventually bring, and their lack of perception might mirror their lack of either significant benefits or costs.

Consequently, one should not be surprised to see special interests working for or against certain public policies. It is work, and work will be undertaken only if the expected gains justify the expenditure of effort. The general public probably does not have that incentive. Special interests do. Perhaps consumer advocacy groups may alter this, although it is not clear that such groups will have the same interests as the general public. While not a perfect solution, this might provide more balance.

Perhaps the best solution, though, is to hoist the flag of caution in these matters. Forewarned is forearmed. By expecting this type of activity, we might be in a better position to deal with it. In addition, the wisdom of the old adage about not mixing business and government, whenever possible, seems to be supported here.

SOCIAL ENTREPRENEURSHIP

One could no doubt interpret or view both the NCL case and the freeway lobbying from many different perspectives or paradigms. Class conflict, corporate greed, Galbraithian choice manipulation, corruption, or even constrained optimization are themes that one might try to develop here (with varying degrees of success), but perhaps the most important theme is entrepreneurship. There are two reasons for this view.

First, entrepreneurial proficiency was, it seems to this author, the decisive factor in determining the outcome in both of these cases. While there is no precise definition of "entrepreneurship," two aspects are quintessential: the ability to perceive opportunities, to perceive or to create possibilities and strategies, and the ability to act on one's insights to actually mobilize, organize, and follow through to fruition.

Both of these elements were important, even decisive, in the motorization of transit and the promotion of freeways. In the case of the NCL campaign, one has to be impressed with the entrepreneurial talent of the motorizers (not necessarily with the results). Members of the auto industry could imagine restructured cities in which it would be easier to sell more autos. The elimination of electric transit was both a goal and a strategy to bring about such a restructuring. People like the Fitzgeralds at NCL were perceptive enough to see profit opportunities in assisting General Motors in this strategy. It matters little in this regard who approached whom. Invention is not the key. Recognizing a good strategy when you see it, or it is presented to you, is. So is knowing how to get the job done.

To appreciate the importance of this element, consider the failure of others to mount similar or opposing campaigns. Where was the "electrification" campaign? Where was General Electric or Westinghouse to play the role of General Motors on the other side? We did identify a trolley-coach promotional group, but their efforts were too little, too late.

One cannot consider the motorization campaign without encountering the auto industry's exceptional perception, as well as its ability to formulate strategies and carry them through. As noted, perhaps the key perception was the understanding that there was far more at stake in the motorization issue than transportation economics. Anyone who failed to perceive this was at a distinct disadvantage in the ensuing struggle.

The same thing can be said for the industry's lobbyists. How many people or groups appreciated the urban-freeway issue in the 1930s or even in 1956? This was not the issue that dominated the headlines, although the impact of the interstate on cities is now generally recognized as one of the more profound developments of the era.[3] There are indications that the general public knew little of the interstate. Of those who did, many thought that it was simply a system necessary to meet present or future travel needs. Still others, including President Eisenhower, seem to have never fully realized the fundamental restructuring of cities that the interstate entailed. It can be argued, however, that the auto industry did recognize the real issue very early on. It saw that the Interstate System could entail a fundamental restructuring of urban areas and life-styles. It was not a narrow transportation or highway issue, but rather a far-reaching reorganization of cities that was at stake. And once again, the battle went to those who perceived the issues and effectively mobilized their forces for the campaign.

The second reason for emphasizing entrepreneurship here stems from the need to expand an appreciation of the range of entrepreneurial activities. A large body of literature has sought to demonstrate how markets can be better understood by emphasizing the role of entrepreneurial decision making in the economy.[4] That appears to be the case here, but if these actions and events are to be interpreted as entrepreneurial, then one must expand its range. In addition to entrepreneurship directed at product innovation, business practices, and so forth, one must include entrepreneurship directed at restructuring the social environment. This would be accomplished through the influencing of public policy or, as in the motorization case, direct manipulation. The range of entrepreneurship must be enlarged to encompass this "social innovation." Both the lobbying for the interstate and the motorization of public transit illustrate this kind of entrepreneurship.

The recognition of this type of entrepreneurship is important, because it raises a serious question regarding its social consequences. In the recent renewal of interest in entrepreneurship and market processes, entrepreneurship has been viewed as the wellspring of competition. Since entrepreneurship is ubiquitous and virtually impossible to monopolize, this view of the economic process finds far more competition in the economy than is suggested by the more traditional structure-conduct-performance methodology. This is an important point, because much economic policy is often based on this important assessment of the degree of competition in the economy.[5] While the link between entrepreneurship and competition is essentially valid for the private economy, it is probably not so in the arena of public policy.

Social entrepreneurship suggests that the same entrepreneurship that fuels competition in the private economy will also lead to attempts at influencing public policy. That is to be expected, but one must wonder if political institutions and regulatory practices are up to the task of dealing with it here. Government always involves a degree of monopoly; that is, it operates on the basis of binding laws and decrees. It is not subject to the check of competition in the same way that market actions are. This makes the marriage of entrepreneurship and public policy a potentially dangerous union. It may be argued that lobbying is open to all, so "competitive lobbying" is a check of sorts. In addition, regulation is, or could be, structured so as to provide a "competitive access" to neutral third-party regulators. Both of the developments considered here, however, tend to belie this notion, and to confirm the wisdom in warnings against mixing government and business.

NOTES

1. There is little argument that *new* electric vehicles were clearly preferable to *new* motor buses, but new motor buses were often preferable to *old* streetcars. This confusion, and sometimes deception, is often encountered in motorization cases. At other times, *old* streetcars were even preferable to *new* motor buses. For example, the public clamored to bring the old streetcars back to the Los Angeles-Glendale-Burbank Line, following an experiment in 1936 entailing the introduction of motor bases. The Glendale newspaper referred to the motor buses as "stink wagons" (*Glendale Star*, August 26, 1937). The Glendale City Council passed a resolution to remove the buses in favor of streetcars (resolution passed June 8, 1937).

2. See, for example, "Statement of GM Corp. Before House Committee on Banking and Currency, Subcommittee on Housing, March 11, 1970, Re Urban Mass Transportation." Presented by Oscar A. Lundin, vice-president, financial staff; and, "Statement of Thomas C. Mann Before House Committee on Banking and Currency, Subcommittee on Housing, March 12, 1970, Re: Federal Assistance for Public Transportation Facilities." Both reproduced at pages 1814–17, and pages 1812–14, respectively, in U.S., Congress, Senate, Committee on the Judiciary, *The Industrial Reorganization Act, Hearings Before the Subcommittee on Antitrust and Monopoly on S. 1167, Part 3*, 93rd Cong. 2d sess., 1974. Also, see *Rapid Transit for the City on Wheels* (booklet prepared by E. C. Houghton and Jesse L. Haugh in the mid 1950s; copy in author's possession). The heads of two NCL-controlled or NCL-affiliated companies argue against a rapid transit measure and for buses on freeways. Also, see the discussion of motor buses on freeways in the AMA-commissioned study referred to in Chapter 5. Wilbur Smith and Associates, *Future Highways and Urban Growth* (New Haven, CT: Wilbur Smith and Associates, 1961), especially p. x. For an account of the Automobile Safety Foundation lobbying against rapid transit in Los Angeles in the 1960s, see Ben Kelley, *The Pavers and the Paved* (New York: D. W. Brown, 1971), p. 47.

3. For a discussion of how the interstate, especially the urban interstate, was viewed then and now, see Gary T. Schwartz, "Urban Freeways and the Interstate System," *Southern California Law Review*, 49 (March 1976), especially pp. 407–12.

4. For example, see Israel M. Kirzner, *Competition and Entrepreneurship* (Chicago: University of Chicago Press, 1973).

5. For a view on the fate of entrepreneurship and capitalism, see Joseph A. Schumpeter, *Capitalism, Socialism, and Democracy* (New York: Harper, 1947). For a discussion of how "social innovation" might alter Schumpeter's analysis and prognosis, see David J. St. Clair, "Entrepreneurship and the American Automobile Industry" (Ph.D. diss. University of Utah, 1979); and David J. St. Clair, "Schumpeter's Theory of Capitalist Development: Revised and Revisited," *Economic Forum* 11 (Summer 1980): 62–78.

Appendix

LABOR COSTS

Serious data limitations with respect to labor costs existed for the pre-1943 period. Payroll figures for each *separate* vehicle were not reported during this period, nor were separate employment figures. Instead, payroll and employment figures for the entire transit industry were aggregated and reported as an industry total. Consequently, it was necessary to estimate payroll figures for each separate vehicle. This required that separate estimates of employment for each vehicle be made, along with separate estimates of average annual wages for each vehicle. The employment figures were estimated by utilizing the average number of employees per vehicle-mile run by each vehicle in the 1943–1945 period and the 1943–1948 period, to estimate the earlier period. The figures from the 1943–1945 (that is, war years) were used in making estimates for 1940–1942, while 1943–1948 figures were used in making estimates for 1935–1939. These average employee-per-vehicle-mile figures were then multiplied by the number of vehicle-miles run during a given year to estimate employment for that vehicle during that year.

Average annual wages for each mode were also not available prior to 1943. A transit-industry average annual wage was available, however, and estimates of each vehicle's average annual wage were estimated from this industry average. In the post-1942 period, trolley-coach and motor-bus wages were both found to have been consistently lower than the industry average wage. On the other hand, streetcar wages were consistently higher than the industry average. Since this was a fairly consistent phenomenon over the entire 1943–1950 period (and even on into the early 1950s), it was assumed that similar differences had characterized the pre-1943 period. Consequently, average annual wages for each of the three vehicles were estimated from the industry average wage on the basis of this assumption. "Average differences" between the industry's average annual wage and each separate vehicle's average annual wage were calculated and rounded off for each year in the post-1942 period. Through this procedure, motor-bus average annual wages were found to have been, on average, $100 below the wage for the industry as a whole. The present study, therefore, assumes that this had also been the case prior to 1943. Trolley-coach average annual wages had been markedly lower during the war so a separate "average differences" (utilizing 1943–1945 data) were calculated for use in estimating the

1940–1942 period. A second set of "average differences" (utilizing 1943–1948 data) were used in estimating the pre-1940 period. Through this procedure, tolley-coach average annual wages were determined to have been $150 below the industry's average annual wage in 1940–1942, and $100 below that average in the pre-1940 period. The streetcar's average annual wage was, on average, $189 above the industry-wide average. This high figure, however, seemed to have been due to unusually rapid wage increases after 1946. Consequently, these years were discounted to avoid distortions, and the average annual wage for the pre-1943 period was assumed to have been only $100 above the reported industry-wide average annual wage. All of the pre-1943 estimates of each vehicle's separate average annual wage were made by adjusting the industry-wide average annual wage by these differences. For example, in 1937 the average wage in the industry was $1,656. Trolley-coach and motor-bus wages were both determined to have been $100 lower, or $1,556, while the streetcar wage was determined to have been $100 higher, or $1,756.

With these estimates of both employment and average annual wages, estimated payroll figures for each vehicle were calculated by multiplying the estimated wage by the estimated employment for each vehicle in each year.

POWER OR FUEL COSTS

Aggregate annual diesel and gasoline expenditure figures were available only after 1942. These were divided by motor-bus vehicle-miles run during each of the years to give a fuel cost per vehicle-mile for motor buses (that is, an average for combined diesel and gasoline bus operations). Since diesel and gasoline expenditures were not reported prior to 1943, this aggregate method could not be used for earlier years. Instead, it was assumed that only gasoline buses were used (most buses still were) and a fuel-consumption rate of 3.5 miles per gallon was assumed. This seemed reasonable in the light of estimates obtained from the Chicago Transit Authority's (CTA) Unit Cost Files,[1] and was consistent with scattered references in the literature as well. This figure was then multiplied by the price of gasoline during a given year to give a fuel cost per vehicle-mile. Gasoline prices were Commerce Department estimates.[2]

The aggregate procedure could not be used to estimate trolley-coach or PCC-streetcar power costs for two reasons. First, in the case of trolley-coaches, there was an unexplained discrepancy in the aggregate data concerning trolley-coach electric-power expenditures. Second, in the case of PCC cars, dividing electric power expenditures by the number of vehicle-miles run would not have adequately estimated *PCC car* power costs, due to the large number of old streetcars in operation. This problem was often encountered elsewhere in attempting to evaluate the PCC car with aggregate data. It was especially serious here, however, because the PCC car was designed to reduce operating costs, including power costs, as well as to improve service.

An alternative means of estimating trolley-coach and streetcar power costs was devised. For trolley coaches, power consumption per vehicle-mile first had to be estimated. This required an assumption as to the number of stops per mile. Six to seven stops per mile was assumed. A 1940 *Transit Journal* article[3] on transit modernization supported this assumption. Trolley-coach power requirements were then estimated at 4.0 kilowatt-hours per vehicle-mile. This estimate was derived from Sebree and Ward's estimate of the relationship between power requirements and the number of stops per mile.[4] This power requirement was then multiplied by the price per kilowatt-hour of electricity. Prices were those actually paid by the transit industry that year and were computed from the aggregate data.

To estimate streetcar power requirements, it was necessary to distinguish between PCC cars and older streetcars, since there were often wide variations in reported power requirements. For example, the CTA reported power requirments of 7.257 kilowatt-hours per vehicle-mile in 1955, and 6.831 kilowatt-hours power mile in 1954.[5] Bauer and Costello reported requirements of four to six kilowatt-hours per vehicle-mile in 1950.[6] (They also estimated the trolley-coach figure at three to five kilowatt-hours.) The discrepancy between these two sources is explicable by noting the difference in what was being measured in each case. The CTA figure was for all streetcars, both PCC and older cars, some of which were over 20 years old. The Bauer and Costello figure was almost certainly for a PCC car.

A better estimate of PCC-car power costs (and cost savings) was obtained from a 1940 *Transit Journal* article by E. A. Palmer.[7] He calculated power requirements for PCC cars at 4.7 kilowatt-hours per vehicle-mile.[8] This figure is certainly consistent with Bauer and Costello's range of four to six kilowatt-hours. In addition, power requirements for pre-1936 (that is, prior to PCC-car availability) streetcars can be estimated from this source. Palmer noted a 30 percent reduction in power requirements by switching from the older cars to the new PCC cars.[9] This would have placed the power requirmenets of the older cars at 6.11 kilowatt-hours per vehicle-mile. This figure, 6.11 kilowatt-hours, was used for 1935, while the 4.7 kilowatt-hours power vehicle-mile was used for all PCC cost estimates after 1935. These figures were then multiplied by electricity prices to yield a power cost per vehicle-mile.

MAINTENANCE MATERIAL COSTS

There are two components of maintenance costs: maintenance labor and maintenance material costs. Because, however, maintenance labor costs were picked up in labor costs, only maintenance material costs had to be estimated. Vehicle maintenance material costs did not present any unusual problems for trolley coaches or motor buses, except for the years after 1947, since aggregate expenditure figures on maintenance material costs were available through 1947. Power and line maintenance material costs however, (for trolley coaches and streetcars) and streetcar vehicle maintenance costs were not reported separately by the ATA or *Transit Journal.* Instead, all electrical operations (trolley-coach, streetcar, and subway and elevated operations) were lumped together in the case of power and line costs; and subways, elevated railways, and streetcars were lumped together for vehicle expenditures. In order to divide these reported aggregate figures into separate vehicle components, "percentage shares" of total electric overhead were estimated for trolley coach, streetcar, and subway and elevated operations. These percentage shares were calculated by dividing each vehicle's route miles (or miles of overhead negative line in the case of trolley coaches) by the total electrified route miles of all electric operations. These percentage shares were then used to divide the reported maintenance material expenditures for all electrical operations into expenditures made for each separate vehicle. The problem of streetcar vehicle maintenance material costs being aggregated with those of subway and elevated railroad costs was handled in the same manner as the power and line problem.

These procedures could not be used for the years after 1947 because of data limitations. This was the case for vehicle as well as power and line maintenance costs. Consequently, it was necessary to use another method for these years. Estimates were derived by extending the "average incremental rate increase" in material costs over the period 1943–1947, on into the post-1947 period. Since only estimates for the next three years had to be made, this simple extrapolation seemed acceptable. The yearly increase in maintenance costs was then added onto the previous year's maintenance material costs. For example, the 1948 estimate was derived by adding the average rate of increase over the 1943–1947 period to material costs of 1947, while the 1949 estimate was the 1947 figure plus the average annual increase times two, and so on.

Serious problems arose with respect to streetcar-track maintenance material costs. The "percentage share" procedure could not be used, because track maintenance costs were not reported separately for streetcars, but were instead combined with subway and elevated railroad maintenance costs. It was felt that the "percentage share" procedure would probably introduce distortions, because the technologies of these three types of operations were quite dissimilar. Streetcars ran on tracks that were usually laid down the center of city streets. As a result, a large part of streetcar maintenance material costs involved the maintenance of the surrounding pavement and its replacement when work was done on the tracks. Subway and elevated railroads, not running on city streets, did not incur this type of cost. They did, however, operate on an elaborate structure located either below or above the street. These structures had to be maintained and therefore involved costs not incurred in streetcar operations. Consequently, there seemed to be no way of accurately allocating these reported track maintenance costs between streetcar and subway or elevated railroad operations. In addition, a further complication arose. The reporting category under which track maintenance costs were reported was called maintenance of "way and structure." Track costs were the main component of this category, but other "structure" maintenance costs may (or may not) have been significant here—for example, the maintenance of buildings used by the transit company. Also, "way and structure" maintenance costs (especially structure maintenance) no doubt included costs properly attributable to trolley-coach or motor-bus operations. There was no way of breaking down these reported aggregate figures.

Consequently, track maintenance costs were not calculated. This omission underestimates streetcar operating costs. The underestimation could be exaggerated, however. I did pick up track maintenance labor costs in the labor cost estimates. Therefore, the underestimation involves only track maintenance *material* costs. The magnitude of this problem can be gauged with CTA data.[10] The CTA used the same reporting category, that is, maintenance of "way and structure." In 1954 the CTA reported maintenance expenditures of 10.17 cents per vehicle-mile. Of this total, 8.28 cents were labor costs, whle 1.89 cents were maintenance material costs. In other words, maintenance labor costs comprised 81.4 percent of the total maintenance costs. This should help in estimating the magnitude of the underestimation of streetcar costs from this omission.

VEHICLE CAPITAL COSTS

Two procedures were employed in estimating vehicle capital costs. First, annual aggregate capital expenditures for rolling stock were available. These annual expenditures could have been divided by the number of new vehicles delivered in a given year (or ordered, in the case of the pre-1943 period) to yield an average cost per new vehicle. This basic procedure had to be altered somewhat, however, due to data limitations. Because of a variable lag between reported vehicle expenditures and their delivery, yearly calculations were not considered reliable. The yearly calculations exhibited wide fluctuations—fluctuations induced solely by the delivery lag after expenditures were made. In order to correct for this problem, the calculations were made over intervals. That is, expenditures for a number of years were divided by the number of vehicles delivered over that period of time. Wherever possible, "natural" periods were used—for example, the war period, the late 1940s, the late 1930s, and so on. Most of estimated purchase prices for motor buses and trolley coaches (for various time intervals) were derived in this manner. No calculations were made with this procedure beyond 1947, however, due to unresolved questions regarding the consistency of the post-1947 data. In addition, only one estimate was made for the streetcar with this method, due to data problems. Streetcar vehicle expenditures were lumped together with expenditures for subway and elevated railroad cars. Since these vehicles utilized a different technology, and since there was no way of separating the expenditures for streetcars from expenditures for subway and elevated vehicles, no calculations were made except for the 1941–1946 period, when no subway or elevated vehicles were purchased. The aggregate date for the 1941–1946 period reflected only streetcar vehicle prices.

The second estimate procedure simply utilized price estimates from the literature. Specifically, I added Hoard's estimate of PCC car prices in 1940,[11] and Bauer and Costello's estimate of motor-bus, trolley-coach, and PCC-car prices in 1950[12] to the figures obtained from the aggregate data. The estimates from Bauer and Costello were assumed valid for the period 1948–1950.

Finally, the discontinuous "jumps" created by these estimating procedures were eliminated by a simple interpolation process. I assumed that the increase in price from one interval to the next occurred through constant annual increases. The average price reported for each interval was then assumed to have been the price for the middle year of that period. It was then assumed that the prices in later years were above average and prices for prior years were below the average. It was also assumed that prices increased annually by a constant amount between the middle years of consecutive intervals.

VEHICLE LIFE EXPECTANCY

Vehicle lives were estimated from two sources. Hoard made the following estimates in 1940: 22-passenger gas bus, 3 years; 40-passenger gas bus, 7 years; 44-passenger gas bus, 10 years; 44-passenger trolley coach, 10 years; 30-passenger trolley coach, 10 years; and PCC car, 20 years.[13] In 1950 Bauer and Costello estimated vehicle lives as follows: streetcars, 25 years; motor buses, 8 years (with perhaps as much as 15 years on new models), and trolley coaches, 15 years.[14]

There were only minor differences between Hoard, Bauer and Costello, and other scattered references to trolley-coach and PCC-car vehicle lives.

Trolley-coach vehicle life was generally reported to have been 10–15 years, while PCC life was generally put at 20–25 years. I therefore assumed that the life of a trolley coach was 10 years during the pre-1945 period, and 15 years in 1945 and subsequent years. The life of a PCC car over the same two periods was assumed to have been 20 years and 25 years respectively.

Motor buses, due to their wide range of sizes and the introduction of diesel buses in the late 1930s, presented a more difficult problem. The figures from Hoard and Bauer and Costello were for gasoline buses. Indeed, Bauer and Costello felt that the diesel bus would never be preferred over the gasoline bus, due, in part, to the shorter life-span and/or higher maintenance costs of diesel buses.[15] In any case, reported lives ranged from 3 to 10 years in 1940, and from 8 to 15 years in 1950 (although the 15 years was somewhat of a conjecture). With these ranges in mind, I assumed that the average motor-bus life expectancy prior to 1945 was 7 years, while the average life expectancy in 1945 and subsequent years was 10 years. These estimates are certainly within the reported ranges and, if anything, probably overestimate the average life expectancy of motor buses, because of the large number of smaller and cheaper buses (with their much shorter life expectancies) that were in service. All of these estimates were used in depreciating the vehicles.

ELECTRIC OVERHEAD COSTS

Newly Constructed Overhead for Trolley Coaches

A very detailed treatment of trolley-coach electric overhead construction costs was found in a 1931 article by L. W. Birch.[16] Birch provided estimates for three types of overhead construction: construction with wooden poles, span construction with steel poles, and bracket-arm construction for one-way operations only. Two-way capability was almost always a desirable characteristic, so only two-way costs were considered. In addition, wooden-pole construction, being the less expensive of the two, was assumed. Birch estimated the cost of constructing a two-way electric overhead with wooden poles at $7,422 per mile in 1931.

Only one other estimate of trolley-coach electric overhead construction costs was available. That estimate, from Bauer and Costello for 1950, estimated costs at between $15,000 and $20,000 per mile.[17] Since I was interested in wooden-pole construction, I took the lower figure, that is, $15,000 per mile of overhead. Since these were the only estimates of overhead construction costs available, a construction cost index was used to estimate costs for one intervening year. This index was published periodically in *Transit Journal* [18] (available through 1941) and was consequently assumed to have been applicable to transit construction costs. With this index, an estimate for overhead construction costs for 1940 was made—$9,901 per mile of overhead.

With these three estimates, estimates for intervening years were made. The 1931 estimate of construction costs was assumed to have been valid for the entire period 1931–1939. This was a simplifying but also realistic assumption. For 1940–1950, I simply interpolated the intervening figures by assuming a constant yearly increase.

Converted Trolley-Coach Overhead

In 1932 Birch[19] noted that conversion of electric overhead was a more desirable option for transit companies considering trolley-coach operations as a replacement for older streetcar operations. These conversion costs depended on the type of overhead already in place, its condition, and whether one, two, or three additional wires had to be added or replaced on the existing overhead. Note that the trolley coach, since it did not have a negative ground in the tracks, had to have a ground wire installed. Birch provided estimates for all three cases, and for both old and new spans. I assumed, for the cost calculations, that two wires were to be added to new spans. In this case, the cost of conversion in 1932 was $1,523 per mile of overhead. In comparison, the cost of *new* construction 1931 was $7,422 per mile, or 4.86 times the cost of conversion in 1932.

Since additional data on the cost of converting overhead were not available from any source for any other year, I estimated these conversion-costs by assuming that they were, in all cases, simply one-fourth of the cost of new overhead construction.

Streecar Electric Overhead

Streetcar electric overhead was roughly equivalent to trolley-coach overhead (the only exception being the third wire on trolley lines). Therefore, the figures derived for trolley coaches were assumed to be good estimates for PCC-car operations; that is, the cost of constructing new trolley-coach overhead was assumed to have been the same as the cost of constructing new overhead for PCC-car operations. Likewise, it was assumed that the cost of converting old streetcar overhead to trolley-coach operations was the same as the cost of refurbishing and reconstructing old streetcar overhead for modern PCC operations. The depreciated costs were, of course, divided by average vehicle-mile per mile of *streetcar* overhead. These assumptions were reasonable on the one hand, and due to data limitations, necessary on the other.

TRACK COSTS

In order to calculate streetcar track costs, it was first necessary to estimate construction costs. Again, as was the case with all of the capital costs estimated above, data were skimpy. I had only two observations of these costs from the literature to utilize, along with the same construction cost index referred to above with respect to electric overhead costs. The first estimate was from a 1931 article by E. P. Goucher.[20] Goucher estimated urban track construction costs at $8.345 per foot. On a per-mile basis, this was $44,061. The second observation was from Bauer and Costello, who estimated track construction costs to have been $100,000 per mile of track in 1950.[21] With these two estimates and the construction cost index previously referred to, annual costs were determined in the same manner as in the case of electric overhead.

VEHICLE SIZE

The estimates of average vehicle size for each year were determined from the aggregate data. Vehicle sizes, however, were almost always reported in ranges—for example, 25 seats or less, 26 to 34 seats, and 35 seats or more. In order to use the data reported in ranges, it was necessary to first estimate an average size (number of seats) *for each range.* This was accomplished by actually calculating these averages for 1940, when each individual purchase and vehicle size was reported for that year in *Transit Journal.*[22] These "range averages" were then used to estimate the total number of seats sold that year by multiplying the range average by the number of vehicles in each range. This figure was then divided by the total number of vehicles sold that year, to give us an average vehicle size for all vehicles of that type sold that year. In the case of streetcars this procedure was not undertaken, since it was assumed that these were exclusively PCC cars, which seated 55 to 60.

This procedure gives only a rough average size of vehicles *sold* in a given year. It does not give an average size for the *stock* of vehicles in use. This latter average would be more useful, but could not be determined. Also, since the average size of motor buses increased faster than the size of trolley coaches or streetcars, this procedure probably *overestimates* the average size of motor buses vis-à-vis the other two vehicles.

NOTES

1. The Chicago Transit Authority's Unit Cost Files were graciously made available to me for inspection in Chicago. The file documents were unnumbered, so all references will be to the file itself.

2. U.S., Department of Commerce, *Historical Statistics of the United States, Colonial Times to 1970* (Washington, DC: U.S. Government Printing Office, 1975), p. 379.

3. "More Riders at Less Cost through Modernization," *Transit Journal* 84 (July 1940): 221–39.

4. Mac Sebree and Paul Ward, *Transit's Stepchild: The Trolley Coach* (Cerritos, CA: Ira L. Swett, 1973), p. 67.

5. CTA Unit Cost File.

6. John Bauer and Peter Costello, *Transit Modernization and Street Traffic Control* (Chicago: Lakeside Press, 1950), p. 82.

7. E. A. Palmer, "80,000,000 Miles Prove Their Worth," *Transit Journal* 84 (August 1940): 269–71.

8. Ibid., p. 271.

9. Ibid.

10. CTA Unit Cost File.

11. George Hoard, "Modernization of a Transit System," *Engineering Experimental Station Series,* Bulletin No. 100, (Seattle: University of Washington, 1940): 15.

12. Bauer and Costello, *Transit Modernization,* p. 81.

13. Hoard, *Modernization,* p. 15.

14. Bauer and Costello, *Transit Modernization,* p. 84.

15. Ibid., p. 88.

16. L. W. Birch, "Many Factors Affect Cost of Trolley Bus Overhead," *Electric Railway Journal* 75 (April 1931): 190.

17. Bauer and Costello, *Transit Modernization,* p. 100.

18. A Construction Cost Index from *Engineering News Record* (no citations) was cited periodically in *Transit Journal.* For example, see *Transit Journal* 88 (January 1941): 9.

19. L. W. Birch, "Converting Street Railway Overhead for Trolley Bus Service," *Transit Journal* 76 (March 1932): 123–126.

20. E. P. Goucher, "A Typical Urban Track Construction," *Electric Railway Journal* 75 (October 1931): 389.

21. Bauer and Costello, *Transit Modernization,* p. 58.

22. "Buses Bought by Transit Companies during 1940," *Transit Journal* 85 (January 1941): 13–15.

Index

About the Author

DAVID J. ST. CLAIR is Associate Professor of Economics at California State University, Hayward.

Dr. St. Clair is the recipient of "The Columbia University Prize in American Economic History in Honor of Allen Nevins" for the best dissertation on U.S. economic history in 1979. He has published in the area of economic history. His articles and reviews have appeared in *The Journal of Economic History* and *Economic Forum*.

Dr. St. Clair holds a B.A. from San Jose State University, San Jose, California, and a Ph.D. from the University of Utah.